Mabo: The Native Title Legislation

PUBLISHED AS A SPECIAL EDITION OF THE UNIVERSITY OF QUEENSLAND LAW JOURNAL

Editor
Margaret Stephenson, Lecturer in Law, T.C. Beirne School of Law, University of Queensland

Editorial Advisory Board
Professor Geoffrey de Q. Walker, Dean, T.C. Beirne School of Law, University of Queensland
Professor R.D. Lumb, T.C. Beirne School of Law, University of Queensland
Professor Alan Fogg, T.C. Beirne School of Law, University of Queensland
Professor Sir William Wade, University of Cambridge
Professor Douglas Kmiec, University of Notre Dame, Indiana
Professor R. Van Caenegem, University of Ghent
Professor N.R.M. Menon, National Law School of India University, Bangalore
Professor G.L. Peiris, University of Colombo
Professor Michael Pryles, Bond University
Professor David Link, University of Notre Dame, Indiana

Editorial Advisers to the Special Edition
Darrell Lumb, Professor of Law, T.C. Beirne School of Law, University of Queensland
Carolyn Sappideen, Associate Professor of Law, T.C. Beirne School of Law, University of Queensland

Editorial Assistants
Alexander Bates
Jane Hunter

The University of Queensland Law Journal has been published since 1948, making it one of the oldest and most prestigious law journals in Australia. It publishes scholarly articles on Queensland law, Commonwealth law, international and comparative law and jurisprudence. The journal is fully refereed and is produced by editors appointed by the Law Faculty Board. The journal is served by an Editorial Advisory Board consisting of eminent Australian and overseas legal scholars.

Mabo: The Native Title Legislation

Edited by M.A. Stephenson

University of Queensland Press

First published 1995 by University of Queensland Press
Box 42, St Lucia, Queensland 4067 Australia

© M.A. Stephenson 1995
Copyright in the individual contributions remains with the authors.

This book is copyright. Apart from any fair dealing
for the purposes of private study, research, criticism
or review, as permitted under the Copyright Act, no
part may be reproduced by any process without written
permission. Enquiries should be made to the publisher.

The typeset text for this book was supplied by the editor.
Printed in Australia by McPherson's Printing Group

Distributed in the USA and Canada by
International Specialized Book Services, Inc.,
5804 N.E. Hassalo Street, Portland, Oregon 97213–3640

Cataloguing in Publication Data
National Library of Australia

Mabo : the native title legislation.

  Bibliography.
  Includes index.

  1. Australia. Native Title Act 1993. 2. Native title —
  Australia. 3. Aborigines, Australian — Land tenure.
  4. Aborigines, Australian — Legal status, laws, etc.
  5. Torres Strait Islanders — Land tenure. 6. Torres Strait
  Islanders — Legal status, laws, etc. I. Stephenson, M.
  A. (Margaret Anne), 1954–

346.940432

ISBN 0 7022 2746 3

Contents

Acknowledgments *vii*
Contributors *ix*
Foreword *xiii*
Introduction *xv*

Parliamentary Responses to the Mabo Decision
   Frank Brennan S.J. *1*
Constitutional Issues and the Native Title Act, 1993 (Cth)
   R.D. Lumb *26*
Native Title and International Law
   Garth Nettheim *36*
Mabo and the Miners — ad infinitum?
   J.R.S. Forbes *49*
Native Title Legislation and Mining
   Hugh Fraser Q.C. *71*
Applications for a Determination of Native Title to the National Native Title Tribunal
   B.A. Keon-Cohen *84*
Pastoral Leases and Reservation Clauses
   M.A. Stephenson *104*
The Commonwealth Native Title Act 1993: A Critique
   P.D. Connolly, Q.C. *120*
Compensation and Valuation of Native Title
   M.A. Stephenson *135*
The Relationship Between the National Native Title Tribunal and the Queensland Native Title Tribunal
   Dominic McGann and David Yarrow *155*
The Land (Titles and Traditional Usage) Act 1993 Western Australia
   Richard H. Bartlett *168*
The Relationship between Native Title and Statutory Title under Land Rights Legislation
   Garth Nettheim *183*

Index *201*

Acknowledgments

Margaret Stephenson initiated and compiled this publication.

The willingness of the authors to participate in this project and their valuable contributions in this important legislation are very much appreciated.

Thanks are due to Betty Rogan for her excellent secretarial assistance and to Alexander Bates and Jane Hunter, editorial assistants, for their diligent efforts. Thanks also go to Barry Maher for typesetting the manuscript. Special thanks and appreciation are due to Professor Darrell Lumb and also to Associate Professor Carolyn Sappideen for their continued guidance, encouragement and advice. Thanks are also due to Dr Clive Turner for his valued assistance.

Publication was made possible by the resources of the T.C. Beirne School of Law, University of Queensland. Thanks are also due to the Dean, Professor Geoffrey de Q. Walker for his active support. The staff of the University of Queensland Press, especially Robert Brown and Sue Abbey, were most helpful at all stages of the project.

Contributors

Richard Bartlett is a Professor of Law at the University of Western Australia and has also held a Chair of Natural Resources Law at the University of Calgary and a Chair at the University of Saskatchewan in Canada. Professor Bartlett has written extensively in the area of mining law, natural resources law and Aboriginal peoples and the law. In *Mabo (No. 2)* the plaintiffs' argument repeated the substance of the Professor's writings in 'Aboriginal Land Claims at Common Law' (1983) 15 UNWALR 295, the subject of which was the concept of native title and its extinguishment. The High Court's conclusions are essentially those of the jurisprudence set forth therein at pages 330-343.

Father Frank Brennan S.J. is both a Jesuit priest and lawyer. He graduated LL.B. from the University of Queensland and LL.M. from the University of Melbourne and obtained a Bachelor of Divinity from the Melbourne College of Divinity. He was founding Director of Uniya—a Christian Centre for Social Research and Action based at Kings Cross and for many years was the Aboriginal Affairs consultant to the Australian Catholic Bishops. He is a member of the Council of the Constitutional Centenary Foundation. He has written extensively on Aboriginal Land Rights and is the author of a number of books including *Land Rights Queensland Style* and *Sharing the Country* and is the co-author of *Finding Common Ground* and *Reconciling our Differences*. In 1989 he won the United Nations Association Media Peace Award. The National Australia Day Council selected him as an Outstanding Achiever in 1993 for his contribution to the Aboriginal community. He is presently a Visiting Fellow with the 'Reshaping Australian Institutions: Towards and Beyond 2001' project in the law program at the Research School of Social Sciences at the Australian National University in Canberra.

The Hon. Mr Justice Peter Connolly C.S.I., C.B.E. recently retired from the bench of the Supreme Court of Queensland after fourteen years as a judge. He is currently President of the Court of Appeal of the Solomon Islands and a Judge of the Court of Appeal of Kiribati. Mr Justice Connolly obtained First Class Honours degrees in Arts and Law and was admitted to the Bar in 1949 and appointed Q.C. in 1963. He is a Past President of the Law Council of Australia, the Australian Bar Association and the Bar Association of Queensland. He has given occasional lectures in a number of subjects, including Constitutional Law, at the University of Queensland Law School since his retirement and has delivered addresses to various societies, including the Sir Samuel Griffith Society.

Dr John Forbes, Reader in Law, holds the degrees BA, LLM (1st Class Honours) from the University of Sydney and PhD (Queensland). He was in practice at the Bar in Brisbane before his academic appointment. He instituted and still conducts a course in the Law of Natural Resources, with other interests in Evidence and Administrative Law. The author of several legal texts, he is Queensland correspondent to the Australian Mining and Petroleum Law Journal.

Mr Hugh Fraser Q.C. was admitted to practice at the Queensland Bar in 1979, having graduated LLB (Hons) from the University of Queensland. He is also a member of the New South Wales Bar, and is admitted to practice as counsel in the Northern Territory. He appeared as counsel in the *Mabo* case in the High Court. He was appointed one of Her Majesty's counsel for the State of Queensland in 1992. His practice includes commercial litigation and advice, including matters relating to mining law, and more recently, cases involving claims of native title.

B. A. Keon–Cohen is a barrister in practice at the Victorian Bar and is a former lecturer in law, Monash University. He was engaged in the *Mabo* case in 1981 and appeared as counsel in the *Mabo* trials before Moynihan J. of the Supreme Court of Queensland and before the High Court. His involvement in Aboriginal Land Rights issues includes his appointment as counsel assisting the *Seaman Enquiry* into Aboriginal land in Western Australia. As a senior officer with the Australian Law Reform Commission he worked on Aboriginal Customary Law Reference. He has advised various Aboriginal organisations on land rights and is currently engaged by communities across Northern Australia in post *Mabo* matters. He co-edited a book entitled *Aborigines and the Law*.

Professor Darrell Lumb who has been with the University of Queensland since 1958 is a noted authority on Australian Constitutional Law. In recent months he has been working on a new edition of the *Constitution of the Commonwealth of Australia*,

Annotated. He has also been writing on the topic of methods of constitutional alteration in the context of the monarchy-republic debate. His interest in constitutional aspects of Aboriginal land rights extends from 1988 when he published 'Aboriginal Land Rights: Judicial Approaches in Perspective' in the Australian Law Journal, and includes his research on the *Mabo* litigation.

Dominic McGann is the former Director of the Aboriginal and Torres Strait Islander Land Interests Program, Department of Lands, Brisbane. He is a lawyer with experience in Aboriginal issues and government policy. He is also a former lecturer in law at both Macquarie University and James Cook University of North Queensland and has published many articles on a wide range of legal issues. He holds the degrees of LL.B. and LL.M. and is currently completing further studies at Bond University.

Professor Garth Nettheim is Chair of the Aboriginal Law Centre and the Diplomacy Training Program at the University of New South Wales. He holds degrees in Law (Syd) and International Relations, (Fletcher School of Law and Diplomacy, USA). Professor Nettheim is a former public affairs producer. He is the author of extensive publications on Aboriginal Legal issues and Aborigines and Torres Strait Islanders, including a contribution in *The Laws of Australia*.

Margaret Stephenson practised as a solicitor in Brisbane before returning to the Law School where she has been a lecturer in Land Law and Contract for several years. She is an editor of the University of Queensland Law Journal and compiled and edited *Mabo: A Judicial Revolution*. She has written several articles on *Mabo* and related issues and has also edited the recently published *Australia: Republic or Monarchy?*

David Yarrow is a Program Officer of the Aboriginal and Torres Strait Islander Land Interests Program, Department of Lands, Brisbane. He is a graduate in science and law from the University of Queensland and is currently completing a Master's degree in law with a significant focus on native title issues.

Foreword

The Right Honourable Sir Harry Gibbs GCMG AC KBE
formerly Chief Justice of the High Court of Australia

This volume is a sequel to *'Mabo: A Judicial Revolution'* which discussed the issues raised by the decision of the High Court in *Mabo v. Queensland (No. 2)* (1992) 175 C.L.R. 1. Although the curious chapter opened by that decision has by no means closed, another chapter has been opened by the passing of the Commonwealth *Native Title Act* 1993. The main purposes of that Act were to recognise and protect the native title whose existence had been discovered in *Mabo v. Queensland (No. 2)*, to validate certain past grants which that decision may have rendered invalid and to provide compensation where native title has been, or is in future, extinguished or otherwise affected.

The Act is no less remarkable than the decision which prompted its passage. It is complex in form and some of its provisions are obscure while others are of doubtful validity. Among the curiosities which it contains are provisions which give 'the common law of Australia in respect of native title' the force of a law of the Commonwealth, which cast on States the burden of compensating native title holders for past acts which on one view may have been done as early as the time of First Settlement and which require certain laws of the States, if they are to be valid, to contain matters specified in the Commonwealth Act.

The High Court will no doubt in time expound the meaning of the doubtful provisions of the Act and resolve the questions that arise as to the constitutional validity of its provisions. However, only time will show whether the provisions which give holders of native title and even claimants a right to negotiate before future acts are done which affect native title and which give a right to compensation will operate as a disincentive particularly to mining exploration and development. Even with time there may still remain in dispute the broader question whether the Act does justice between the Aboriginal people and other Australians, and between those Aboriginal people who can establish that they hold native title and those who cannot.

Like the earlier volume, this book contains a valuable and balanced discussion of questions which are of great importance to the future of Australia.

Introduction

The *Native Title Act* 1993 is the Commonwealth Government's legislative response to the High Court's 1992 decision in *Mabo v. State of Queensland (No. 2)* (1992) 175 C.L.R. 1. The Commonwealth *Native Title Act* became law on 1 January 1994. This legislation gives statutory effect to much of the decision in *Mab*o while also introducing new elements in relation to native title and providing a framework in which native title can operate. A brief summary of the objectives and main features of the *Native Title Act* 1993 (Cth) is as follows.

The Act is designed to achieve four main objectives. These are the recognition and protection of native title, the regulation of future dealings affecting native title, the establishment of a means to deal with native title claims such as the Tribunal and court processes, and the validation of past acts if they have been invalidated because of the existence of native title. The Act also includes provision in Section 10 for a National Aboriginal and Torres Strait Islander Land Fund designed to assist in the indigenous purchase of land. The issues arising from the Land Fund were still a matter of political debate at the time of writing.

The common law principle of 'native title' as established by the High Court in *Mabo* is recognised by the *Native Title Act* 1993 (Cth). The Act establishes a Native Title Tribunal, the functions of which include the determination of claims involving the existence of native title, the determination of compensation payable for extinguishment or impairment of native title, the ascertaining of whether a government may grant an interest in land held under or claimed for native title, and whether a government may compulsorily acquire land where native title exists.

The Act validates titles granted by, and other 'past acts' undertaken by the Commonwealth Government; and permits titles granted by, and other past acts undertaken by State Governments to be validated by the States. Such validation can occur only in relation to titles issued up to 31 December 1993 and other 'past acts' occurring prior to 1 July 1993. The validity of such titles and other 'past acts' may have been in doubt because of the provisions of the *Racial Discrimination Act* 1975 (Cth). Such validation of existing titles may mean an automatic extinguishment, impairment or suspension of native title rights subject to appropriate compensation payments being made to the native title holders.

New rights in addition to those identified by the High Court in *Mabo* are recognised for native title holders in the legislation. Native title is treated as the equivalent to freehold for the purposes of acquisition by the Crown or in relation to any dealing with the land by the Crown. The *Native Title Act* 1993 (Cth) stipulates that from 1 January 1994, any grant of an interest by a government may be made over land subject to native title, only if that grant could have been made over freehold land. Thus a government can deal with native title only in the same way that it can deal with freehold, and that is by formal acquisition procedures under the relevant Compulsory Acquisition legislation. Consequently, land over which native title exists would have to be formally acquired before a pastoral lease, for example, could be granted. Although the High Court recognised a State's sovereign power to deal with land, this power has been restricted in that governments can no longer extinguish native title without complying with the procedures in the *Native Title Act* 1993 (Cth). The *Native Title Act* 1993 (Cth) gives greater rights to native title holders or those registered as claimants of native title over and above those recognised in *Mabo*, in that prior to the formal acquisition or grant of any interest in the land the title holders are given a 'right to negotiate' (section 26) in relation to any proposed acquisition or grant, including an exploration or mining interest.

If no agreement is reached between the native title holders or claimants and the Crown then the matter will be referred to an 'arbitral body'— either the National Native Title Tribunal or a corresponding State/Territory body. The arbitral body or Tribunal may refuse to allow the grant or acquisition to proceed. Such determination may, however, be overturned by a State or Commonwealth minister in the State or national interest. A State/Territory arbitral body will correspond to the National

Native Title Tribunal only if the Commonwealth determines that the State/Territory body meets Commonwealth criteria. Native title holders may choose whether they take their claim to the Tribunal, to the State/Territory body concerned, or to another court. However, 'an approved determination of native title' can be made only by the National Native Title Tribunal, by the correspondingly recognised State/Territory arbitral body, or by the Federal Court, or the High Court. Subject to appeal or review, such an approved determination would override any differing determination by another body or court.

Compensation will be payable to native title holders for any loss or impairment of their native title, whether caused by the validation of titles issued prior to the legislation or by government making grants of interests in land subject to native title after the passing of the *Native Title Act* 1993 (Cth). The Act provides that compensation will be payable by the government involved, either Commonwealth or State. The *Native Title Act* 1993 (Cth) also recognises that native title may be claimed over waters and offshore places, as it may be claimed over the land mass of Australia.

It is obvious that there are a number of issues of importance arising from the Commonwealth *Native Title Act* 1993. These include the concept of native title and its contents, determinations of native title, past and future dealings with native title land, the extinguishment of native title and the constitutional and international law issues. Many of these issues are discussed in the articles in this book.

Father Frank Brennan S.J. examines the Parliamentary responses to the *Mabo* decision and provides an enlightening overview of the Federal Parliament's legislation. He emphasises that the non-discrimination principle, a principle in accord 'with the contemporary values of the Australian peoples', is the cornerstone of both the *Mabo* decision and the *Native Title Act* 1993 (Cth) and he considers that this legislation will ensure that in the future native title land will be dealt with by governments and third parties in a non-discriminatory way and in a fashion similar to that accorded ordinary title holders.

Leading constitutional lawyer, Professor Darrell Lumb, analyses the constitutional issues relating to the validity of the

Commonwealth *Native Title Act* 1993. He notes that this legislation has a major impact on the management of State Crown land especially with regard to future dealings. Professor Lumb is particularly concerned with the scope of the race power (section 51(xvi)) and the impact of the Commonwealth *Native Title Act* 1993 on the legislative power of the States. His primary focus is on the capacity of the Commonwealth Parliament to enact legislation which involves an intrusion into a State's power of management over areas of Crown land, and which is directed against the legislative powers of the States and fetters their legislative capacity to modify the common law operating within their boundaries.

The background international law upon which the *Racial Discrimination Act* 1975 (Cth) was based and which assisted the High Court in reaching its decision in *Mabo v. Queensland* (1992) 175 C.L.R. 1 is reviewed by acknowledged Australian expert on Australian native title, Professor Garth Nettheim. He sees the Commonwealth *Native Title Act* 1993 as a reflection of international principles designed to eliminate discriminatory practices based on race and to ensure that the generally applicable standards of human rights are to be observed. Professor Nettheim considers that had Australia not reversed the non-recognition of native title and had it not supported that reversal by the enactment of national native title legislation, the Government would have been vulnerable to adverse commentary in the international fora for the denial of human rights standards.

The effect of the *Native Title Act* 1993 (Cth) on mining is of importance. Commentary on mining is provided by Dr John Forbes. Dr Forbes also focuses on the evidentiary requirements and difficulties of proof likely to arise in contested cases under the Commonwealth's Native Title legislation. He warns that judicial and quasi-judicial methods of government action are suitable only when all parties are likely to have reasonably equal opportunities to obtain evidence, and he cites sources indicating that non-claimant parties may not have equal access to appropriate evidence in all cases. Further details of the impact that the *Native Title Act* 1993 (Cth) could have on the mining industry in the future are presented by Hugh Fraser Q.C. He argues that the Native Title legislation will add significantly to the lead time for mining projects, with a shift in the power to control mining from the States and Territories to the Commonwealth.

An assessment of the impact of the Native Title legislation from the perspective of a claimant desiring to bring an application for native title before the National Native Title Tribunal is provided by Bryan Keon-Cohen. The author's experience in the Tribunal's jurisdiction allows his analysis from a practical viewpoint. He argues that the Act is a preferable alternative to bringing common law actions to determine native title.

An issue, the subject of much speculation, concerns pastoral leases and reservation clauses contained therein. The pertinent question here is whether a reservation in a pastoral lease to allow indigenous inhabitants to pursue their traditional lifestyle upon the leased land will have the effect of preserving native title or whether such title will be impaired or extinguished. This is considered by Margaret Stephenson. The creation of a new legislative right to compensation in the *Native Title Act* 1993 (Cth) for both past and future extinguishment or impairment of native title rights is further reviewed by Margaret Stephenson.

A critique of the workings of the Commonwealth *Native Title Act* 1993 is provided by the Hon. P.D. Connolly Q.C. He finds that some of the procedural aspects of this legislation are a little disturbing particularly as the Tribunal is able to hold meetings in private and give directions concerning who should be present, notwithstanding a party's right of representation.

Details of legislation by two States, Queensland and Western Australia, reflecting differing responses and approaches to native title have also been included. The relationship between the National Native Title Tribunal and the Queensland Native Title Tribunal is explored by Dominic McGann and David Yarrow who conclude that the Queensland legislation addresses native title in a comprehensive way. Background to the operation of the *Native Title (Queensland) Act* 1993 is included. Professor Richard Bartlett argues that the Western Australian legislation, the *Land (Titles and Traditional Usage) Act* 1993, rather than bringing certainty and stability to the resource industry has brought legal and resource insecurity. He concludes that the Act harms the industry it was passed to help. He offers strong argument against the Western Australian legislation, based, *inter alia*, on a firm belief in justice for all. Also included with regard to State legislation is the relationship between native title and statutory title under land rights legislation. Professor Nettheim explores the question as to whether title to land granted by the various land rights Acts, some passed before *Mabo (No. 2)* and some after, is consistent with the continued existence of native title or whether that title is inconsistent so as to impair or even extinguish native title.

The *Native Title Act* 1993 (Cth) removes uncertainty that may have existed in relation to the validity of titles granted in the past. However, it does restrict the States and Territories in the management of land, waters and resources and the ability to grant licences, titles and permits in the future. While this legislation has done much to deal with the legal issues left unresolved by the High Court decision in *Mabo* there remain several areas that have not been addressed, namely: whether leases with reservation of rights in favour of Aboriginal communities extinguish native title; how to value the special relationship that Aboriginal people have for their land; whether the Aboriginal community's customary rules would allow transferability of title or whether commercial development of traditional lands would be permitted, and the precise content and nature of Aboriginal title; and the nature of the traditional connection which needs to be proved.

This book seeks to address some of the new challenges raised and further frontiers to be bridged under the *Native Title Act* 1993 (Cth).

Update

At the time this book was in press the High Court on 16th March 1995 handed down its judgment in *The State of Western Australia v. The Commonwealth* (F.C.95/010).

The High Court's unanimous decision confirmed that the Commonwealth *Native Title Act* 1993 is valid save for Section 12 of the Act, see Professor Lumb's article (Constitutional Issues and the *Native Title Act*, 1993 (Cth)) pages 33 and 34. Section 12 was found by the Court to be severable from the *Native Title Act* 1993 (Cth). Section 12 of the Act states that the common law of Australia in respect of native title has the force of the law of the Commonwealth. The High Court's decision means that States could amend the common law in so far as it is not inconsistent with the Commonwealth *Native Title Act* 1993 and the *Racial Discrimination Act* 1975 (Cth).

This decision also confirmed Professor Richard Bartlett's view that the Western Australian legislation, the *Land (Title and Traditional Usage) Act* 1993 (WA), was invalid as it was inconsistent with the Commonwealth *Native Title Act* 1993 and with section 10 of the *Racial Discrimination Act* 1975 (Cth), see pages 168 to 182. Interests purported to be granted (or future acts undertaken) over native title land pursuant to the Western Australian legislation will have the effect described by the *Native Title Act* 1993 (Cth). Depending on the circumstances in which grants (or acts) were made, such interests could be classified as impermissible future acts that could be invalid to the extent that they affect native title (section 22) or if subject to the negotiation regime such interests could be totally invalid (section 28). 'Future' grants or acts would not generally extinguish native title as the provisions of the Commonwealth *Native Title Act* 1993 must be complied with before this can occur (section 11). All acts and grants undertaken pursuant to the Western Australian legislation should be carefully examined.

The High Court found it unnecessary to decide the effect of the *Racial Discrimination Act* 1975 (Cth) on the validity of the State laws authorising the doing of executive acts which purportedly extinguish or impair native title after the *Racial Discrimination Act* 1975 (Cth) came into operation.

Parliamentary Responses to the Mabo Decision

Frank Brennan, S.J.[*]

1. Legislating in a Non-Discriminatory Way

The Commonwealth Parliament passed the *Native Title Act* 1993. Most of the Act came into effect on 1 January 1994. Part 10 (to establish a National Aboriginal and Torres Strait Islander Land Fund) is being repealed and replaced by the Indigenous Land Corporation and Land Fund (ATSIC Amendment) Bill 1994, providing $45 million per annum for indigenous land purchases. The Bill is expected to pass in the Autumn 1995 sittings. There is a National Native Title Tribunal (hereinafter referred to as N.N.T.T.) which operates pursuant to the Act. The N.N.T.T. regulations set down the forms and procedures for native title determination applications and compensation applications. The Minister for Aboriginal and Torres Strait Islander Affairs has made initial determinations of which Aboriginal organisations are representative Aboriginal and Torres Strait Islander bodies for the purposes of the Act. The N.N.T.T. has published a plain English 'Applicants' Guide' for lodgement of applications.

Introducing the legislation the Prime Minister told Parliament it had four key aspects:

1. ungrudging and unambiguous recognition and protection of native title;
2. provision for clear and certain validation of past acts including grants and laws if they have been invalidated because of the existence of native title;
3. a just and practical regime governing future grants and acts affecting native title;

---

[*] Barrister, Visiting Fellow in Law, Research School of Social Sciences, Australian National University, Canberra; Member Constitutional Centenary Foundation.

4. rigorous, specialised and accessible tribunal and court processes for determining claims to native title and for negotiation and decisions on proposed grants over native title land.[1]

By the time the legislation was returned to the House of Representatives from the Senate, it contained one hundred and fifteen amendments. The basic framework of the Bill remained intact. The fundamental balance between Aboriginal interests and those of miners and pastoralists was also maintained. There were five major policy changes. First, though the legislation puts beyond doubt the validity of all titles granted to miners and pastoralists since 1975, any future dealings in land pursuant to the *Native Title Act* 1993 (Cth) will have to be consistent with the *Racial Discrimination Act* 1975 (Cth) (hereinafter referred to as *R.D.A.*). Secondly, because of the complexity of the legislation and its novelty, the Parliament has provided for a Parliamentary Joint Committee on Native Title to monitor and review the operation of the legislation. Thirdly, the Aboriginal and Torres Strait Islander Social Justice Commissioner, Mr Michael Dodson, will provide an annual report to the government on the operation of the legislation and its effect on the exercise and enjoyment of human rights of Aboriginal peoples and Torres Strait Islanders. Fourthly, the holders of existing commercial, agricultural, pastoral and residential leases are assured automatic renewal of their leases without the need to negotiate with persons claiming to be native title holders. Fifthly, Aborigines who establish a native title claim need not have the title vested in a body corporate. They may choose to hold the title as a group of individuals, setting up a corporation just for the receipt of payments.

The Government had proposed further pro-industry amendments but they failed because the Coalition decided to oppose all amendments 'on principle'. In the absence of those amendments, fishermen may be required to negotiate with Aboriginal native title holders for access to areas between the high and low water mark.[2] Miners may face the prospect of tribunals reviewing decisions to grant mining interests even if there has not been a material change in the circumstances between the mining company and the Aboriginal native title holders.³ State Governments and developers were hopeful that any arrangements between governments and developers entered into 'in good faith' before 1 January 1994 could proceed without the need for land use matters being referred to any native title holders.⁴

In the *Mabo* decision, Brennan J. (Mason C.J. and McHugh J. concurring) in the lead judgment said the common law would not accept 'an unjust and discriminatory doctrine' which refused to recognise the rights and interests in land of the indigenous inhabitants of settled colonies. He thought such discrimination contrary not only to the expectations of the international community but also to 'the contemporary values of the Australian people'.⁵ Even though the Federal Coalition could not see its way clear to support the Commonwealth *Native Title Act* 1993, all members of the House of Representatives and the Senate were committed to the principle of non-discrimination. Dr Hewson, the former leader of the Opposition, when publishing the Coalition's formal policy on *Mabo* said:

> The essence of the Coalition's alternative is to reflect the proper role of the Commonwealth Government in: working with the States to validate existing land titles via complimentary legislation and ensuring just terms compensation is paid in cases where native title is extinguished in a manner inconsistent with the *Racial Discrimination Act*; and acknowledging that under the *Racial Discrimination Act*, while States are free to develop their individual responses in recognition of the High Court's *Mabo* decision in relation to future land grants, they must do so in a non-discriminatory way.⁶

He said the Coalition would continue to uphold the *R.D.A.* 'to ensure that all Australians including indigenous Australians are treated on a non-discriminatory basis'.⁷ He, as much as the Prime Minister, insisted, 'there should be no relaxation of the *Racial Discrimination Act* except to the extent that may be necessary to validate past grants and then only on the proviso that compensation is paid on a non-discriminatory basis'.⁸

The principle of non-discrimination on the basis of race is now common ground among all political parties and espoused by all elected politicians at the national level. It is a principle fully in accord 'with the contemporary values of the Australian people'. Even though the Coalition was prepared to allow the States primary control over land management even in relation to native title lands, Dr Hewson insisted, 'they have to do that under two constraints: firstly they have to do that by recognising native title and, secondly they have to do that subject to the *Racial Discrimination Act*'.[9] Non-discrimination is the cornerstone of the *Mabo* decision and the *Native Title Act* 1993 (Cth). Parliament was prepared to go one step further giving native title holders 'a right to be asked about actions affecting their land' in view of 'their deeply felt attachment to land'.[10]

The preamble of the *Native Title Act* 1993 (Cth) provides that 'in future, acts that affect native title should only be able to be validly done if, typically, they can also be done to freehold land and if, whenever appropriate, every reasonable effort has been made to secure the agreement of the native title holders through a special right to negotiate'.

2. Commonwealth Recognition of Native Title

Since 30 June 1993, the common law of Australia in respect of native title has had the force of a law of the Commonwealth.[11] Native title can be extinguished only in accordance with the *Native Title Act* 1993 (Cth). Faithful to the High Court decision, the Act defines native title as:

> The communal, group or individual rights and interests of Aboriginal peoples or Torres Strait Islanders in relation to land or waters, where:
> (a) the rights and interests are possessed under the traditional laws acknowledged, and the traditional customs observed, by the Aboriginal peoples or Torres Strait Islanders; and
> (b) the Aboriginal peoples or Torres Strait Islanders, by those laws and customs, have a connection with the land or waters; and
> (c) the rights and interests are recognised by the common law of Australia.[12]

These rights can include hunting, gathering and fishing rights.[13]

In the original *Native Title Bill* the Commonwealth was proposing that upon determination of native title the title would be vested in a corporation, as is the case for all other land rights legislation throughout Australia. However, in response to

Aboriginal objections, extensive amendments were made permitting native title holders a choice between vesting title in the common law holders themselves or in a body corporate acting as trustee for the common law holders.[14] Some traditional owners of land in the Northern Territory have been objecting to the Commonwealth procedure vesting grants in land trusts managed by land councils. In *Pareroultja v. Tickner*,[15] traditional owners failed in a Federal Court action claiming that the grant of an interest in land to a land trust pursuant to the *Aboriginal Land Rights (Northern Territory) Act* 1976 (Cth) was contrary to the *R.D.A.* and would be an unwarranted extinguishment of native title. Lockhart J. (O'Loughlin and Whitlam JJ. concurring) concluded, 'The grant of land to a land trust does not extinguish native title; it protects it'.[16] Though the traditional owners were refused special leave to appeal to the High Court, Mason C.J. spoke for the full bench when he said, 'we are not to be taken as necessarily agreeing with the conclusion of the Federal Court that the grant of an estate in fee simple to a Land Trust under the *Aboriginal Land Rights (Northern Territory) Act* 1976 (Cth) is consistent with the preservation of native title to the land the subject of that grant'.[17]

3. Validation of Invalid Past Acts

Except for native title holders, all persons holding interests in land in Australia derive their rights from a Crown grant. Undoubtedly most grants were and are valid. Valid grants of freehold and valid leases permitting the lessee the right of exclusive possession undoubtedly extinguish native title. Leases containing reservations permitting continued Aboriginal access for traditional purposes need not extinguish native title, impairing it to the extent of any inconsistency. In the past, the Crown, whether in right of the Commonwealth, a State or Territory, may have purported to make a grant which was invalid. The *Native Title Act* 1993 (Cth) distinguishes between grants which were invalid because the grantor had failed to take into account the existence of native title and grants which are invalid for reasons unrelated to the existence of native title. It is only the former class of invalid grants which are validated by the *Native Title Act* 1993 (Cth). The effect of the validation of these 'past acts' varies.

The *Native Title Act* 1993 (Cth) sets up four categories (A-D) of past invalid grants which failed to account for native title. Freehold grants, commercial leases, agricultural leases, pastoral leases and residential leases are category A-past grants.[18] Once validated, these grants extinguish native title. The affected native title holders are entitled to compensation on just terms payable by the government which made the original grant invalidly and then validated the grant. Any other invalidly granted leasehold interests, except for a mining lease, will upon validation, extinguish native title only to the extent of any inconsistency between the validated leasehold interest and the native title.[19] Any invalidly issued mining lease subject to validation by the *Native Title Act* 1993 (Cth) does not extinguish native title. Native title is merely suspended for the term of the lease. Any invalidly granted interest in land which is not freehold or a lease of any description, does not extinguish native title upon validation. Once again native title is simply suspended for the life of the interest to the extent of any inconsistency.

The net effect of the validation provisions of the *Native Title Act* 1993 (Cth) is that all Crown grants are guaranteed validity regardless of the existence of native title on land at the time the Crown grant was first purportedly granted. There may still be some Crown grants which are invalid for reasons extraneous to the existence of native title. Understandably the *Native Title Act* 1993 (Cth) is silent on the validation of such grants. The effect of their invalidity is determined by the ordinary law of property and trusts.

Residual doubts about the validity of grants made by the Crown since the *R.D.A.* came into effect have been resolved by this comprehensive validation scheme whereby any invalid Commonwealth grants have been validated. The Commonwealth Act permits State Parliaments to legislate, regardless of the *R.D.A.*, such that State governments can validate their grants in similar circumstances. Where such grants are validated thereby extinguishing native title, compensation is payable to the past native title holders. Compensation is payable on just terms.

4. A Regime Governing Future Crown Grants on Native Title Land

The *Native Title Act* 1993 (Cth) is designed to ensure a return to certainty in future dealings with all lands and waters in Australia. Native title holders of land are to be dealt with in the same way as the holders of ordinary title in each jurisdiction. A native title holder in the Australian Capital Territory or at Jervis Bay, is to be treated in the same way, or at least in no more disadvantageous way, than an ordinary lease holder. In all other areas, the native title holder is to be dealt with in a non-discriminatory way, similar to that of an ordinary freeholder.[20] Native title land can no longer be treated as if it were simply vacant Crown land. But neither is such land locked up and frozen from future development. Third parties wanting to deal with native title land have to deal on the same terms and conditions as they would with an ordinary title holder.

Before there has been a determination of native title holders, low impact future acts[21] such as minor licences and permits for activities such as bee keeping can continue. They do not extinguish native title nor do they require the payment of compensation. Once native title is established or determined, such licences or permits could be granted only if they are similarly able to be granted on ordinary title land. This would usually require an agreement with the title holder.[22]

Commercial, agricultural, pastoral and residential leases can be renewed, re-granted, or extended on native title land provided they are subject to the same terms and conditions, and do not create greater proprietary interests than were created by the initial lease.[23] Expired mining leases can be renewed without negotiation only if the miner had a legally enforceable right to renewal.[24] Where renewal of any mining interest is subject to the discretion of the Crown, the miner will have to negotiate with the native title holders.

The distinctive right granted to native title holders by the *Native Title Act* 1993 (Cth) is the right to negotiate when a government party proposes to do a permissible future act to an onshore place which is subject to native title.[25] When the government party proposes to grant, vary or extend a mining lease or to acquire compulsorily native title land under a Compulsory Acquisition Act so as to confer rights on a third party, the negotiation regime comes into play.[26] States do not have to comply with the negotiation process before acquiring compulsorily native title land for public purposes such as infrastructure development. They simply have to act in a non-discriminatory way. Native title holders have no special rights to negotiate and no power to stop activities licensed by government on waters in which they have an interest. When government does license an activity such as fishing, native title holders may engage in the activity 'for the purpose of satisfying their personal, domestic or non-commercial communal needs'.[27]

Native title holders have not been given a veto similar to that enjoyed by Aboriginal land holders in the Northern Territory. Under the principle of non-discrimination, native title holders are guaranteed that government cannot interfere with their native title rights (whether or not they be proprietary) except in the same way in which government has power to interfere with the rights of a freeholder. Developers seeking access to native title land are required to negotiate an agreement. A permissible future act is one which can occur on native title land as it can on freehold land or the equivalent. Any interference with native title by a permissible future act is to be compensated on just terms.

Having given notice of an intention to do a permissible future act, the government may proceed after two months notice if there is no registered native title claimant in relation to any of the land or waters that will be affected by the act.[28] When government is of the view that an act, such as the issue of a prospecting permit, would not directly interfere with the community life of title holders or involve major disturbance to their land, the government may seek determination by an expedited process.[29] If no objection is received within two months, the arbitral body is then to determine whether the act is one attracting the expedited procedure. In all other cases the parties will be guaranteed at least four months to negotiate an exploration agreement, and six months to negotiate a full blown mining agreement. The Commonwealth minister has power to exclude any act from the right to negotiate procedures.[30]

5. Tribunal and Court Processes for Determination of Native Title and Approval of Development Applications

An application for determination of native title may be brought by the relevant Commonwealth, State or Territory minister, any person holding an interest in the land and any person claiming to hold native title, either alone or with others.[31] Applicants seeking determination by the N.N.T.T. make application to the Registrar who accepts it unless of the opinion that the application is frivolous or vexatious or that *prima facie* the claim cannot be made out.[32] Once an application is registered, the Registrar notifies all persons whose interests may be affected. If there are no objections, or if the tribunal is able to mediate all objections, the N.N.T.T. makes a determination which is lodged in the Federal Court for registration on the Native Title Register. If mediation is unsuccessful, the application is determined by the Federal Court which can obtain assistance from assessors.[33]

Native title claimants may choose to have their determination of native title decided by the N.N.T.T. or by an approved State or Territory arbitral body, if there is one. The States and Territories have an option to set up their own arbitral bodies. Should a State or Territory set up a recognised body, it will determine all development applications when native title holders fail to reach agreement with miners or government seeking compulsory acquisition of native title land for the benefit of a third party. There is some latitude permitted to States and Territories to modify the negotiation regime. Alternative State procedures will receive Commonwealth approval only if they provide: appropriate notification to native title holders who then have the right to object; access to mediation; determination by a tribunal with a qualified legal practitioner; and participation in the determination by at least one member of the State arbitral body or the N.N.T.T.[34] Ordinarily a Mining Wardens Court would satisfy these procedures provided the warden was joined by a member of the arbitral body.

Should the parties fail to reach agreement after mediation within the prescribed time limits the arbitral body makes a determination having regard to various factors, including the effect of the proposed act on the native title rights, the way of

life of the native title parties, and any public interest.[35] The
State minister then has the power to overrule the determination
of the recognised State body if the minister considers it 'to be in
the interests of the State'.[36] This right to negotiate is therefore
not a *veto*. Even if the independent tribunal agrees with the
native title holders in their objections to a mining development
proceeding, the State government can override the Aboriginal
objections in the State interest. There would be little prospect of
judicial review of any ministerial override.

The Commonwealth legislation is posited on the presumption
that all States and Territories will set their own tribunals for the
determination of future dealings on native title land. Should a
State decide not to do so, the N.N.T.T. will perform the function,
and the Commonwealth minister will have the power to override
the Tribunal if it is considered to be in the State interest. If
compensation arises because of acquisition of land under a
Compulsory Acquisition Act, the body making the determination
of compensation may have regard to any principles or criteria set
down in such an Act for determining compensation.[37]

6. Fiduciary Duty and the Wik Claim

In *Mabo*, the plaintiffs claimed that the Queensland Government
was under a fiduciary duty, or alternatively bound as a trustee, to
the Meriam people to recognise and protect their rights and
interests in the Murray Islands. Justice Toohey was the only one
of the majority who pursued this issue at any length, concluding
that such a general fiduciary duty was owed by the Crown. He
was elliptical in the way he related the Crown's duty to
parliamentary sovereignty. I have suggested elsewhere[38] that a
valid act of Parliament could never constitute a breach of an
obligation owed by the Crown. Rather it would constitute an
accurate delimitation of the extent of the fiduciary duty according
to law.

On 30 June 1993, about one hundred Aborigines identified as
the Wik peoples, commenced proceedings against the State of
Queensland and Comalco, claiming the *Comalco Act* 1957 (Qld),
agreement and leases were invalid. The Wik plaintiffs have
claimed that the *Comalco Act* 1957 (Qld) is invalid on the

grounds that it purports to grant rights to exploit resources of the sea bed beyond the territorial limits of Queensland, which have at all material times been within the sole preserve of the Commonwealth. Furthermore, they claim the Comalco agreement and the bauxite leases are invalid, being a breach of the Crown's fiduciary duty to the Wik people and having been finalised contrary to the rules of procedural fairness.

Presumably, any provisions of the *Comalco Act* 1957 (Qld) with invalid extra-territorial effect would be severable from, or be able to be read down from, provisions which otherwise would be within power and which would work as an effective limitation on the ambit of any fiduciary duty owed previously by the Crown to the native title holders of onshore lands. The valid provisions of the Act would include the Comalco Agreement's onshore provisions 'having the force of law as though it were a statutory enactment'. For the Wik people to succeed they would have to establish that a fiduciary duty owed by the Crown is a judicially enforceable fetter on the legislative competence of a Parliament whose law making function is not in theory instituted or controlled by the Crown, though of course most Bills are initiated by ministers of the Crown. The Wik people therefore confront major hurdles in establishing their claim. Their claim is not within the confines of the *Mabo* decision. Their claim of fiduciary duty augmented by breach of the rules of procedural fairness even goes beyond the limits set down by Justice Toohey.

Under the *Native Title Act* 1993 (Cth), a law of a State or Territory may validate past acts attributable to the State or Territory if the act was invalidated only by virtue of the existence of native title. Presumably the Wik people are arguing that the Crown owed them a fiduciary duty whether or not native title existed. It is difficult to postulate such a duty owed to indigenous persons in relation to dealings with land when those indigenous persons are not the holders of native title. Justice Toohey envisaged a wide ambit for such a fiduciary duty. In part, he relied upon the writings of Professor Paul Finn. In the light of *Mabo*, Professor Finn has said:

> In Queensland mining arrangements entered into many years ago have been attacked on the ground that they constitute breaches of a

separate, a discrete, fiduciary duty owed by the State to a particular Aboriginal community. This concept of a distinct fiduciary relationship with indigenous peoples raises issues of a complexity which I cannot canvass here. I would, however, venture this much. First, if, as has been suggested, it is based on the bare ground of the vulnerability of our indigenous people to the power of the State, its effect is to perpetuate an offensive paternalism in the State–indigenous people relationship which should have no place in our society. Secondly, if it means no more than that the State has a distinctive responsibility to the indigenous people it is perfectly explicable—but in terms of the general governmental trust embracing all of the people of this country about which I have been speaking. A legacy of *Mabo* is the recognition that Aboriginal communities can and may possess rights not possessed, and, importantly, not able to be possessed, by the non-Aboriginal community. In virtue of this alone they occupy a distinctive place within our community and we properly should recognise this to be so. And what this should mean for our State institutions—Parliaments, Executives, and the like—is that, because as part of our community there is a distinctive class with its own separate rights, the State itself in acting in the interests of all Australian people, must act fairly to that class—to the Aboriginal peoples—where their distinctive interests are affected by any exercise of public power. This can necessitate preferential treatment.

To acknowledge this much as a constitutional imperative of the State and its institutions is to recognise an obligation which has been disregarded callously in our history. But to ask more of the fiduciary idea—and in particular to use it, not to condition how public power is exercised, but rather to deny that power at all—is an attack on the notion of an Australian community which should be resisted for so long as we wish to conceive of ourselves as joined together, despite our differences, in a single nation. I should add that what I have said here is by no means inconsistent with a significant level of self-determination being accorded our indigenous people.[39]

More recently in *Coe v. The Commonwealth*,[40] Mason C.J. once again has left open the question of the extent of any fiduciary duty.

7. The *Racial Discrimination Act* 1975 (Cth) and Special Measures

The preamble of the *Native Title Act* 1993 (Cth) sets out considerations taken into account by the Parliament in enacting the law. The preamble states:

> The law, together with initiatives announced at the time of its introduction and others agreed on by the Parliament from time to time, is intended, for the purposes of ... the *Racial Discrimination Act* 1975, to be a special measure for the advancement and protection of Aboriginal peoples and Torres Strait Islanders...

In the second reading speech the Prime Minister relied upon a number of benefits to explain the categorisation of a special measure:

> Special processes for determining native title; protection of native title rights; just terms compensation for any extinguishment of native title; a special right of negotiation on grants affecting native title land; designation of Aboriginal and Torres Strait Islander organisations to assist claimants; and establishment of a National Land Fund.[41]

A validation scheme would not be so classifiable. In any event the question is academic given that the *Native Title Act* 1993 (Cth), being a later specific Commonwealth statute, to the extent of any inconsistency with the *R.D.A.*, overrides that Act, thereby partially lifting the fetter on State governments and Parliaments being able to discriminate against native title holders on the basis of their race, but only to the extent permitted by the later specific Commonwealth statute. Section 8 of the *R.D.A.* provides that Part II of that Act does 'not apply to, or in relation to the application of, special measures to which paragraph 4 of Article 1 of the Convention applies'. There are some exceptions but they are not relevant to this matter. The relevant paragraph of the Convention states:

> Special measures taken for the sole purpose of securing adequate advancement of certain racial or ethnic groups or individuals requiring such protection as may be necessary in order to ensure such groups or individuals equal enjoyment or exercise of human rights and fundamental freedoms shall not be deemed racial discrimination,

provided, however, that such measures do not, as a consequence, lead to the maintenance of separate rights for different racial groups and that they shall not be continued after the objectives for which they were taken have been achieved.

In September 1993, the Commonwealth Government had issued its outline of proposed legislation suggesting the suspension of the *R.D.A.* saying:

> The Bill will provide that, notwithstanding any other law (including the *Racial Discrimination Act*), the Act or a law of a State or Territory is able to validate past grants affecting native title (and acts and laws) where such grants were in whole or in part invalidated by the combination of the existence of native title and the operation of any law.[42]

It was common ground that there would be payment of compensation to native title holders whose interest in land had been unwittingly extinguished by the issuing of Crown grants since 1975. The outstanding concern had been with the question of procedural fairness and the question of whether the issue of Crown grants over native title land since 1975 would be invalid pursuant to section 9 of the *R.D.A.* This concern was often overstated by commentators comparing native title holders with registered, known freeholders rather than with other unknown, unknowing title holders.

If the Crown has acted in the same way as it would have in relation to any other unknown and unknowing title holder, regardless of their race, the subsequent Crown grants would not be invalidated by section 9 of the *R.D.A.* That section would operate only to invalidate grants made as a result of the Crown's racially discriminatory disregard of Aboriginal rights and interests. Such valid grants made since 1975 would have extinguished or impaired native title. The only matter outstanding would be compensation.

Some commentators have argued that all Crown grants over native title land since 1975 are invalid given that there has been a want of procedural fairness because of ignorance of both government and native title holders about the state of the law; that ignorance impacting only on Aborigines and relating only to a form of title dependent on the racial identity of the title holders. In response to the Federal Government's September outline, the Aboriginal groups proposed a system for 'upfront validation' of land titles 'without suspending the *Racial Discrimination Act*' but with provision for negotiation of dual purpose land use, thereby facilitating co-existence of native title and compensation for any resultant impairment. This proposal was rejected by the Prime Minister in his statement of 18 October 1993.

To put beyond doubt the scope of the *R.D.A.*, the *Native Title Act* 1993 (Cth) provides that the *R.D.A.* does not impact on grants issued between 1975 and 1993.[43] It is not to the point to argue that the validation regime is part of a special measure under section 8 of the *R.D.A.* If the Commonwealth *Native Title Act* 1993 were being enacted and the High Court's *Mabo* decision were given at the same time the *R.D.A.* was passed, there would have been no need for a validation regime. A validation regime to make right Crown grants to non-Aborigines between the time of the *R.D.A.* and the implementation of *Mabo* over a decade later, cannot be for the advancement of Aboriginal native title holders, as they are thereby deprived of the power to negotiate terms and conditions for co-existence of native title.[44]

In *Gerhardy v. Brown*,[45] the High Court considered the South Australian *Pitjantjatjara Lands Rights Act* 1981 and concluded that the key provisions were a special measure pursuant to section 8 and therefore not inconsistent with Part II of the *R.D.A.* With regard to the special measures question, Mason J. said, 'In considering this question we need to recall that the object of legislation of this kind is not merely to restore to an Aboriginal people the lands which they occupied traditionally, but also to provide that people with the means to protect and preserve their culture'.[46] The purpose of a validation regime is, if anything, the reverse. Wilson J. expressed the view that the:

> State Act bears upon its face the clear stamp of a special measure such as is contemplated by the Convention. The emphasis upon traditional ownership and the functions of Anangu Pitjantjatjaraku ... are plainly directed to enabling the Pitjantjatjaras to protect and preserve their culture, a culture which, as the Premier observed in the House of Assembly in the course of the second reading speech 'is still largely intact'.[47]

Brennan J. said, 'A special measure must have the sole purpose of securing advancement'.[48] He was satisfied that:

> The purpose of the *Land Rights Act* is to provide the support - undisturbed and full access to the Pitjantjatjaras' traditional country - with the intention of advancing the Pitjantjatjaras in order to ensure their ability to enjoy and exercise, equally with others, their human rights and fundamental freedoms. That is a purpose of the kind prescribed by Art. 1(4).[49] ... The purpose of securing advancement for a racial group is not established by showing that the branch of government or the person who takes the measure does so for the purpose of conferring what it or he regards as a benefit for the group if the group does not seek or wish to have the benefit. The wishes of the beneficiaries for the measure are of great importance (perhaps essential) in determining whether a measure is taken for the purpose of securing their advancement.[50]

So what if the native title holders say that they do not want the validation regime? Brennan J. does make the point that the characterisation of a special measure depends on a political assessment by a political branch of government and that 'a municipal court must accept the assessment made by the political branch of government which takes the measure'.[51] But he does say the Court needs to determine 'whether the political branch acted reasonably in making its assessment'.[52]

It would be difficult to argue that the political branch of government was acting reasonably in the interests, and for the advancement of native title holders, by legislating a validation regime which extinguishes native title retrospectively granting only compensation. Deane J. said, '[i]f the relevant question were whether it had been shown that the rigid formality of section 19 of the State Act is necessary to achieve a purpose of the kind referred to in Article 1(4) of the Convention, I would be of the view that it had not been shown that it was'.[53] Deane J. could 'see no proper grounds for doubting that [the provisions of section 19] were enacted in good faith for the same purpose as that which characterizes the central provisions of the State Act'.[54] But Deane J. would require some convincing that a regime for extinguishing native title was for the sole purpose of advancing the interests of those native title holders.

There is no way that a court would determine that the validation regime was enacted for the same purpose as the other provisions of the *Native Title Act* 1993 (Cth). The former is purely for the benefit of non-Aboriginal title holders; the latter is for the benefit of Aborigines and developers. Even though Parliament has characterised the validation regime as part of a special measure, the High Court would, if required to determine the issue, rule it not to be. The legislation does not depend for its validity upon such characterisation. If valid, it would simply prevail over the *R.D.A.* to the extent of any inconsistency.

The Government was not prepared to accept a proposed amendment by the Democrats that the preamble of the Act stated 'It is the intention of the Parliament that the *Racial Discrimination Act* 1975 shall prevail over the provisions of this Act'. Neither were they agreeable to an amendment proposed by the Aboriginal negotiators that 'Nothing in this Act authorises any conduct whether legislative, executive or judicial, that is inconsistent with the operation of the *Racial Discrimination Act*'. Section 7(1) provides, 'Nothing in this Act affects the operation of the *Racial Discrimination Act* 1975'. Sub-section 1 is expressed not to affect the validity of past acts by or in accordance with the Act.[55]

8. Western Australia's Attempt to Go It Alone

The Western Australian Parliament passed the *Land (Titles and Traditional Usage) Act* 1993 before the Commonwealth Parliament passed its *Native Title Act* 1993. Under the Western Australian Act, common law native title is replaced by statutory rights of traditional usage which generally are to be 'equivalent in extent to the rights and entitlements that they replace'.[56] The preamble of the Western Australian Act says:

> It is desirable in the interests of all the people of Western Australia, both Aboriginal and non Aboriginal, that those rights be recognised by and derived from the written laws of Western Australia so that those rights can be administered as part of the single system of land titles and land management and in particular, so that appropriate compensation can be provided if those rights are extinguished or impaired.

The original Western Australian Bill, in clause 19(1), contained a provision that 'the existence of rights of traditional usage in relation to land does not create any proprietary rights in, on, above or below the land'. The legislation then proceeded to deal with native title rights and their statutory equivalents as non-proprietary rights and interests. The Western Australian legislation amends the *Mining Act* 1978, the *Land Act* 1933, the *Petroleum Act* 1967, the *Petroleum (Submerged Lands) Act* 1982, the *Petroleum Pipelines Act* 1969, the *Public Works Act* 1902, and the *Pearling Act* 1990, treating the holders of statutory rights of traditional usage in a manner distinct from that accorded to holders of ordinary proprietary titles. In view of section 10 of the *R.D.A.*, all these procedures will have to be appropriately qualified so as to operate in a non-discriminatory way. Presumably the original clause 19(1) was removed in light of legal advice about the effect of section 9 of the *R.D.A.* which would have invalidated the original legislation.

Once it is conceded that native title rights are in some circumstances proprietary, it is necessary that those enjoying statutory rights equivalent to native title rights be treated in a non-discriminatory way when it comes to dealings with their interests. Withdrawing the original clause 19(1) during the course of debate, Premier Richard Court told Parliament:

> As I have stated repeatedly, the primary intention of the Bill is to ensure that the substance of the native title rights is not diminished in the conversion from the common law rights to statutory rights. In this regard whether the rights are legally categorised as common law or statutory, proprietary or personal is not the issue: it is the content, the substance of the rights, which is the essential issue. The High Court recognised this. The six majority judges could not agree whether native title rights held by the Meriam people were proprietary or personal, but they nevertheless agreed on the substance of those rights.[57]

The proposed amendments to the development Acts set out a regime which is designed to ensure that the statutory rights of traditional usage in no way interfere with mining development projects enjoying government approval in much the same way as they did prior to the *Mabo* decision. The Commonwealth has rightly insisted on the need for consultation, independent tribunal review, and ultimate government decision processes. The Western Australian Government has decided to omit any involvement by an independent tribunal and to ensure as far as possible that ministerial discretions are not reviewable in the courts. This is to be achieved by requiring the Commissioner for Aboriginal Planning to determine if there is an Aboriginal group having an interest in land for development purposes. This responsibility has to be cast upon the Commissioner because the Government is opposed to a universal registration and claims system. Presumably some judicial review of the Commissioner's decision to include or exclude Aborigines from the interested group would be possible. The Commissioner then reports to the minister to whom the administration of the *Land (Titles and Traditional Usage) Act* 1993 (WA) is committed. That minister then makes a recommendation to the Minister for Mines.

This dual ministerial role has been designed to ensure as far as possible that the courts could never interfere with what is seen to be a purely political decision which in no way allows an affected Aboriginal group judicial review on the basis of denial of natural justice. The measures designed to ensure the exclusion of judicial review reveal the underlying policy of this legislation. The rights of traditional usage, unlike native title rights, are not to enjoy ungrudging and unambiguous recognition. These rights are to be enjoyed at the Government's pleasure.

The mining provisions of each Act contain a provision that 'any advice, recommendation or certificate of the responsible Minister is not liable to be challenged, reviewed or called in question by a court on account of anything which the responsible Minister has done or failed to do for the purposes of this section' (section 94H (5), *Mining Act* 1978 (WA)). The Minister for Mines even has the power to shorten the statutory period allowed the responsible minister to perform his or her functions. The legislation stipulates that mining wardens are 'not concerned with rights of traditional usage that may be claimed in respect of land to which an application for a mining tenement relates'.[58] As if this were not enough protection for the politicians making non-reviewable decisions regarding rights of traditional usage by Aborigines, the Minister for Mines has power to declare that the responsible minister has no role whatever to play in determining an application for a particular kind of mining tenement, in respect of an area of Crown land, as well as in relation to an application for a particular mining tenement.

Once the Western Australian provisions are put through the non-discrimination sieve of section 10 of the *R.D.A.*, native title holders will be entitled to access to a tribunal similar to that accessible by ordinary freeholders. Given the Western Australian Government's failure to set up an arbitral body or a recognised State body for the mediation and determination of mining applications with an appropriate regime, native title holders in Western Australia will enjoy continued access to the N.N.T.T. for determination of native title claims and development applications. The Commonwealth Act was amended during the Senate stage of debate so as to ensure that the replacement statutory rights in Western Australia would be included in the definition of native title.[59]

9. Queensland's Co-operative Response

At the other end of the spectrum of responses to the Commonwealth legislation is the *Native Title (Queensland) Act* 1993 which has been passed but is yet to be proclaimed.[60] The Queensland Act validates past acts in accordance with the Commonwealth legislation. It provides for the establishment of the Queensland Native Title Tribunal and sets down procedures so as to ensure that the Queensland Native Title Tribunal and the Mining Wardens Courts can be recognised bodies and arbitral bodies for the purpose of the Commonwealth *Native Title Act* 1993.

The Queensland legislation also contains a two year interim procedure for compulsory acquisition of native title land and the ongoing operation of mining legislation in Queensland before definitive registration of claimants and determination of native title holders throughout the State. The owners of land under State *Mining Acts* include the holders of native title who are entitled to every right and privilege enjoyed by other owners of land.[61] The practical difficulty in this interim period will be for miners to determine who are the native title holders so they may extend to them the same rights and privileges as are extended to other owners of land who are registered. Not until a register is complete can a developer be guaranteed immediate certainty about whom to notify and consult.

10. Co-operative Responses by Other Jurisdictions

At the other end of the spectrum of responses to the Commonwealth legislation are the Native Title Acts of Queensland, New South Wales, the Australian Capital Territory and the Northern Territory.[62] These laws validate past acts in accordance with the Commonwealth legislation. They provide either for the use of the Commonwealth Tribunal (as in the Australian Capital Territory and the Northern Territory) or for the establishment of the State Tribunals and set down procedures so as to ensure that the State Tribunal or Land and Environment Court and the Mining Wardens Courts can be recognised bodies and arbitral bodies for the purpose of the Commonwealth *Native Title Act* 1993.

11. Conclusion

On 13 April 1994, special leave to appeal to the High Court was refused in *Pareroultja v. Tickner*.[63] Legal challenges to the validity of the Western Australian and Commonwealth legislation are reserved before the High Court. Though the Western Australian legislation may be valid, its racially discriminatory provisions will be rendered non-discriminatory by the operation of section 10 of the *R.D.A.* To the extent of any inconsistency with the *Native Title Act* 1993 (Cth), the latter provisions will prevail. In so far as the Western Australian Government is not minded to appoint acceptable arbitral bodies, the N.N.T.T. will discharge all appropriate functions in Western Australia. Meanwhile jurisdictions such as Queensland, anxious to legislate and administer the State consistent with the terms of the Commonwealth legislation, will maintain supervision of developments on native title land through their own tribunal system which will be little more than a modified Mining Wardens Court. Presumably all jurisdictions including Western Australia will do likewise once the next round of constitutional challenges is complete. Native title is now part of the Australian legal landscape. The principle of non-discrimination is firmly entrenched in the philosophy of all political parties, Commonwealth legislation and High Court jurisprudence. Land management is accepted as primarily a State responsibility. The Commonwealth has a role in setting appropriate standards for the recognition of Aboriginal rights and interests. Aborigines denied a right of veto of development on their land will enjoy a limited right to negotiate. An efficient and fair system for the registration of native title will be in the interests of developers as much as for the convenience and protection of native title holders.

Notes

1. (1993) Commonwealth Parliamentary Debates 2878 (H. of R.); 16 November 1993.
2. Native title holders of land are guaranteed that future acts can occur on their land only in the same way as such acts would be permitted on ordinary freehold land. By a draftsman's oversight, areas between the high and low water mark were defined as land, not water (*Native Title Act* 1993 (Cth)(hereinafter *N.T.A.*s.253). The Government had proposed that waters be defined to include 'the shore, or subsoil under or airspace above the shore, between high water and low water'. As fishing licences cannot be issued over freehold land, governments will not be able to issue fishing licences between the high and low water marks of native title land. Fishermen will have to negotiate private agreements with the native title holders.
3. Under *N.T.A.* s.40, when an arbitral body has resolved an issue between the parties at the exploration stage, the parties can only seek to vary the decision at the mining stage with leave of the arbitral body. In response to industry concerns, the Government proposed that the arbitral body be able to grant leave only 'if there has been a material change in the circumstances relating to the issue'.
4. Section 25 permits renewal of third party interests in native title land without the need for negotiation with native title holders only if the holder of the interest has a legally enforceable right of renewal. The Government proposed a much wider provision:

   (1) If an act is a future renewal act (defined in subsections (3) and (4)):
      (a) the act is valid; and
      (b) the non-extinguishment principle applies to the act; and
      (c) if any native title holders would be entitled to compensation under subsection 17(2) for the act on the assumption that it was a past act mentioned in that sub-section—the native title holders are entitled to compensation for the act in accordance with Division 5.

   Recovery of compensation
   (2) The native title holders may recover the compensation from:

(a) if the act is attributable to the Commonwealth—the Crown in right of the Commonwealth; or
(b) if the act is attributable to a State or Territory—the Crown in right of the State or Territory.

Future renewal act—options etc.

(3) A future act is a **'future renewal act'** for the purposes of this section if:
   (a) it takes place:
      (i) in exercise of a legally enforceable right created by the making, amendment or repeal of legislation before 1 July 1993 or by any other act done before 1 January 1994; or
      (ii) in giving effect to, or otherwise because of, an offer, commitment, arrangement or undertaking made or given (other than in legislation) in good faith before 1 January 1994, and of which there is written evidence created at or about the time the offer, commitment, arrangement or undertaking was made; and
   (b) it is not the making, amendment or repeal of legislation.

Future renewal act—extensions etc.

(4) A future act (the **'later act'**) is also a **'future renewal act'** for the purposes of this section if:
   (a) an act (the **'earlier act'**) that took place before 1 January 1994 created interests in a person and the later act creates interests in:
      (i) the same person; or
      (ii) another person who has acquired the interests of the first person (by assignment, succession or otherwise);
      in relation to the whole or part of the land or waters to which the earlier act relates; and
   (b) the interests created by the later act take effect before or immediately after the interests created by the earlier act cease to have effect; and
   (c) the interests created by the later act permit activities of a similar kind to those permitted by the earlier act.

The later act was never to create a greater interest than the earlier act. Such an amendment would have ensured that valid interests would have been automatically renewable in the same way as invalid interests validated by native title legislation of the Commonwealth, States or Territories. It would also have permitted governments to honour undertakings made to developers before 1 January 1994 for the grants of future interests.

5. (1992) 175 C.L.R. 1, 42.
6. Dr. J. Hewson, Media Release, 168/93, 18 November 1993.
7. *Ibid.*
8. *Ibid.*
9. (1993) Commonwealth Parliamentary Debates 4544 (H. of R.); 22 December 1993.
10. The Prime Minister, The Hon. P.J. Keating, Second Reading Speech, (1993) Commonwealth Parliamentary Debates 2880 (H. of R.); 16 November 1993.

11. *N.T.A.*s.12. See opinion of Dennis Rose Q.C., Acting Solicitor-General of Australia, (1993) Commonwealth Parliamentary Debates 5438 (Senate); 16 December 1993: 'Issues as to the existence or content of native title in particular cases, in so far as native title would have Commonwealth statutory force, would be matters arising under [a law] made by the Parliament ... within the meaning of section 76(ii) of the Constitution, and so federal jurisdiction could be validly conferred on the High Court and the Federal Court in such matters'.
12. *N.T.A.* s.223(1).
13. *Id.* s.223(2).
14. *Id.* ss.55-60.
15. (1993) 117 A.L.R. 206.
16. *Id.* 216 per Lockhart J.
17. (1993) 117 A.L.R. 206.
18. *N.T.A.* s.229.
19. *Id.* ss.15, 230.
20. *Id.* s.253.
21. Defined *Id.* s.234.
22. *Id.* s.21.
23. *Id.* s.235(7).
24. *Id.* s.25(1).
25. *Id.* Part 2, Division 3, Subdivision B, ss.26-44.
26. *Id.* s.26.
27. *Id.* s.211(2)(b).
28. *Id.* ss. 28, 30.
29. *Id.* ss. 32, 237.
30. *Id.* s.26(3)(b).
31. *Id.* s.61(1).
32. *Id.* s.63(1).
33. *Id.* ss.74, 80-87.
34. *Id.* s.43(2).
35. *Id.* s.39(1).
36. *Id.* s.42.
37. *Id.* s.51(2).
38. F. Brennan, 'Mabo and the Racial Discrimination Act' in J. Flew (ed.), *Essays on the Mabo Decision* (Sydney: Law Book Co, 1993), 86-102.
39. P. Finn, 'The Abuse of Public Power in Australia: Making our Governors Our Servants', Cunningham Lecture, Academy of the Social Sciences in Australia, 16 November 1993.
40. (1993) 68 A.L.J.R. 110.
41. (1993) Commonwealth Parliamentary Debates 2879 (H. of R.); 16 November 1993.
42. Mabo: Outline of Proposed Legislation on Native Title, Commonwealth of Australia, September 1993, para 21.
43. *N.T.A.* ss.11(2), 14(1), 19(1).
44. *Ibid.*
45. (1985) 57 A.L.R. 472.
46. *Id.* 497.
47. *Id.* 504.
48. *Id.* 521.
49. *Id.* 522.
50. *Id.* 521.

51. *Id.* 523-4.
52. *Id.* 524.
53. *Id.* 535.
54. *Ibid.*
55. *N.T.A.* s.7(2).
56. *Land (Titles and Traditional Usage) Act* 1993 (WA) s.7(2).
57. The Premier of Western Australia, R. Court, Legislative Assembly, 18 November 1993.
58. *Mining Act* 1978 (WA) s.94L.
59. *N.T.A.* s.223(3).
60. The only other State to have legislated is Victoria. Its *Land Titles Validation Act* 1993 received royal assent on 17 August 1993. Most provisions are yet to be proclaimed. The New South Wales Government has circulated an 'exposure draft' *Native Titles Bill*. The Northern Territory has passed a *Confirmation of Titles to Land (Request) Act* 1993 and the *McArthur River Project Agreement Ratification Amendment Act* 1993.
61. *Native Title (Queensland) Act* 1993 s.152.
62. *Native Title (Queensland) Act* 1993, *Native Title (New South Wales) Act* 1994, *Native Title Act* 1994 (ACT) and *Validation of Titles and Actions Act* 1994 (NT).
63. (1993) 117 A.L.R. 206, No.S 156 of 1993, 12-13 April 1994.

Constitutional Issues and the Native Title Act, 1993 (Cth)

R.D. Lumb[*]

1. Introduction

The *Native Title Act* was passed by the Federal Parliament in December 1993.[1] The Bill, as passed by the House of Representatives, was amended by the Senate. Some of these amendments were proposed by the Government, others by the Western Australian Greens, and others by the Australian Democrats. The Opposition did not support the Bill at any stage as it took the stance that legislation on the matter of native title was primarily a matter for the States, some of which had already legislated in the area.[2] The legislation does not, therefore, reflect bipartisan support.

In so far as it affects the States, the *Native Title Act* 1993 (Cth) is based on the inconsistency provision of the Constitution, section 109. It attempts to create an inconsistency between its major sections and State legislation *in futuro*,[3] but it also operates retrospectively.[4]

Its major sections in this respect are section 10 (protection of native title), section 11 (prohibition of extinguishment of native title except pursuant to the Act), section 12 (giving the common law of native title the force of a law of the Commonwealth) and sections 22 and 23 (impermissible and permissible future acts). Constitutionally, its general thrust is to invoke the decision of the High Court in *Mabo (No. 1)*[5] (where inconsistency was found to exist between a Queensland Act and the *Racial Discrimination Act* 1975 (Cth)).

The head of power to which the *Native Title Act* 1993 (Cth) relates is section 51(xxvi) generally known as the race power, but

---

[*] Professor of Law, University of Queensland.

it also attempts to 'adopt' the *Racial Discrimination Act* 1975 (Cth).[6] This has the effect of invoking section 8 of the latter Act (which gives effect to article 1(4) of the 'Discrimination Convention'[7]) by treating the *Native Title Act* 1993 (Cth) as a special measure for the advancement of the Aboriginal race.

In *Gerhardy v. Brown*[8] it was held that the source of Commonwealth power for the enactment of the *Racial Discrimination Act* 1975 (Cth) was the external affairs power (section 51(xxix)) and not the race power. Consequently the *Native Title Act* 1993 (Cth) may have the effect of utilizing the external affairs power as a basis for some of its provisions, for example by equalising the treatment of Aboriginals and non-Aboriginals in some cases, but more significantly by granting greater rights to Aboriginals compared with non-Aboriginals in other cases ('reverse discrimination'). However, because it is a later Act, the *Native Title Act* 1993 (Cth) would take precedence over the earlier Act where there was any direct inconsistency. Therefore the major constitutional support for the legislation is to be found in the race power.

Apart from the question of 'characterisation', that is of determining whether the Act comes under the race power, constitutional questions relating to inter-governmental immunities also arise. These include the questions whether section 106, protecting State Constitutions, has been infringed and whether implied federal principles protecting the States, most recently recognised in the *Queensland Electricity Commission* case[9] (including the questions of discriminatory laws and laws of general operation which impair the capacity of the States, or a State, to function as governments) have been breached. An associated question is whether section 12 of the Act in giving the common law, as at 1 July 1993, the force of a law of the Commonwealth is an attempt to fetter the legislative capacity of a State to modify the common law operating within its boundaries.

2. The Race Power

The legislation is to a large extent about 'vacant' Commonwealth and State (or 'government') land. In area, State Crown land far exceeds Commonwealth Crown land. The word 'vacant' is a compendious expression for describing land not already alienated in freehold or leasehold, or set aside and used for public purposes.

The legislation distinguishes between various types of past grants (by establishing certain categories, the major ones extinguishing, the minor ones not extinguishing native title). In relation to past acts, grants in category A (freehold and most major leaseholds) are, in the case of Commonwealth grants, validated, and in the case of State grants, may be validated by State laws.[10] A right of compensation, uncertain in scope, is given to native title holders (as members of groups or corporate bodies).[11] In relation to future dealings, substantial restrictions are imposed (through a court and tribunal system) on the making of grants where native title exists *or* is claimed.

Initially, the question is whether these provisions fall under section 51(xxvi). It is accepted that a law may come under a section 51 head of power even though it also deals with matters falling within the residual powers of the States.[12] The Act deals with native title claims and determinations of such claims.

Native title is defined in terms of the High Court's analysis of that concept in *Mabo (No. 2)*.[13] One holding in that case was that the title is a burden on the radical title of the Crown which existed at the time of settlement or of annexation of a territory to Australia (as in the case of the Torres Strait Islands). Other aspects of the High Court reasoning in *Mabo (No. 2)* are the requirement of a continuing connection with the land by the native group and the recognition of extinguishment of native title by governments.[14]

As stated earlier, the legislation has a major effect on the management of State Crown land (although, strangely, that phrase does not appear in the legislation). Apart from validation of titles, its major impact is in relation to future dealings by States and the Commonwealth with land which is the subject of a determination of native title or of a claim to native title.

Apart from the compensation provisions relating to future dealings, the *Native Title Act* 1993 (Cth) also confers a right on native title holders to sue States for compensation for past acts which may have been invalid because of the existence of native title and have not been validated in accordance with the Act.[15] Other grounds of action are not affected. This raises questions of a potential liability of State Governments to be sued for acts going back to the time of settlement (subject to any Statute of Limitations or equitable defences). A major cause of action would be for breach of fiduciary duty,[16] alleging failure of State and Colonial Governments to fulfil their obligations of good faith to Aboriginal groups in their dealings with land occupied by those groups.

One specific question which arises in relation to the characterisation question is this: do the provisions of the Act amount to an intrusion into the powers of management (including derivation of revenue) over areas of State Crown land which may be subject only to *limited* rights of native usage (more in the nature of a profit à prendre), which are less than freehold ('ordinary title')? If the radical or residual title of a State Crown is subject to regulation to a constitutionally impermissible extent, then the law to that extent could be said to fall outside the race power.

In *Mabo (No. 2)*, several justices of the High Court referred to the Privy Council case of *Amodu Tijani v. Secretary, Southern Nigeria*.[17] The significant passage in the Privy Council's judgment is as follows:

> [The] title ... is prima facie based, not on such individual ownership as English law has made familiar, but on a communal usufructuary occupation, which may be so complete as to reduce any radical right in the Sovereign to one which only extends to comparatively limited rights of administrative interference.[18]

The Judicial Committee was referring to the 'White Cap' lands held by native chiefs in Lagos. In *Mabo (No. 2)* the native title at issue was (basically) the gardening rights of Torres Strait Islanders in the Murray Islands. The nature of the rights of Aboriginals on the mainland is still to be ascertained, but these rights may be of a different nature from those of the groups mentioned above, and could be limited to traditional rights of fishing, hunting and gathering.[19] This raises the question of the capacity of the Commonwealth Parliament under the race power to deal with State Crown land as though a claim of native title eliminated State management powers in relation to such land, or allowed a Commonwealth body to make a determination as to the nature of State powers over the land. The part of the *Native Title Act* 1993 (Cth) affecting future dealings[20] could be construed as having this effect on State land. In these circumstances, the radical or residuary titles of the State Crowns expressed in the concept of management and control, derived initially from Imperial legislation passed at the time of responsible government granting to the Australian colonies legislative power over their 'wastelands'[21] and incorporated in some State Constitution Acts,[22] would not be within the race power because such State management powers are outside the scope of native title.

If it were argued that the title of the State Crown was within the race power as being 'incidental' thereto, such an argument would be met by invoking the principle outlined in the *Second Uniform Tax* case[23] that a Commonwealth head of power cannot be 'stretched' to intrude on the constitutional relations between a State and its own residents. In that case it was held that the taxation power (section 51(ii)) could not be used to modify the relationship between a State and its taxpaying citizens. In relation to State Crown land it can be argued that the race power cannot be used to modify the relationship of the State Crown as manager of its lands, with its citizens, to the extent to which that relationship is not covered by the concept of native title.

However, even if the question of characterisation is decided in favour of the Commonwealth the question still remains whether the legislation breaches any express or implied prohibitions on the exercise of Commonwealth power.

3. Constitutional Prohibitions

(a) Express Prohibitions
Section 106 of the Constitution has the effect of preserving State Constitutions. In the *Australian Railways Union* case[24] the High Court referred to that section as imposing a brake on the power of the Commonwealth Parliament, exercising a section 51 head of power, to intrude upon a topic specifically given to a State Parliament by its own State Constitution. In that case it was recognised that a law enacted pursuant to section 51

(xxxv)—the arbitration power—could not be utilised to impose an obligation on a State to appropriate monies to satisfy an award made by the Commonwealth Arbitration Commission, as this power of appropriating State revenue was a specific power given to the States under their Constitutions.[25] The power of management and control of State Crown land is given to State Parliaments by Imperial legislation or their own Constitution Acts, although this is of course under the *Engineers* principle[26] subject to inconsistent Commonwealth legislation enacted under the race power, but only to the extent to which that legislation deals with 'native title'.

The major 'suspect' sections of the *Native Title Act* 1993 (Cth), in the light of the doctrine of constitutional prohibitions, are section 20(2), which grants a right of compensation to native title holders against States which do not validate past acts under the Commonwealth scheme; section 22, which deals with 'impermissible' acts, these acts being defined to include acts of legislatures;[27] section 23 dealing with 'permissible' future acts; and section 43 which relates to the recognition by a Commonwealth Minister of State systems which give a right to negotiate equivalent to the Commonwealth system.

In one or other aspect, it is strongly arguable that in the light of the *Australian Railways Union* case[28] these sections breach section 106 in relation to a State's management of its radical or residual title (including the revenue derived from it).[29]

(b) Implied Prohibitions

In *Melbourne Corporation v. The Commonwealth*[30] (the *State Banking* case), Dixon J. outlined the principles which prevented the Commonwealth from using a legislative power to place burdens on State functions. He pointed out that the *prima facie* rule is that the power to legislate with respect to a given subject enables the Parliament to make a law which, upon that subject, affects the operations of the States and their agencies. This principle, however, was subject to certain implied limitations or qualifications:

> [To] my mind, the efficacy of the system logically demands that, unless a given legislative power appears from its content, context

or subject matter so to intend, it should not be understood as authorizing the Commonwealth to make a law aimed at the restriction or control of a State in the exercise of its executive authority. In whatever way it may be expressed an intention of this sort is, in my opinion, to be plainly seen in the very frame of the Constitution.[31]

In *Koowarta v. Bjelke-Petersen*,[32] Stephen J. referred to the *Melbourne Corporation* case[33] in these terms:

> There no doubt also exist limitations to be implied from the federal nature of the Constitution and which will serve to protect the structural integrity of the State components of the federal framework, State legislatures and State executives ...[34]

In *Queensland Electricity Commission v. The Commonwealth*,[35] Mason J. summed up the law as follows:

> This review of the authorities shows that the principle is now well established and that it consists of two elements:
>
> (1) the prohibition against discrimination which involves the placing on the States of special burdens or disabilities; and
> (2) the prohibition against laws of general application which operate to destroy or curtail the continued existence of the States or their capacity to function as governments ...
>
> The second element of the prohibition is necessarily less precise than the first; it protects the States against laws which, complying with the first element because they have a general application, may nevertheless produce the effect which it is the object of the principle to prevent.[36]

Mason J. also referred to the *Tasmanian Dam* case[37] where the prohibition was again examined, although in the circumstances of that case the principle was not applied to prevent the application of the *World Heritage Properties Conservation Act 1983* (Cth) to State forestry land. Specifically, Mason J. said that apropos of his own judgment and that of Brennan J. in that case:

> It is against impairment of the capacity of the State to function as a government, rather than against interference with or impairment of any function which a State government undertakes, that this aspect of the prohibition is directed.[38]

In *A.C.T.V. v. Commonwealth*[39] Brennan and McHugh JJ. considered that certain sections of the *Political Broadcasts and Disclosures Act* 1991 (Cth) relating to State elections were invalid because they infringed State Constitutions and the implied prohibition recognised in the *State Banking* case and other cases.[40] It may be argued that the States are not discriminated against by the *Native Title Act* 1993 (Cth) because the Act also binds the Commonwealth Crown. But although the Commonwealth may remove the restrictions imposed on it by passing later inconsistent legislation, the States cannot do the same because of the operation of section 109. In any case the constitutional prohibition, in its reference to discrimination, does not refer to discrimination between governments but between State government and citizen. The regulatory and prohibitory sections of the Act do not apply to other holders of titles, that is freeholders and (most) leaseholders (except in an indirect sense) but single out government title and transactions effected by governments.

There is the further question that sections of the Act which in effect amount to a forced transfer of a State's management rights over its land may be an acquisition of property from a State.[41] If that is the case, the State would be entitled to 'just terms' on the basis of section 51(xxxi).

(c) Fettering the Legislative Capacity of State Parliaments

Section 12 of the *Native Title Act* 1993 (Cth) provides that, subject to the Act, the common law of Australia in respect of native title has, after 30 June 1993, the force of a law of the Commonwealth. Apart from purporting to retrospectively invalidate State legislation (such as the Western Australian native title legislation which received the royal assent before the Commonwealth Act came into force) this section has the effect of preventing State Parliaments from amending the common law on native title as it operates within their boundaries. It has already been stated that the Commonwealth Parliament is not so disabled. In so far as the common law is treated as part of the legal system of the States[42] this section could be regarded as also falling foul of the principle of implied prohibitions directed, as it is, against the legislative power of State Parliaments.[43]

4. Conclusion

It is difficult to escape the conclusion that a number of constitutional problems raised by the *Native Title Act* 1993 (Cth) would have been avoided if a genuine co-operative arrangement (such as has been achieved with the Corporations Law and the Off-shore Settlement schemes) had been entered into by the Commonwealth and State Governments. The rushing of the legislation through the Parliament without such co-operation has weakened the substance and processes of federalism.

Notes

1. No. 110 of 1993. Various sections of the *Native Title Act* 1993 (Cth) raise constitutional questions. The major ones are examined in this article. However questions relating to the exercise of judicial power are not dealt with.
2. *Land Titles Validation Act* 1993 (Vic); *Land (Titles and Traditional Usage) Act* 1993 (WA). See also *Native Title (Queensland) Act* 1993 which adopts the Commonwealth Act or, rather, an earlier version of the Commonwealth Bill. For that reason it has not yet been proclaimed.
3. See, for example, *Native Title Act* 1993 (Cth) (hereinafter referred to as N.T.A.) s.22.
4. See, for example, *id.* ss.11(2), 12, 19(1), 20(2).
5. *Mabo v. State of Queensland* (1988) 166 C.L.R. 186.
6. See *N.T.A.* s.7(1).
7. *The Convention on the Elimination of all Forms of Racial Discrimination* (given effect to by the *Racial Discrimination Act* 1975 (Cth)).
8. (1985) 159 C.L.R. 70.
9. *Queensland Electricity Commission v. Commonwealth* (1985) 159 C.L.R. 192.
10. *N.T.A.* s.15.
11. *Id.* s.20.
12. See *Actors and Announcers Equity Association of Australia v. Fontana Films Pty. Ltd.* (1982) 150 C.L.R. 169, 192 per Stephen J.
13. *Mabo v. Queensland* (1992) 175 C.L.R. 1.
14. See *Coe v. Commonwealth* (1994) 68 A.L.J.R. 110, 119 per Mason C.J.
15. *N.T.A.* s.20(2). For the definition of a past act see especially s.228(2)(b).
16. A claim raised in current proceedings in the Federal Court of Australia known as the *Wik* claim.
17. [1921] 2 A.C. 399.
18. *Id.* 409-10.
19. See *N.T.A.* s.223(1) and (2). *Delgamuukw v. R.*, (B.C.C.A.), (1993) 104 D.L.R. (4d) 470, 520. R.D. Lumb, 'Mabo and Aboriginal Title in Queensland' (1993) 14 *Queensland Lawyer* 15.

20. Part 2 Division 3. This is so particularly with regard to the power of a State to reserve or set aside its land for public purposes (with which the *Native Title Act* 1993 (Cth) interferes).
21. *Waste Lands (Australia) Repeal Act* 1855, 18 & 19 Vict. c.56 s.4 (Vic and NSW), s.5 (SA and Tas), 53 & 54 Vict. c.26, s.3 (WA).
22. *Constitution Act* (Vic) No. 8750 of 1975, s.17. *Constitution Act* (Qld) 1867, ss.30, 40.
23. *Victoria v. Commonwealth* (1957) 99 C.L.R. 575, 614.
24. *Australian Railways Union v. Victorian Railways Commissioners* (1930) 44 C.L.R. 319. See also *Re Tracey, ex parte Ryan* (1989) 166 C.L.R. 518, *A.C.T.V. v. Commonwealth* (1992) 177 C.L.R. 106, 162-4 per Brennan J. and 241-4 per McHugh J.
25. Cf. the *Garnishee* Case (*New South Wales v. Commonwealth*) (1932) 46 C.L.R. 155 where the words 'notwithstanding anything contained in this Constitution or the constitutions of the several states' in s.105A(5) of the Constitution were held to override the State immunity in relation to enforcement of State debts under the Financial Agreement.
26. *Amalgamated Society of Engineers v. Adelaide Steamship Co. Ltd.* (1920) 28 C.L.R. 129.
27. See also *Mabo v. Queensland (No. 1)* (1988) 166 C.L.R. 186, 197 per Mason C.J. on the application of s.107 of the Constitution.
28. (1930) 44 C.L.R. 319.
29. See text accompanying notes 20 and 21.
30. (1947) 74 C.L.R. 31.
31. *Id.* 83. See also *Re State Public Service Federation* (1993) 113 A.L.R. 365, 391, per Mason C.J., Deane and Gaudron JJ.
32. (1982) 153 C.L.R. 168.
33. (1947) 74 C.L.R. 31.
34. *Id.* 216. See also *Queensland Electricity Commission v. Commonwealth* (1985) 159 C.L.R. 192, 217 per Mason J.; *Federal Commissioner of Taxation v. E.O. Farley Ltd.* (1940) 63 C.L.R. 278, 304 per Dixon J.
35. (1985) 159 C.L.R. 192.
36. *Id.* 217.
37. *Commonwealth v. Tasmania* (1983) 158 C.L.R. 1.
38. (1985) 159 C.L.R. 192, 216-7.
39. (1992) 177 C.L.R. 106.
40. *Id.* 162-4, 241-4.
41. Cf. *McClintock v. Commonwealth* (1947) 75 C.L.R. 1.
42. But see *Breavington v. Godleman* (1988) 169 C.L.R. 41, 135 per Deane J.
43. See especially, *Native Title Act* 1993 (Cth) s.211 (requirement of removal of prohibitions on native title holders). See also note 27.

Native Title and International Law

Garth Nettheim[*]

International law was an element that led to the belated recognition and protection by the common law of what has become known as 'native title' in Australia. It was also an element in the protection of native title against action by State and Territory governments, and in the evolution and design of the *Native Title Act* 1993 (Cth). Lastly, international law provides standards by reference to which Australian law may be evaluated.

International Law and Common Law

Prior to 3 June 1992 there had been no judicial recognition of the pre-existing rights of the indigenous peoples of Australia to their lands and resources.[1] The issue had arisen directly for consideration in only one case, *Milirrpum v. Nabalco*,[2] and the response of Blackburn J. in the Supreme Court of the Northern Territory was to deny judicial recognition. He did so on the basis of a number of judicial statements in prior Australian cases and in the Privy Council,[3] and on the basis of supposed distinctions, in the circumstances of British colonisation, between Australia and other colonies in which pre-existing rights had been acknowledged. In *Mabo v. Queensland (No. 2)*[4] the High Court, in its first opportunity directly to address the issues, held by a six to one majority that the common law of Australia does accommodate and protect such native title, subject to the power of governments to extinguish native title by subjecting the land to inconsistent grants to others or to inconsistent public uses.

International law was influential in the decision in two principal ways. Members of the High Court noted the close correlation between, on the one hand, principles of English

---

[*] Professor of Law and Chair, Aboriginal Law Centre, University of New South Wales.

common law concerning the legal regime operating within new British colonies and, on the other hand, the principles of international law concerning acquisition by European powers of sovereignty over colonies. The international law principles concerning acquisition of sovereignty by 'discovery' and 'occupation' were linked to the classification in English common law of some colonies as 'settled', as distinct from colonies acquired by 'conquest' or 'cession'.[5]

Within the common law it proved necessary for the High Court to disentangle questions of the acquisition of British sovereignty over the Australian colonies (which it described as non-justiciable within the Australian court system) from questions as to the legal consequences of that acquisition of sovereignty for the pre-existing land rights of the existing inhabitants. It was also necessary to distinguish doctrines of international law from doctrines of common law. In particular, while the international law concept of *terra nullius* had been extended to apply to territories inhabited by 'backward peoples' so as to permit acquisition of sovereignty by 'discovery' and 'occupation', the High Court held that such an extension did not, in the common law, require or justify disregard for the territorial rights of the prior inhabitants.[6]

Modern international law was also directly relevant in assisting the High Court majority to choose between the long accepted reading of Australian common law as not accommodating native title and an alternative reading which would accord more closely with the common law as developed in other former British colonies. While their Honours were concerned lest recognition of native title would 'fracture a skeletal principle of our legal system',[7] their conclusion was that native title could be recognized on terms which would avoid any such drastic consequence. Brennan J. in particular was assisted by reference to modern international human rights standards, particularly standards against discrimination on the basis of race.

> Whatever the justification advanced in earlier days for refusing to recognize the rights and interests in land of the indigenous inhabitants of settled colonies, an unjust and discriminatory doctrine of that kind can no longer be accepted. The expectations of the

international community accord in this respect with the contemporary values of the Australian people. The opening up of international remedies to individuals pursuant to Australia's accession to the Optional Protocol to the International Covenant on Civil and Political Rights ... brings to bear on the common law the powerful influence of the Covenant and the international standards it imparts.

The common law does not necessarily conform with international law, but international law is a legitimate and important influence on the development of the common law, especially when international law declares the existence of universal human rights. A common law doctrine founded on unjust discrimination in the enjoyment of civil and political rights demands reconsideration. It is contrary both to international standards and to the fundamental values of our common law to entrench a discriminatory rule which, because of the supposed position on the scale of social organization of the indigenous inhabitants of a settled colony, denies them a right to occupy their traditional lands.[8]

While international human rights standards assisted the High Court majority to conclude that Australian common law does recognize and protect surviving native title, the recognition was on terms that also acknowledged the power of governments to extinguish that title,[9] and to do so without compensation.[10] Had *Mabo v. Queensland (No. 2)* stood alone there would have been nothing to prevent Australian governments from continuing to extinguish native title without compensation as they and their predecessors had done over the previous two centuries.

International Law and the Racial Discrimination Act

Mabo v. Queensland (No. 2) does not stand alone and needs to be read with *Mabo (No. 1)*[11] in which a majority of the High Court held that 1985 Queensland legislation designed to extinguish any surviving native title in the outer Torres Strait Islands was ineffective because of the *Racial Discrimination Act 1975* (Cth) (hereinafter referred to as the *R.D.A.*) section 10(1). The *R.D.A.* had been enacted to authorise Australian ratification of the *International Convention on the Elimination of All Forms of Racial Discrimination*, and it implemented in Australian law the major obligations of State Parties to that Convention.[12] In particular, the Queensland Act was seen as discriminating on the basis of race in relation to rights in Article 5(a) of the Convention:

(v) The right to own property alone or in association with others.
(vi) The right to inherit.

Their Honours also referred to the *Universal Declaration of Human Rights*, Article 17:

1. Everyone has the right to own property alone as well as in association with others.
2. No one shall be arbitrarily deprived of his property.

The combination of the subsequent affirmation of native title in *Mabo (No. 2)* and the *R.D.A.* as applied in *Mabo (No. 1)* thus immeasurably strengthened the legal position of native title against action by State and Territory governments. However, it would do so only as long as the federal 'safety net' provided by the *R.D.A.* was maintained. The efficacy of that federal 'safety net' was under threat during the course of the 'Mabo debate' in 1993.[13]

The *R.D.A.* commenced operation on 31 October 1975. *Mabo (No. 2)* was decided on 3 June 1992. Actions by governments between those dates, particularly grants of interest over land, may have been invalid if, at the time, there was surviving native title over the same land. State and Territory governments and industry groups called on the Commonwealth Government to legislate to validate doubtful titles, and, for this purpose, to displace the operation of the *R.D.A.* Aboriginal and Torres Strait Islander representatives sought to defend native title as far as possible and, for this purpose, to minimise any displacement of the *R.D.A.* They were substantially successful.[14]

The eventual outcome was the *Native Title Act* 1993 (Cth) which set out: (1) to recognize and protect native title; (2) to validate, and to authorise State and Territory legislatures to validate, past actions which would have been invalid because of the existence of native title; (3) to set up expeditious processes for determining the existence of native title and/or assessing compensation; and (4) to provide that future dealings with native title land should be on the same basis as dealings with freehold title land, with an additional 'right to negotiate' in respect of mining proposals and some compulsory acquisition proposals.

The *Native Title Act* 1993 (Cth) also provides for a national fund to support purchases of land on behalf of the vast majority of indigenous Australians who have no prospect of asserting native title. The *Native Title Act* 1993 (Cth) contemplates complementary State and Territory legislation. Most States and Territories are proceeding to enact such legislation.[15] Western Australia has chosen, instead, to enact its own legislation, extinguishing native title and substituting much weaker statutory 'rights of traditional usage'.[16] The Western Australian State Act is under constitutional challenge in the High Court by Aboriginal organizations. That State is itself challenging the validity of the *Native Title Act* 1993 (Cth). The actions were listed together for argument in the High Court in September 1994.[17]

International Law and the Native Title Legislation

How does the new regime of common law and native title legislation conform to international law?

The general body of international human rights law is very clear in opposing discrimination on the basis of race. The norm against discrimination on this basis is articulated in the *Charter of the United Nations* itself, in Article 2 of the *Universal Declaration of Human Rights*, in Article 2(2) of the *International Covenant on Economic Social and Cultural Rights*, in Article 2(1) of the *International Covenant on Civil and Political Rights*, and, of course, in the *International Convention on the Elimination of All Forms of Racial Discrimination*. Australia has ratified the two Covenants and the Convention. In addition, it is considered by many that the norm against discrimination on the basis of race has now become established as a principle of customary international law.[18]

While the two Covenants do not expressly cover the right to own property, the *Universal Declaration* does and so does the *International Convention on the Elimination of All Forms of Racial Discrimination*. As noted, these instruments provided the primary basis for the invalidation, via the *R.D.A.*, of Queensland legislation in *Mabo (No. 1)*. None of these instruments deals specifically with indigenous people though, of course, as individuals they are as entitled as others to the full range of human rights. Most indigenous peoples, however, combine a collective approach to land holding and land use together with a much more holistic relationship to the land itself. The need to accommodate the special vulnerability of the world's indigenous peoples has led to the evolution of more specific international standards (just as many national governments have developed special legislation or agreements for indigenous peoples).

The International Labour Organization (hereinafter referred to as the ILO) in 1989 adopted a new Convention Number 169 concerning 'Indigenous and Tribal Peoples in Independent Countries'. (Australia is considering whether to ratify the Convention.) Part II of the Convention deals with Land, and comprises Articles 13–19, the texts of which are set out in Appendix 1. The United Nations is also beginning to develop standards through the work over several years of the Working Group on Indigenous Populations. At its twelfth Session in July 1994, the Working Group completed consideration of its Draft Declaration on the Rights of Indigenous Peoples. The Draft Declaration, as it emerged from the 1993 Session, contains a number of provisions about land and resources which are set out in Appendix 2.

Both instruments require recognition of the special significance of land for indigenous peoples (ILO 13; UN 25). Australian law recognizes this special significance in a number of ways under land rights legislation,[19] heritage legislation[20] and the common law principles enunciated in *Mabo (No. 2)*. Similar recognition is found in provisions of the native title legislation (Commonwealth, State and Territory) providing an additional 'right to negotiate' in respect of certain future acts, criteria and processes for arbitral decisions concerning proposals for such future acts, and criteria and processes for determination of native title and compensation.

ILO Number 169, Article 14(2) and (3) declares a duty on State Parties to identify indigenous peoples' lands, to protect their rights and to establish adequate procedures to resolve land claims. Australian law did not meet these standards, except for the variable patchwork of land rights Acts, prior to the decision of the High Court in *Mabo (No. 2)*. The native title Acts now provide even more 'adequate' procedures to resolve land claims, to identify the lands of indigenous Australians and to guarantee effective protection. ILO 14(1) and UN 26 both require recognition of indigenous ownership, occupation and use, on indigenous terms. This is largely achieved by some land rights Acts, *Mabo (No. 2)* and native title Acts.

Both instruments require protection against unauthorised intrusion on indigenous peoples' lands (ILO 18; UN 26). This is generally the position under most land rights Acts, *Mabo (No. 2)* and the native title Acts. Both instruments require recognition of indigenous peoples' own laws as to transmission of rights in respect of land among their own members (ILO 17(1); UN 25 and 26). This is achieved in some land rights Acts, *Mabo (No. 2)* and native title Acts. Both instruments require protection of indigenous peoples' lands from alienation to non-indigenous peoples or at least require consultation (ILO 17(2) and (3); UN 25 and 26). This is achieved in Australian law under most land rights Acts, *Mabo (No. 2)* and the native title Acts.

Of course, much of the land of indigenous peoples throughout the world has been taken from them in the past. While the international instruments look mainly to the future, some of their provisions may be relevant to past dispossession. Both instruments provide firmly against removal of indigenous peoples from their land other than with their free and informed consent, after agreement on just and fair compensation, and where possible, with the option of return (ILO 16; UN 10). Such rights are now substantially respected in Australian law. However, any proposal to remove indigenous Australians from their lands is likely to be at the instigation of governments. Governments may repeal their own legislation and override common law principles. State and Territory governments are limited only by any superior Commonwealth legislation, but the Commonwealth is limited only by the constitutional requirement of 'just terms' compensation concerning any acquisition of property. More specific constitutional recognition, as in Canada, is desirable.

ILO 19 speaks of provision of additional land for indigenous peoples who may need it, and also of provision of means to develop indigenous peoples' lands. This requirement — and, to some extent, the restitution of lost lands or compensation — may be accommodated by funding for purchase of lands for indigenous peoples. Funds for such purposes have been available to the Aboriginal and Torres Strait Islander Commission (ATSIC), and to the New South Wales Aboriginal Land Council. A nationwide scheme is to be established under the *Native Title Act* 1993 (Cth) provision in section 210 for a National Aboriginal and Torres Strait Islander Land Fund.[21]

In light of the strongly articulated antagonism of sections of the Australian mining industry to any control by indigenous peoples over mineral exploration and exploitation, it is relevant that both instruments affirm the rights of indigenous peoples to the natural resources pertaining to their lands and their right to participate in the use, management and conservation of these resources (ILO 15; UN 30). Where the State retains ownership of such resources, ILO 15(2) requires consultation. UN 30 requires consent. Both instruments require compensation. Australian law now generally requires consultation but stops short of requiring consent, as even the so-called 'veto' under the *Aboriginal Land Rights (Northern Territory) Act* 1976 (Cth) may be overridden by a proclamation of the Governor-General in the national interest. Detail in other land rights Acts (and in mining and other legislation) varies. The common law as declared in *Mabo (No. 2)* had nothing to say about resources but, when combined with the *R.D.A.*, would require that native title holders have the same rights and protection as holders of other forms of title. This is now expressly prescribed in the *Native Title Act* 1993 (Cth),[22] and an additional 'right to negotiate' is provided.[23]

Conclusion

If Australia had not reversed the non-recognition of native title, in *Mabo (No. 2)*, and if it had not supported that reversal by the enactment of national native title legislation, the Government would have been vulnerable to adverse commentary in international fora for the denial of generally applicable human rights standards. With the *Mabo (No. 2)* decision and the *Native Title Act* 1993 (Cth) the nation is close to compliance even with the more specific requirements of ILO Convention 169 and the current language of the UN Draft Declaration. If a future Commonwealth government should elect to dismantle this régime, international odium would be inevitable.

APPENDIX 1

International Labour Organization Convention No 169 concerning Indigenous and Tribal Peoples in Independent Countries[24]

Article 13

1. In applying the provisions of this Part of the Convention governments shall respect the special importance for the cultures and spiritual values of the peoples concerned of their relationship with the lands or territories, or both as applicable, which they occupy or otherwise use, and in particular the collective aspects of this relationship.
2. The use of the term 'lands' in Articles 15 and 16 shall include the concept of territories, which covers the total environment of the areas which the peoples concerned occupy or otherwise use.

Article 14

1. The rights of ownership and possession of the peoples concerned over the lands which they traditionally occupy shall be recognised. In addition, measures shall be taken in appropriate cases to safeguard the right of the peoples concerned to use lands not exclusively occupied by them, but to which they have traditionally had access for their subsistence and traditional activities. Particular attention shall be paid to the situation of nomadic peoples and shifting cultivators in this respect.
2. Governments shall take steps as necessary to identify the lands which the peoples concerned traditionally occupy, and to guarantee effective protection of their rights of ownership and possession.
3. Adequate procedures shall be established within the national legal system to resolve land claims by the peoples concerned.

Article 15

1. The rights of the peoples concerned to the natural resources pertaining to their lands shall be specially safeguarded. These rights

include the right of these peoples to participate in the use, management and conservation of these resources.
2. In cases in which the State retains the ownership of mineral or sub-surface resources or rights to other resources pertaining to lands, governments shall establish or maintain procedures through which they shall consult these peoples, with a view to ascertaining whether and to what degree their interests would be prejudiced, before undertaking or permitting any programmes for the exploration or exploitation of such resources pertaining to their lands. The peoples concerned shall wherever possible participate in the benefits of such activities, and shall receive fair compensation for any damages which they may sustain as a result of such activities.

Article 16

1. Subject to the following paragraphs of this Article, the peoples concerned shall not be removed from the lands which they occupy.
2. Where the relocation of these peoples is considered necessary as an exceptional measure, such relocation shall take place only with their free and informed consent. Where their consent cannot be obtained, such relocation shall take place only following appropriate procedures established by national laws and regulations, including public inquiries where appropriate, which provide the opportunity for effective representation of the peoples concerned.
3. Whenever possible, these peoples shall have the right to return to their traditional lands, as soon as the grounds for relocation cease to exist.
4. When such return is not possible, as determined by agreement or, in the absence of such agreement, through appropriate procedures, these peoples shall be provided in all possible cases with lands of quality and legal status at least equal to that of the lands previously occupied by them, suitable to provide for their present needs and future development. Where the peoples concerned express a preference for compensation in money or in kind, they shall be so compensated under appropriate guarantees.
5. Persons thus relocated shall be fully compensated for any resulting loss or injury.

Article 17

1. Procedures established by the peoples concerned for the transmission of land rights among members of these peoples shall be respected.

2. The peoples concerned shall be consulted whenever consideration is being given to their capacity to alienate their lands or otherwise transmit their rights outside their own community.

3. Persons not belonging to these peoples shall be prevented from taking advantage of their customs or of lack of understanding of the laws on the part of their members to secure the ownership, possession or use of land belonging to them.

Article 18

Adequate penalties shall be established by law for unauthorised intrusion upon, or use of, the lands of the peoples concerned, and governments shall take measures to prevent such offences.

Article 19

National agrarian programmes shall secure to the peoples concerned treatment equivalent to that accorded to other sectors of the population with regard to:

(a) the provision of more land for these peoples when they have not the area necessary for providing the essentials of a normal existence, or for any possible increase in their numbers;

(b) The provision of the means required to promote the development of the lands which these peoples already possess.

APPENDIX 2

Working Group on Indigenous Populations United Nations Draft Declaration on the Rights of Indigenous Peoples

Article 10

Indigenous peoples shall not be forcibly removed from their lands or territories. No relocation shall take place without the free and informed consent of the indigenous peoples concerned and after agreement on just and fair compensation and, where possible, with the option of return.

Article 25

Indigenous peoples have the right to maintain and strengthen their distinctive spiritual and material relationship with the lands, territories, waters and coastal seas and other resources which they have traditionally owned or otherwise occupied or used, and to uphold their responsibilities to future generations in this regard.

Article 26

Indigenous peoples have the right to own, develop, control and use the lands and territories, including the total environment of their lands, air, waters, coastal seas, sea-ice, flora and fauna and other resources which they have traditionally owned or otherwise occupied or used. This includes the right to the full recognition of their laws, traditions and customs, land-tenure systems and institutions for the development and management of resources, and the right to effective measures by states to prevent any interference with, alienation of or encroachment upon these rights.

Article 27

Indigenous peoples have the right to the restitution of the lands, territories and resources which they have traditionally owned or otherwise occupied or used, and which have been confiscated, occupied, used or damaged without their free and informed consent. Where this is not possible, they have the right to just and fair compensation. Unless otherwise freely agreed upon by the peoples concerned, compensation shall take the form of lands, territories and resources equal in quality, size and legal status.

Article 30

Indigenous peoples have the right to determine and develop priorities and strategies for the development or use of their lands, territories and other resources, including the right to require that States obtain their free and informed consent prior to the approval of any project affecting their lands, territories and other resources, particularly in connection with the development, utilization or exploitation of mineral, water or other resources. Pursuant to agreement with the indigenous peoples concerned, just and fair compensation shall be provided for any such activities and measures taken to mitigate adverse environmental, economic, social, cultural or spiritual impact.

Notes

1. There had been some legislative recognition of native title in several jurisdictions, notably through the *Aboriginal Land Rights (Northern Territory) Act* 1976 (Cth), the *Pitjantjatjara Land Rights Act* 1981 (SA), the *Maralinga Tjarutja Land Rights Act* 1984 (SA), the *Aboriginal Land Act* 1991 (Qld) and the *Torres Strait Islander Land Act* 1991 (Qld).
2. (1971) 17 F.L.R. 141.
3. *Attorney-General (NSW) v. Brown* (1847) 1 Legge 312; *Cooper v. Stuart* (1889) 14 App. Cas. 286; *Williams v. Attorney-General (NSW)* (1913) 16 C.L.R. 404; *Randwick Corporation v. Rutledge* (1959) 102 C.L.R. 54. Such statements were characterised as *obiter dicta* in *Mabo v. Queensland (No. 2)* (1992) 175 C.L.R. 1, 103-104 per Deane and Gaudron JJ.
4. (1992) 175 C.L.R. 1.
5. *Id.* 32 per Brennan J., 77-78 per Deane and Gaudron JJ.
6. *Id.* 31–40, 43–45 per Brennan J.; 78-83 Deane and Gaudron JJ.; 179-182 Toohey J.
7. *Id.* 29-30, 43 per Brennan J.; also 104 Deane and Gaudron JJ.
8. *Id.* 42 per Brennan J.
9. *Id.* 63-71, 75-76 per Brennan J.; 89–90, 110–112, 116–118 Deane and Gaudron JJ.; 192–198 Toohey J.
10. *Id.* 15-16 per Mason C.J. and McHugh J.
11. *Mabo v. Queensland* (1988) 166 C.L.R. 186.
12. The validity of key sections of the *R.D.A.* had earlier been upheld by the High Court in *Koowarta v. Bjelke–Petersen* (1982) 153 C.L.R. 168 as an exercise of the Commonwealth Parliament's legislative power with respect to 'external affairs' under the Constitution s.51(xxix).
13. For accounts of that debate, see Dr J. Gardiner–Garden, Background Paper No 23, 1993 'The *Mabo* debate — a chronology' (Department of the Parliamentary Library, Parliament House, Canberra); Tim Rowse, 'How we got a Native Title Act' (1993) 65 *Australian Quarterly* 111.
14. G. Nettheim, 'The Uncertain Dimensions of Native Title' (1993) 65 *Australian Quarterly* 55, 59–62.
15. *Native Title (Queensland) Act* 1993 (Qld); *Validation of Titles and Actions Act* 1994 (NT); *Native Title (New South Wales) Act* 1994 (NSW).
16. *Land (Titles and Traditional Usage) Act* 1993 (WA).
17. *The State of Western Australia v. Commonwealth of Australia; Biljabu & Ors v. The State of Western Australia; The Wororra Peoples & Ors v. The State of Western Australia.*
18. *Koowarta v. Bjelke–Petersen* (1982) 153 C.L.R. 168, 220-221 per Stephen J.; 234-235 Mason J.
19. For example, various provision of the *Aboriginal Land Rights (Northern Territory) Act* 1976 (Cth).
20. For example, the *Aboriginal and Torres Strait Islander Heritage Protection Act* 1984 (Cth).
21. New legislation to replace s.210 was introduced in the Commonwealth Parliament in June 1994 - the *ATSIC Amendment (Indigenous Land Corporation and Land Fund) Bill*, 1994.
22. N.T.A. ss. 23, 235, 240 and other provisions.
23. *Id.* Part 2, Division 3, Subdivision B.
24. (1989) 28 International Legal Materials 1382, 1387-1388.

Mabo and the Miners — *ad infinitum?*

J.R.S. Forbes*

In the previous article '*Mabo* and the Miners'[1] I considered implications of the *Mabo* decision[2] for the natural resources industries. These points were made: that the decision was judicial legislation which could scarcely operate without some normal statute-making; that the concepts of native custom and continuing connection with land were vague and manipulable; that *Mabo* probably did not affect Crown title to minerals; and that 'expert' as well as 'lay' evidence in such cases may be of dubious weight and disproportionately available to claimants. At the time of the first article '*Mabo* and the Miners'[3] almost nothing about *Mabo* in practice was known, and even now (in 1994) most of the legal, economic, fiscal and curial realities remain to be revealed. Probably *Mabo* was never meant to be more than an impulse to legislators to legislate, although Queensland[4] and several other States already had 'land rights' laws in place. The complexities of the *Native Title Act* 1993 (Cth) are virgin territory. Present predictions will no doubt have to be modified in the light of unpredictable events.

Sequelae for the High Court

Mabo has provoked criticism of the High Court for sudden and excessive judicial legislation. As a former Federal Court judge puts it: 'The court has constructed, from really nothing, a completely new doctrine'.[5] Critics claim that the Court has compromised its judicial role and there have been calls for closer scrutiny of High Court appointments in future. Other critics have focused upon the (self-described) 'emotive' language of Deane and Gaudron JJ.[6] which would have been better left to propagandist politicians or lobbyists. However, it was not entirely novel. In 1983 Gaudron J.'s predecessor spoke *ex cathedra* of

---

* Reader in Law, University of Queensland.

'unprovoked aggression, conquest, pillage, rape, brutalisation [and] attempted genocide' in the history of Aboriginal affairs.[7] A few judicial checks and balances have recently appeared. A claim of 'genocide' in a '*Mabo*-style' action claiming a large portion of New South Wales was struck out by Mason C.J.,[8] and in a similar case in the Queensland Supreme Court a judge pruned the list of defendants, observing that he 'could understand [Premier] Goss being offended at being named as a mass murderer'.[9]

The *Native Title Act* 1993 (Cth) aside, the most striking sequel to *Mabo* was a remarkable effort by Chief Justice Mason to defend that decision in particular and judicial legislation in general. (One wonders what the reaction would have been if the dissenting judge, Dawson J., had toured the country expounding *his* view of the proper limits of judicial power.) The Chief Justice defended the decision on two grounds. The first defence was that some degree of judicial legislation is part and parcel of the common law. This truism was adorned with heavy patronage of anyone so 'ignorant'[10] or so addicted to 'fairy tales'[11] as to question it. However, the Chief Justice ignored the real issue, namely the difference between incremental development over many years and a sudden, major *volte-face*.[12] Not all commentators missed the logical leap: 'Of course judges make law. Even the most conservative lawyer accepts that. [But there is a vast difference between] an evolutionary process [and] a sudden or unexpected break'.[13] Another protested: 'Each time a court applies a principle to new facts it is to a degree developing the law, but sweeping new proclamations of policy ... that require Acts of Parliament to put them into effect are quite outside the judicial function'.[14] The Chief Justice's second defence is more intriguing: 'I think that in some circumstances, governments ... prefer to leave the determination of controversial questions to the courts rather than [to] ... the political process. *Mabo* is an interesting example'.[15] Unfortunately we are not told how the legislative judge decides that government has 'left it' to him or her. But can the unspoken thought-process be other than this: 'Parliament has not legislated. I think it should have. So I will'?

The Chief Justice's retrospectives did not deal with complaints[16] that *Mabo* contains sweeping *dicta*[17] about native title on the entire Australian continent despite the facts: that there was no such issue before the Court; that there was no proper evidence about the mainland;[18] and that several parties affected were not joined in the action.[19] These unusual aspects of *Mabo* raise an incidental but not unimportant question: in abolishing *terra nullius* does *Mabo* also repeal pre-existing axioms of natural justice? It is at once piquant and reassuring that one of the defects found by Mason C.J. in the *Wiradjuri Claim* was a failure to join all interested parties.[20]

The Federal *Native Title Act* 1993

As the first article '*Mabo* and the Miners'[21] predicted, the Commonwealth felt compelled (or encouraged) to legislate about *Mabo*, and in some respects to extend it. The decision itself contains just one fleeting reference to mining[22] but the *Native Title Act* 1993 (Cth) selects mining titles for special attention. Alone among the major Crown grants they do not extinguish native title.[23] (Where a residence has been built upon a pre-1994 mining lease the residence area may be 'dissected' and exempted from the 'non-extinguishment' principle[24] but this does not apply to land occupied by other buildings or improvements.)

The *Native Title Act* 1993 (Cth) is non-committal about Crown title to minerals, merely saying that 'a State may confirm any existing ownership of natural resources' provided that it does not thereby impair competing native title.[25] Patently, this does not resolve the issue but for reasons given in the earlier article '*Mabo* and the Miners'[26] it is submitted that if native title to minerals ever existed, it was extinguished long before the enactment of the *Racial Discrimination Act* 1975 (Cth).[27] However, there are at least two actions pending which include claims to minerals - the Wik claim against Comalco and other parties in the Federal Court[28] and an action by the Burri Gubbi group in the High Court.[29] Whether native title to minerals exists or not, new developments have to contend with the 'right to negotiate' and compensation provisions in sections 26–54 of the Act.[30] Native title holders *and claimants* normally have four months to negotiate with an intending explorer, and six months with an intending lessee.[31] In return for their consent they may seek payments based on income or profits of the venture.[32] If four (or six) months elapse without agreement either party may ask the Native Title Tribunal to arbitrate. The Tribunal may approve the proposal, disallow it, or allow it upon conditions set by the Tribunal.[33] The broad statutory guidelines for making these decrees include seven items of primarily Aboriginal concern.[34] The Tribunal is to 'take all reasonable steps' to decide within a further four (or six) months.[35] As backlogs develop, Tribunal members may well persuade themselves that it is not 'reasonable' to expect a decision within those time limits. Possibilities of capitulation by would-be developers aside, present estimates of the additional delay vary between twelve and twenty-four months.[36] Commonwealth spokesmen are at pains to point out that the 'right to negotiate' is not a veto, but it remains to be seen whether this is a distinction without a difference. The President of the Tribunal has already advertised the fact that, irrespective of proof, native title can effectively be obtained by registered agreement or by default.[37] Aboriginal interests are still pressing for a veto *strictu sensu*.[38]

A decision of the Tribunal may be set aside by the minister on public interest grounds[39] but the special interest politics which would inevitably besiege such a decision are a strong deterrent. In the absence of a more or less voluntary agreement a successful explorer must run the 'right to negotiate' gauntlet twice—first, when seeking an exploration licence, and again when applying for a mining lease, by which time the objectors' visions of a profit share will be more sharply focused.

The renewal of a mining tenement would not be caught by the 'right to negotiate' if renewal were an 'option or right ... created by' the original concession.[40] But renewal of mining titles is generally a matter of *discretion*.[41] More pertinent, then, is section 228(4) which deems a renewal to be a 'past act' (and so exempt from the 'right to negotiate') if it covers no new land,[42] if there is no time lapse between the old and new terms, and if the activities allowed by the renewal are 'of a similar kind to those permitted' originally. Those who rely upon this provision should beware of 'tacking on' new areas or significantly different conditions, as sometimes occurs in mining practice. While State laws allow conditions to be varied upon renewal[43] there may now be a serious question whether the revised terms are sufficiently 'similar [in] kind' to escape the 'negotiation' process.

Notwithstanding recent revivals of Rousseau's romantic State of Nature[44] and claims of mystical attachments to land there are distinct signs that commercial considerations will enliven 'rights to negotiate' under Part 2 Division 3 of the *Native Title Act* 1993 (Cth).[45] In the Northern Territory the Jawoyn and the Dominion Mining Ltd. have become joint venturers, as have Mount Isa Mines Ltd. and a subsidiary of the Aboriginal and Torres Strait Islanders' Commission in the much larger McArthur River project.[46] A Jawoyn representative boasted of using the 'big stick' of *Mabo* in his negotiations.[47] Such blandishments may render proof of native title to minerals unnecessary.

Mining companies have been warned to confine negotiations to the 'big unions' of Aboriginal affairs.[48] Bureaucratic nature being what it is, it will not be surprising if an oligopoly of 'native title brokers'[49] commends itself to the central Government[50] although some native groups in the Northern Territory have challenged the hegemony of the Central and Northern Land Councils.[51] In one instance[52] it was necessary to obtain a Federal Court order directing a Land Council to provide legal aid to a tribe of whose claim the Council did not approve. So far remarkably little has been heard about ensuring that all title holders receive, equitably and efficiently, a proper share of the government grants, compensation and other fruits of the native title movement. Some of the zeal displayed elsewhere could usefully be directed to this area.[53] There is also a question whether public sector emoluments and allowances absorbed in a labyrinth of 'representative' organisations will leave enough for distribution among those for whom the structure is said to exist.[54]

Adjudication of Native Title Claims

Section 12 of the *Native Title Act* 1993 (Cth) declares the 'common law of Australia in respect of native title' to be a law of the Commonwealth, but the Act makes no attempt to codify the implications of *Mabo*.[55] As the federal Minister for Energy observed, it will take time for the select adjudicators to reveal 'how these cases are run and what kind of ambit people are looking at in terms of compensation'.[56] The first High Court decision in the line of *Mabo*[57] has discouraged actions for collateral political purposes and claims to vast and ill-defined areas, but it remains to be seen how tribal memories and anthropologists' theories will produce 'precise'[58] metes and bounds acceptable to Registrars of Titles.

Disputed claims to native title and for compensation will be adjudicated in the Federal Court.[59] Compensation for some past dealings which extinguished native title falls directly upon the taxpayer.[60] The Court will also hear appeals on points of law touching the 'right to negotiate'.[61] Unopposed claims[62] and objections to new developments on established (or alleged[63]) native title land will be processed by a National Native Title Tribunal[64] or approved State counterpart.[65] Some aspects of the Wik claim have already been referred to the national Tribunal.[66] Tribunal decisions become orders of the Federal Court when registered there.[67] Constitutional questions may arise with respect to unopposed or consent orders made by non-judicial personnel,[68] but old distinctions between federal judicial power and executive functions have lost their magic[69] and in this instance the High Court will hardly stifle its own child.[70]

Wardens Courts will have limited jurisdiction over native title issues when the *Native Title (Queensland) Act* 1993 comes into force.[71]

While it is difficult to speak of tradition in a court established less than twenty years ago the Federal Court, for present purposes, is constituted in a most unusual way. It is exempt from the rules of evidence[72]— a provision which is common in tribunals, but certainly not in regular courts. Instead, the Court is directed to follow procedures which are 'fair, just, economical, informal and prompt'[73]—a formula which has become a mantra among promoters of new tribunals.[74] The Court must 'take account of the cultural and customary concerns of Aboriginal peoples'.[75] It would obviously be bound to do so if normal evidence of those things were presented, so unless that provision is otiose it creates some new, vague *corpus* of judicial notice.

Mabo aside, judicial notice[76] and judges' own inquiries[77] are very limited sources of legitimate evidence at common law.

These are not the only departures from normal court procedure. The Court is to be assisted[78] by a professional 'super witness' and potential *de facto* adjudicator[79] described as an assessor. Preliminary proceedings before an assessor may be treated as evidence in the Court[80] and 'as far as is practicable ... assessors are to be selected from Aboriginal peoples'.[81] These provisions are widely seen as a considerable advantage to claimants[82] and as a commensurate handicap to respondents. However, in the light of evidential problems considered below,[83] they may not make respondents' prospects much worse in practice.

The composition of the National Native Title Tribunal is governed by section 110. The President, recently appointed, is a Federal Court judge. Australian politicians have a deep and abiding belief that the citizenry will more readily defer to a tribunal or administrative inquiry headed by someone entitled 'Justice'. On several occasions in its short history the Federal Court has served to confer that title on persons who really exercise quasi-judicial or non-judicial functions. Non-Presidential members of the Tribunal will include 'assessors' (as described above), people with 'special knowledge in relation to Aboriginal ... societies', and others chosen by the federal executive. The Tribunal may prohibit the disclosure of evidence[84] but presumably natural justice will require it to disclose to all parties any material which it collects for itself from reports and other sources mentioned in section 146.[85] Despite early rumours to the contrary there is a right to legal representation in the Tribunal.[86]

Perhaps it is still possible for our oldest courts, the State Supreme Courts, to retain significant jurisdiction over what is, after all, part of the common law relating to land.[87] These are still courts most appropriately described as superior courts of general jurisdiction. They are not confined to piecemeal statutory jurisdiction and they still handle the criminal jurisdiction, State and Federal, where the scrutiny of evidence is most exacting. Their judicial traditions (well over a century in every instance) extend far beyond the Federal Court's life of twenty years. Appointments to State courts probably receive closer professional scrutiny. Special-purpose (or single issue) tribunals, even when they are not staffed by selected enthusiasts, rapidly become part of the 'club' or 'industry' concerned.[88]

Procedural Amendments

It is submitted that two procedural amendments to the *Native Title Act* 1993 (Cth) should be made forthwith. First, it should be made clear that a non-claimant party may apply to have an application struck out as disclosing no reasonable cause of action before any other proceedings in the Court or the Tribunal. At present there are elaborate safeguards for a claimant whose application is rejected as hopeless by the Registrar, but there are none for a respondent who wishes to contend that an application should have been rejected *in limine*.

Secondly, it should also be provided that, where there is an 'extinguishment' issue, the Tribunal (or Court) should determine that issue before taking evidence of relevant native customs and attachments. In sharp contrast to the relatively nebulous and time-consuming evidence of 'customs and traditions', evidence on an extinguishment issue will normally be short, precise and documentary in nature. Time and money should not be spent upon other issues until it is clear that any native title to the subject land has not been extinguished by past acts of the Crown.

Evidence in Native Title Actions

Let it be clear that nothing in this article is concerned to question the wisdom of dispositions of land and money which governments have increasingly made to Aborigines and Islanders in the past two decades. This section on evidence attempts to make just three points: (1) judicial and quasi-judicial methods of government action are suitable only when all parties are likely to have reasonably equal opportunities to obtain relevant evidence; (2) there are statements by lawyers and anthropologists which indicate that non-claimant parties will not have equal access to appropriate evidence, be it lay ('traditional') testimony or expert evidence - except upon extinguishment issues; and (3) *if* these statements and predictions are substantially correct, the distributive process should not be presented to the public as judicial activity, except where extinguishment issues or specific points of law are involved.

In the first article '*Mabo* and the Miners'[89] I observed: 'There is little point in exegesis which ignores the manner in which native title may be proved ... or which glosses over difficulties likely to arise in contested cases'.[90] This fundamental question still demands proper attention. The emphasis here is on weight and availability as distinct from technical admissibility. Discussion of the latter would be pointless when neither the Court nor the Tribunal is bound by the rules of evidence.

Lay Evidence

The earlier article '*Mabo* and the Miners'[91] suggested that 'lay' evidence in support of applications would often be self-serving and remote hearsay, extremely difficult to cross-examine or seriously assess, even if (in the 'club' atmosphere which special tribunals develop), it were 'correct' to attempt such an exercise. As a former Supreme Court judge has pointed out, alleged laws and customs 'are likely to be recalled in a manner favourable to the claimants which is, after all, simply human nature'.[92] Evidence for applicants may self-levitate by finding its way into assessors' reports.[93] As the 'lay' evidence will usually not be based on any written record, a standard technique of cross-examination, based on prior inconsistent statements, will seldom be available.

Previous reference has been made[94] to an article in which Queen's Counsel, experienced in Northern Territory 'land rights' cases,[95] described species of hearsay which are received in that jurisdiction, including 'group evidence' which lends itself to 'collaboration and concoction'.[96] According to Professor Maddock evidence of dreams about desired acquisitions has been seriously considered in the Northern Territory.[97] But folk legends are not static and sometimes they are historical nonsense.[98]

If and when cross-examination is tolerated[99] it will remain very hard to test direct evidence (let alone hearsay) if the opponent has no access to alternative versions. It is uncertain whether the new adjudicators will take well-tried precautions in dealing with assertions which are easy to make and well nigh impossible to check,[100] and with evidence of 'experts' whose scientific detachment is questionable. They were taken by Moynihan J., the Supreme Court judge who actually heard the evidence in *Mabo*, but the High Court paid remarkably little attention to his pointed comments on matters of credit. (Perhaps an enigmatic remark that the primary findings 'unavoidably contain areas of uncertainty'[101] marks the burial place of those comments.) Moynihan J. suspected that evidence of certain 'immemorial customs' owed a good deal to 'The Drums of Mer', a travelogue by a popular writer of the 1940s.[102] He also questioned a lavish use of interpreters: 'On a number of occasions I soon gained the impression that the witness both understood and could speak English ... The arrangement gave the opportunity to ... hear the question twice and time for the witness to collect his or her thoughts and to collaborate ... on an answer'.[103] Moynihan J. was 'not impressed with the creditability of Eddie Mabo' who seemed 'quite capable of tailoring his story to whatever shape he perceived would advance his cause'.[104] The most careful perusal of the High Court judgments will not alert the reader to these comments (and others of more than passing interest) by the only judge who saw and heard the witnesses.

Expert Evidence

Land rights litigation has given birth to a new expert witness industry comprising anthropologists[105] and professors of Aboriginal history. The first article '*Mabo* and the Miners'[106] suggested that the common law's traditional reservations about expert evidence should apply *a fortiori* to inexact sciences prone to ideology.[107] It also dared to suggest that the *Mabo* judgments encourage gentle treatment of claimants' evidence 'even if the investigation of native title remains in the ordinary courts ... *a fortiori* if it is moved to special tribunals'.[108] It noted[109] comments by Graham Hiley Q.C. upon the 'resentment' and 'alienation from his peers' facing an anthropologist who dared to cast doubt on a native title claim.[110] Hiley also writes:

> To the best of my recollection an expert anthropologist has never been called to give evidence in a land claim except on behalf of the claimants or by counsel assisting the Land Rights Commissioner ... It seems that parties other than the claimants usually find some difficulty in retaining an anthropologist who has the appropriate experience ... and who is willing and able to positively testify against the claim ... During the Jawoyn claim, when counsel assisting did in fact seek to call an anthropologist who had some experience with the Jawoyn people the attempt to call him was met with repeated and strenuous objections ... There has been an understandable reluctance by anthropologists to be seen to be advising parties other than Aborigines.[111]

Hiley adds that access to primary materials, that is what an applicant's anthropologist claims to have found or to have been told by his or her clients, is difficult to obtain. This is another factor tending to make applications *ex parte* in reality if not in form.

Despite strong temptations to self-censorship there is substantial evidence supporting Hiley Q.C. and some of it is in the impressive form of statements against interest. In March 1993 the President of the Australian Anthropological Society, Nic Peterson, was reported as saying that 'most anthropologists are more comfortable working for Aborigines than in some situation where they could be construed as working against their interests'.[112] He was not the first of this profession to say so. In 1991, at the Kakadu inquiry, an anthropologist in the employ of the Northern Land Council declared that the primary duty of experts like himself was 'to represent the people they work with'. The chairman of the inquiry then asked the witness whether he and his colleagues would use their professional position to offer false or incomplete evidence. After an equivocal exchange the witness said he would lose his job if he disagreed with the Land Council's position.[113] In such circumstances there need not be positive falsehood; embarrassing information may simply be suppressed.

The admissions of Nic Peterson and his colleagues are in keeping with the *Revised Principles of Professional Responsibility* of the American Anthropological Association, to which many Australian anthropologists belong:

> Anthropologists' first responsibility is to those whose lives and cultures they study. Should conflicts of interest arise, the interests of these people take precedence over other considerations ... Anthropologists ... must consider carefully the social and political implications of the information they disseminate.[114]

No exception is made for occasions when sworn evidence is required. Plainly these directives expose anthropologists to embarrassment if they are at all sceptical about native title claims. Scepticism would also expose them to prejudice in the public sectors upon which they depend for employment—universities, government departments, Land Councils and kindred institutes where pressures to be 'correct' are likely to be strong. An anthropologist or other social scientist who breaks ranks may be denied access to the very people and places he or she must contact in order to prosper in his or her calling and to become an influential expert witness. It is hardly surprising that anthropologists 'as a rule, do not make their services available to objectors to a claim'.[115]

Dr Peter Sutton, a specialist in Aboriginal affairs, acknowledges that 'the closed ranks of anthropologists [are] denying [miners] access to ... scientific expertise'.[116] His colleague, Professor Maddock, is more specific:

> The suspicion that anthropologists who give evidence for Aboriginal claimants are hopelessly biased is strengthened by the difficulty objectors to land claims have in getting anthropological advice. The defence lawyers in the Gove case, for example ... ended up with nothing better than a retired missionary. In the Alligator River claim, the mining company Peko-EZ strongly contested parts of the claim, but the research on which they relied was carried out by a solicitor who apparently had no training in anthropology.[117]

Professor Maddock notes that witnesses are usually employees of, or consultants to the Land Council which sponsors the claim.[118] In normal litigation this would not enhance their credit but special tribunals develop cultures of their own. Maddock goes so far as to say that probable bias 'arises from the nature of anthropological research'.[119] Dr Sutton adds these particulars:

> The problem with a sociological diagnosis, as opposed to a medical one, is that in our culture a medical diagnosis has very little to do with a physician's politics, while a sociological diagnosis can have quite a lot to do with an anthropologist's politics.[120]

The writer recalls an American 'expert' who was a potential witness in a land rights case. There was no pretence of professional detachment. In conference the witness candidly identified with the claimant 'team', volunteering emotive and partisan views on relevant aspects of Australian history.

It is easy to imagine the state of personal injury litigation if the medical profession sent to Coventry any member who dared to give evidence for defendants. Out of court 'agreements' would be common but would they commonly be free and fair?

Mining executives fear that if they manage to obtain expert evidence they will be 'dismissed as bigoted and racist' simply for opposing claims.[121] Any access which they do gain to relevant facts, opinions or counter-legends is apt to be expensive. The going rate for a consultant anthropologist is said to be about $500 a day, and influential 'lay' witnesses with indigenous associations command between $100 and $200 a day.[122] At a conference in Queensland in 1993 a Federal Government adviser urged Aboriginal delegates to go forth and research their 'rights' without delay. One need not presume that the word 'research' was used as a euphemism for something more creative but it does seem that the scope for reliable reconstruction is limited. Maps of such tribal areas as can now be recalled are hotly disputed, even when they are based on many years of field research.[123] Two scholars in this field observe that Land Councils 'have the resources, contacts and influence to ... establish the extent of traditional territories in [their] regions' but they and their lawyers find it convenient 'to negotiate claims without any self-imposed limits'.[124] One of them recommends that native title issues be settled without 're-inventing knowledge or elaborating traditions that are imperfectly known'.[125]

The caveats and admissions set out above suggest that these comments of a senior journalist are not to be dismissed out of hand:

> Most of the people who have undertaken the study of anthropology in relation to Australian Aborigines have been people who ... tend to believe that their subjects have a grievance and they sympathise with it ... So when it comes to the giving of evidence on land claims it is going to be difficult to find trained anthropologists ... who are not strongly biased in favour of the claims. [S]ome individuals with a clear political agenda have been active and influential in these matters for many years. (Likewise) there are historians who believe that any invention is justified in the service of what they see as the Aboriginal cause.[126]

In some eighteen months since that article appeared in a national newspaper the present writer has seen no denial of its substance, let alone a reasoned refutation. On the other hand, since the first draft of this article was prepared there have been several statements by lawyers and further admissions by an anthropologist which support the thesis that access to evidence by non-claimants will be markedly inferior to that enjoyed by applicants for native title.

Perhaps the best prospects of obtaining rebuttal evidence will be in cases where several groups compete for the same area. The Wik claim at Weipa faces competition;[127] so do several other cases brought in *Mabo's* name.[128] In these circumstances the experts may not be *quite* so sure where their 'first responsibility' lies and the lay witnesses will not be univocal. But even then there may be a compromise division of spoils rather than absolution for respondents or taxpayers. Besides, evidence which seeks to displace one alleged native title in favour of another will not usually bring much joy to non-claimants.

It will be interesting to see how often the existence and content of native title depends on the *ex parte* evidence of a claimant's anthropologist or historian. Will proof of title really be the 'arduous process' that one interested historian predicts?[129] Applicants in the Wik-Comalco case asserted invalidity of all land grants in Queensland since 1859 on the basis of one historian's favourable opinion. This drew sharp criticism from Drummond J.,[130] but other courts (not to mention tribunals) may be less robust. A resources industry spokesman predicts that '... under the tribunal system ... [there]

will develop a loose interpretation of the *Mabo* decision and certainly the federal legislation provides room for that ... I think that if claims are made they will tend to be granted'.[131] This prediction accords with Maddock's survey of Northern Territory cases in the 1980's: '[I]t has been usual for the Commissioner to recommend that most or all of the land claimed be granted'.[132]

Perhaps the best chance of an even contest will occur when there is an issue of extinguishment before 1975. In such a case that issue should be tried first; the evidence will usually be much less woolly and it will be equally available to each party.[133] It remains to be seen whether the onus of proof here will be placed on the party claiming title or the party resisting the claim. The claimant should bear the onus because non-extinguishment is part and parcel of the affirmative case.[134]

Is it really too late for some conductor of this non-symphony to rattle the podium and cry '*da capo*'? If the collective wisdom requires an expansive and primarily economic 'reconciliation' is it necessary to wrap just a minor part of it in complex pseudo-litigation? Taxpayers will in any event contribute to the National Aboriginal and Torres Strait Islander Land Fund,[135] which, in conjunction with the *Aboriginal Land Rights (Northern Territory) Act* 1976 (Cth) and State legislation may well produce more 'native title' than the *Mabo* doctrine ever will. (The Minister's guess is that *Mabo* title will benefit only five per cent of the vaguely defined class of beneficiaries.)[136] Taxpayers will also pay direct for any '*Mabo*' titles extinguished since 1975 and for the legal services consumed by title claimants and objectors to new developments. It cannot be assumed that governments will rigorously test claims for compensation. Governments have political doctrine and expediency to consider and they are better placed than mining companies to make the country pay for their compromises. The Commonwealth was not a zealous guardian of the common weal in *Mabo*, as Sir Anthony Mason has noted.[137]

Taxpayers will pay indirectly as well; if resource industries find it expedient to pay handsomely for quick releases from 'negotiations' they will pass on the costs one way or another, or the international balance of payments will bear them. The first official utterance of the President of the National Native Title Tribunal points out that, under pressures of time, costs or fear of defended litigation, native title can be constructed without putting the evidence (such as it may be) to the rather benign tests envisaged by the *Native Title Act* 1993 (Cth).[138] Later it may be exchanged for a conventional title which could well be more valuable than the original acquisition.[139]

If access to evidence in native title cases is nearly so unequal as well-informed critics predict,[140] would it not be simpler, cheaper and more candid to abandon litigation for a simpler system of land funds and other benefits within the country's capacity to pay? Unlike *Mabo* title such benefits are not restricted by history or evidential chance to people outside the cities and towns. A frankly administrative scheme might be better for all concerned (hopeful tribunalists, 'experts' and practitioners aside) than a patchwork in which pseudo-litigation legitimises part of the expenditure and disposition of public property. It would be neither conciliatory nor economical to have a complex court and tribunal system spending much of its time issuing judgments which are really *ex parte* orders, or rubber-stamping agreements made by complaisant governments or by private concerns in fear of costs, long delays or unhelpful 'assessors', or simply resigned to the fact that 'as a rule, (appropriate experts) do not make their services available to objectors to a claim'.

Notes

1. J.R.S. Forbes, 'Mabo and the Miners' in M.A. Stephenson and S. Ratnapala (eds.), *Mabo: A Judicial Revolution* (Brisbane: University of Queensland Press, 1993), 206–225.
2. *Mabo v. Queensland (No. 2)* (1992) 175 C.L.R. 1.
3. Forbes, *supra* note 1, 206.
4. *Aboriginal Land Act* 1991 (Qld).
5. D. F. Jackson Q.C., 'The Lawmaking Role of the High Court' (1994) 11 *The Australian Bar Journal* 197, 211.
6. *Mabo v. Queensland (No. 2)* (1992) 175 C.L.R. 1, 120.
7. *Tasmania v. The Commonwealth* (1983) 158 C.L.R. 1, 180 per Murphy J.
8. *Coe v. The Commonwealth* (1993) 68 A.L.J.R. 110.
9. 'Writ on Land Rights to Stay', *Courier Mail*, 24 March 1994, 17.
10. 'Chief Justice Attacks Mabo Critics',The *Australian*, 6 November1993, 3.
11. 'It's Time to Rule Legal Fairy Tales Out of Court', The *Australian*, 8 November 1993, 11.
12. As more recently manifested in the Court's abolition of the privilege against self-incrimination with respect to corporations: *Environment Protection Authority v. Caltex Refining Co. Pty. Ltd.* (1994) 68 A.L.J.R. 127.

13. 'Lawmaking and the Judiciary' (editorial), *Financial Review* (Sydney), 10 November 1993.
14. 'Mason Must Defend Court's Role' (quoting Professor G. de Q. Walker), The *Australian*, 14 July 1993, 9.
15. Sir Anthony Mason, 'Putting Mabo in Perspective' (1993) 28, *Australian Lawyer* 23. See also 'Chief Justice Defends Ruling as Lawful, The *Australian*, 2 July 1993, 2.
16. S.E.K. Hulme Q.C., 'Aspects of the High Court's handling of Mabo' in *The High Court of Australia in Mabo*, Association of Mining and Exploration Companies, W.A. (1993) 23, 24, 48 ff.
17. What are technically *dicta* are effectively legislation; see now *Native Title Act* 1993 (Cth) (hereinfter referred to as *N.T.A.*).
18. However, members of the Court took 'judicial notice' of a good deal of history and anthropology which did not concern the Murray Islands. One comment on this phenomenon is as follows: [S]ome of the judges, at least, are convinced of a view of the history of white settlement ... which has been established mainly by propagandist historians desperately rewriting the past in order to gain control of the present ... The Court ... was presented with a series of briefs by propagandists and advocates of a particular view of Australia prepared by historians, lawyers, and others who played no public role in the case ... ': 'High Court's Role Now Irrevocably Politicised' , The *Australian*, 13–14 November 1993, 2.
19. The Commonwealth, originally a party 'ran dead': Cf. Sir Anthony Mason, 'Putting Mabo in Perspective' (1993) 28 *Australian Lawyer* 23 where Mason C.J. stated: 'The Commonwealth was prepared to leave the matter to the Court without offering any argument itself'.
20. *Coe v. The Commonwealth* (1993) 68 A.L.J.R. 110, 111.
21. Forbes, *supra* note 1, 206.
22. *Mabo v. Queensland (No. 2)* (1992) 175 C.L.R. 1, 69 per Brennan J., suggesting that exploration licences may not extinguish native title.
23. *N.T.A.* ss.15(1)(d), 231 (definition of 'category C past act'), 238(8) (non-extinguishment principle), 242(2) (mining lease references include a licence) and 253 (definition of 'mine').
24. *N.T.A.* s.245(3).
25. *N.T.A.* s.212(1) and (3).
26. Forbes, *supra* note 1, 206.
27. Forbes, *supra* note 1, 211–212.
28. Application No. QG 104 of 1993.
29. Action No. 341 of 1993.
30. This will not apply to freehold land or land which has already been proved to be clear of native title.
31. *N.T.A.* s.35(a).
32. *N.T.A.* s.33.
33. *N.T.A.* s.38(1).
34. *N.T.A.* s.39.
35. *N.T.A.* s.36(1)(a).
36. 'Mining Chiefs Renew Mabo Fears', The *Australian*, 8 February 1994 , 39; 'Mabo Fears Send Mine Investors Elsewhere', The *Australian*, 28 February 1994, 19.

37. 'Rights Not Reliant on Title: Judge', The *Australian*, 16 May 1994, 1; French J., 'Introductory Notes for Mediation Conference', 14 May 1994, (Wiradjuri claim to Wellington Common) National Native Title Tribunal (mimeo 9), 4.
38. 'Miners Warn Against Black Push', The *Australian*, 17 January 1994, 2; 'Keating Refuses to Strike Mabo Rights Off Agenda', The *Australian*, 27 January 1994, 2; 'Keating Confirms Stance on Veto', The *Australian*, 28 January 1994, 4.
39. *N.T.A.* s.42.
40. *N.T.A.* s.26(2)(c).
41. *Mineral Resources Development Act* 1990 (Vic) s.31(2); *Mining Act* 1992 (NSW) s.114(1); *Mining Act* 1978 (WA) s.78(2); *Mineral Resources Act* 1989 (Qld) s.7.43.
42. *Semble* part of the original area may be deleted, as in *Hopevale Aboriginal Council v. Cape Flattery Silica Mines Pty. Ltd.*, 23 March 1992, (unreported) Court of Appeal (Queensland) noted in (1992) 11 *A.M.P.L.A. Bulletin* 67.
43. As permitted, for example, by the *Mineral Resources Act* 1989 (Qld) s.7.49.
44. On latter day myth-making in the style of Rousseau see R.B. Edgerton, *Sick Societies: Challenging the Myth of Primitive Harmony* (Toronto: Maxwell Macmillan, 1992).
45. 'Aboriginal Leader Calls for Mine Joint Ventures', *Courier Mail*, 23 March 1994, 23.
46. 'Aborigines, MIM in Giant Joint Venture', *Courier Mail*, 23 April 1994, 39.
47. 'From Bula to Boardroom', The *Australian*, 16–17 April 1994, 34, quoting Mr Ah Kit. 'He warned that if Dominion discovered a viable ore body it might also find previously unregistered sacred sites in the same area.' A native title claim in the area failed before the Northern Territory Land Rights Commissioner in 1989.
48. 'Aboriginal Leader Calls for Mine Joint Ventures', *Courier Mail*, 23 March 1994, 23. Northern Territory Land Councils receive 18 percent of mining royalties as well as direct government funding: 'Mabo's Land', The *Australian*, 8 February 1994, 43.
49. It was reported that a Land Council in the Kimberleys has blocked local negotiations, even on a small scale: 'Crocodiles Caught in Jaws of Dispute', The *Australian*, 21 February 1994, 11.
50. Cf. *N.T.A.* Part 11 (representative bodies).
51. 'Tribal Guide Through a Legal Maze', The *Australian*, 11 February 1993, 13; 'How to Kill the Golden Goose', *Sunday Mail* (Brisbane), 7 March 1993, 57; *Pareroultja & Ors v. Tickner* (1993) 117 A.L.R. 206.
52. *Majar v. Northern Land Council* (1991) 37 F.C.R. 117.
53. 'A.T.S.I.C. Urges Tighter Control of Funds', The *Australian*, 30 August 1993, 2; 'Auditor Slams Land Council', The *Australian*, 15 December 1993, 4; 'Black Agency Collapse Spurs Inquiry', The *Australian*, 29 December 1993, 3; 'Staff "Squander Black Funds on Luxury Goods"', The *Australian*, 22 April 1994, 1; 'Millions Wasted: Auditor', *Courier Mail*, 2 December 1993, 1; 'Black Leaders Should Tighten Finances: Goss', *Courier Mail*, 4 December 1993, 5 ; 'Minister Says Black Councils Will be Sacked', *Courier Mail*, 26 February 1994, 11; 'Shape Up or Be Sacked, Warner Warns Black Councils', *Courier Mail*, 20 April 1994, 1; 'Audits Not Complete Probe Told', *Sunday Mail* (Brisbane), 19 September 1993,

23; 'Prosecutions May Follow Investigation', *Sun-Herald*, (Sydney), 20 February 1994, 5.
54. 'Fourth World Shame', *Courier Mail*, 25 May 1994, 6: quoting a woman 'with 25 years experience in indigenous health care' complaining that 'crumbs (are received) at grass root level' and that too much public money is 'gobbled up in administration'.
55. *N.T.A.* s.223 does not take this matter much further.
56. 'Uranium Miners Urged to Improve Green Credentials' (Senator Collins), The *Australian*, 28 December 1993, 1.
57. *Coe v. The Commonwealth (The Wiradjuri Claim)* (1993) 68 A.L.J.R. 110 (Mason C.J.).
58. *Id.* 111.
59. *N.T.A.* ss.74, 81.
60. *N.T.A.* ss.17(4), 20(3).
61. *N.T.A.* s.169.
62. *N.T.A.* s.70.
63. Mere claimants of title may lodge objections if they are registered as claimants under s.186. See also *N.T.A.* s.29(2)(b).
64. *N.T.A.* ss.26 ff, 107 ff.
65. *N.T.A.* s.251(1).
66. 'Wik Get Tribunal Hearing', The *Australian*, 12 March 1994, 8. (Reference from the Federal Court at Brisbane.)
67. *N.T.A.* s.167.
68. *N.T.A.* ss.70, 73. Cf. *Thompson Australia Holdings Pty. Ltd. v. Trade Practices Commission* (1981) 148 C.L.R. 150 and *R.D. Werner & Co. Inc. v. Bailey Aluminium Products Pty. Ltd.* (1987) 16 F.C.R. 488, 495 per Northrop J.
69. *Harris v. Caladine* (1991) 172 C.L.R. 84 (admixture of judicial and administrative functions in the Family Court).
70. See, however, the High Court's reversion to a stricter view of the 'separateness' of federal judicial functions, in the *Human Rights Commission case*, February 1995. (*Brandy v. Human Rights and the Equal Opportunity Commission and Others* (FC 95/006).
71. See sections 25-27 of the Queensland Act, yet to be proclaimed.
72. *N.T.A.* s.82(3).
73. *N.T.A.* s.82(1).
74. See for example the title to Chapter 7 of a Report recommending the creation of an Administrative Appeals Tribunal (to be known as 'QICAR') in Queensland: Electoral and Administrative Review Commission—'Report on Review of Appeals from Administrative Decisions', Vol I August 1993, 'Fair, Simple, Flexible, Quick and Cost Effective—How QICAR Will Work'.
75. *N.T.A.* s.82(2).
76. *Holland v. Jones* (1917) 23 C.L.R. 149, 153 per Isaacs J.; *R v. Dodd* [1985] 2 Qd. R. 277, 280-281 per Demack J.; *Gordon M. Jenkins & Associates Pty. Ltd. v. Coleman* (1989) 87 A.L.R. 477.
77. *Middleton v. Freier* [1958] Qd.R. 351; *Kristeff v. R* (1969) 42 A.L.J.R. 233.
78. *N.T.A.* s.83.
79. Officially of course an assessor is 'not to exercise any judicial power of the Court': *N.T.A.* s.82(3).
80. *N.T.A.* s.86.
81. *N.T.A.* s.218, inserting a new s.37A into the *Federal Court Act* 1976 (Cth).

82. The Electoral and Administrative Review Commission (Qld), adopting a submission by a former President of the Victorian AAT that tribunals be 'agenda free', has recently rejected the 'representative' tribunals (comprising sectional interests): Report on Tribunals September 1993, 55. Of such bodies it has been said: 'The result is in practice, as we all know, that a (representative) is a partisan and an advocate rather than a Judge ... It is not easy to imagine a less satisfactory tribunal, viewed as a judicial body': *In re Skene's Award* (1904) 24 N.Z.L.R. 591, 597–598 per Denniston and Chapman JJ.
83. See sub-heading 'Evidence in Native Title Claims'.
84. *N.T.A.* s.155.
85. A duty which the Federal Court (O'Loughlin J) held was not discharged when the federal Minister placed a 'stop' order on the 'Hindmarsh Bridge' development in South Australia, on the basis of secret evidence by Aboriginal women, contained in a sealed envelope, and not seen even by the Minister: *Courier Mail*, 16 February 1995, 5.
86. *N.T.A.* s.143. 'Other persons' may also appear. Proposals to exclude lawyers from the tribunal were quickly and quietly dropped when Aboriginal interests protested.
87. *N.T.A.* s.12.
88. On 21 November 1994 the writer attended sittings of a 'land rights' tribunal at which one expert witness for the claimants conducted the examination in chief of another expert witness for the same parties!
89. Forbes, *supra* note 1.
90. *Ibid.*
91. *Id.* 212.
92. 'Native Title Decision Bogus', *Courier Mail*, 14 September 1993.
93. *N.T.A.* s.86.
94. Forbes, *supra* note 1.
95. Detailed discussion of the *Aboriginal Land Rights (Northern Territory) Act* 1976 (Cth), largely the creation of the barrister who was unsuccessful in *Milirrpum v. Nabalco Pty. Ltd.* (1971) 17 F.L.R. 141, is beyond the scope of this article. For an account of several proceedings under that Act see K. Maddock, *Your Land Is Our Land* (Australia: Penguin Books, 1983), Chs. 5 and 8.
96. G. Hiley Q.C., 'Aboriginal Land Claims Litigation' (1989) 5 *Australian Bar Review* 187, 194–195. See also Maddock, *supra* note 92, 93.
97. 'I Dreamed It So I Owned It', *Courier Mail*, 6 July 1993, 9.
98. In a Northern Territory story (Captain) Cook founded Sydney and Darwin and oppressed the Aborigines ... In a Victoria River story the first white arrival was Ned Kelly ... but then Cook came along, killed Ned Kelly and robbed the Aborigines: The *Australian*, 27–28 November 1993, 18 (letter, Dr Geoffrey Partingdon, Flinders University, referring to an essay by K. Maddock, 'Myth, History and a Sense of Oneself' in J.R. Beckett (ed.), *1988 Past and Present: Construction of Aboriginality* (Canberra: Aboriginal St. Press, 1988).
99. In the Tribunal cross-examination requires leave: *N.T.A.* s.156(5).
100. Such as self-serving claims against deceased estates.
101. *Mabo v. Queensland (No. 2)* (1992) 175 C.L.R. 1, 115 per Deane and Gaudron JJ.

102. Findings of Moynihan J. of the Queensland Supreme Court delivered 16 November 1990, entitled 'Determination Pursuant to a Reference of 27 February 1986 by the High Court of Australia to the Supreme Court of Queensland to hear and determine all issues of fact raised by the pleadings'. Vol. I (mimeo 227), 60.
103. *Id.* 66.
104. *Id.* 70, 79.
105. 'The content of the land rights legislation itself has largely been engineered by anthropologists in concert with lawyers': P. Sutton, 'Anthropology Outside the Universities in Australia' *American AS Newsletter* June 1982, 12, 21.
106. Forbes, *supra* note 1, 206.
107. See the comments by a magistrate and a professor of forensic psychology on routine unilateral evidence in a certain 'criminal compensation' tribunal: 'Sex Crimes and Dollar Signs': '... on the other side is only the taxpayer', The *Australian* (Weekend Review), 23-24 April 1994, 1.
108. Forbes, *supra* note 1.
109. *Id.* 216.
110. Hiley Q.C., *supra* note 93, 194–5.
111. G. Hiley Q.C., 'Aboriginal Land Rights in the Northern Territory' (1985) *A.M.P.L.A. Yearbook* 491, 505–506.
112. 'The Mabo Factor—Learning from the Past', quoting Nic Peterson, The *Australian*, 5 March 1993, 23.
113. R. Brunton, 'Down to Earth' (1992) Vol. 45 No. 1 *IPA Review* 1.
114. *American AS Newsletter* June 1990, 44.
115. Maddock, *supra* note 92, 83.
116. Sutton, *supra* note 102, 21.
117. K. Maddock, 'Involved Anthropologists'. In E. Wilmsen (ed.), *We Are Here* (Berkley: University of California Press, 1989), 155, 167.
118. K. Maddock, *supra* note 92, 153.
119. *Id.* 168.
120. Sutton, *supra* note 102, 22.
121. 'Mabo's Land', The *Australian*, 8 February 1994, 43.
122. 'The Mabo Factor—Learning from the Past', The *Australian*, 5 March 1993, 23.
123. 'Tribal Guide Through a Legal Maze', The *Australian*, 11 February 1993, 13 (map by Dr Stephen Davis showing that the tribal lands which can be established do not agree with the boundaries drawn by A.T.S.I.C. and Land Councils); 'Government Hits Tribal Map', *Courier Mail*, 2 April 1994, 14.
124. S.L. Davis and J.R.V. Prescott, *Aboriginal Frontiers and Boundaries in Australia* (Melbourne: Melbourne University Press, 1992), 2.
125. The *Australian*,16 February 1993, 10 (letter, J.R. Prescott).
126. P.P. McGuinness, 'Strict Assay is Needed on This Mother Lode', The *Australian*, 8 December 1992, 40.
127. 'Tribes in Land Tussle', *Courier Mail*, 24 August 1993, 1; 'More Land Claims Over Weipa Leases' (1993) *Australian Journal of Mining* 5.
128. 'Aboriginal tensions Erupt Over Land Rights', The *Australian*, 5 January 1993, 3; 'Tribal Guide Through a Legal Maze' (some Land Council areas partition tribal areas), The *Australian*, 11 February 1993, 13; 'Perkins Hits Out Over Mabo Claims', *Sydney Morning Herald*, 5 June 1993.
129. 'The Spirit of Mabo in Danger of Extinction', The *Australian*, 11 October 1993, 11.

130. 'Judge Blasts Lawyers Over Wik Claims', *Courier Mail*, 22 December 1993, 2.
131. 'Mabo's Land' (quoting P. Ellery), The *Australian*, 8 February 1994, 43.
132. Maddock, *supra* note 92, 83.
133. On 14 February 1995 the National Native Title Tribunal struck out a claim by the Waanyi, on the basis that native title was extinguished by pastoral leases granted by the Queensland Government in the late nineteenth century. (*In the Matter of the Native Title Act 1993 and in the Matter of the Waanyi* Application No. QN94/9.)
134. *Coe v. The Commonwealth* (1993) 68 A.L.J.R. 110, 119.
135. *N.T.A.* ss.17(4), 23(5), 24(2), 25(2), 54 and Part 10.
136. 'Dispossessed Aborigines Get 1.4 Billion for Land', The *Australian*, 11 May 1994, 19.
137. Sir Anthony Mason, 'Putting Mabo in Perspective' (1993) 28 *Australian Lawyer* 23.
138. French J., 'Introductory Notes for Mediation Conference' 14 May 1994 (Wiradjuri claim to Wellington Common) National Native Title Tribunal (mimeo 9), 4.
139. *N.T.A.* s.21(3).
140. Information given to the writer in April-May 1994 by practitioners in Darwin and members of the Sydney and Brisbane Bars with experience in Nothern Territory land rights cases strongly confirmed the impressions of evidential imbalance expressed in the text above.

Native Title Legislation and Mining

Hugh Fraser Q.C.[*]

1. Introduction

The 'native title' law in force in Queensland, and indeed in all parts of Australia, derives essentially from two sources. The first source is, of course, the decision of the High Court in *Mabo*.[1] The common law usually develops incrementally. *Mabo* was different. As Deane and Gaudron JJ. pointed out, the propositions in the earlier Australian cases[2] that upon settlement of New South Wales the unqualified legal and beneficial ownership of all land in the colony vested in the Crown and that the land was then unoccupied or uninhabited for the purposes of the law 'were regarded as either obvious or well settled' and 'accorded with the general approach and practice of the representatives of the Crown in the colony after its establishment'.[3] Their Honours described these as 'fundamental propositions which have been endorsed by long established authority and which have been accepted as a basis of the real property law of the country for more than one hundred and fifty years'.[4] Similarly, Brennan J. (with whose reasons for judgment Mason C.J. and McHugh J. agreed) acknowledged that to state that the common law accepted that the antecedent rights and interest in land possessed by the indigenous inhabitants survived the change in sovereignty involved the overruling of the earlier cases.[5] For reasons of this kind, some commentators have referred to *Mabo* as 'judicial legislation'.[6]

Further comment on these interesting and controversial issues is, however, beyond the scope of this paper which is more directly concerned with legislation in the conventional sense that

---

[*] Barrister, Queensland Bar.

is the second, and more recent, source of the law relating to native title, the Commonwealth's *Native Title Act* 1993. The relevant provisions of this Act commenced on 1 January 1994. The *Land (Titles and Additional Usage) Act* 1993 (WA) has been in force in Western Australia since 2 December 1993. State legislation upon this subject has been slow to commence to operate.[7] The constitutional validity of essential elements of the *Native Title Act* 1993 (Cth), and the validity of the Western Australian legislation, are the subject of challenges which were litigated in the High Court in September 1994. This paper proceeds on an assumption that the relevant provisions of the *Native Title Act* 1993 (Cth) will survive, and the position in Western Australia is not considered further.

With the commencement of the operation of State legislation, the procedures relevant to the grant of future mining tenements which are dealt with below will be different. For example, under the Queensland Act, the Wardens Court will become the 'arbitral body' which, subject to the right of the State minister to overrule its determinations, will determine whether mining tenements which are claimed to affect native title may be granted.[8] It has not been made clear whether the delay in the commencement of the State legislation has been caused by matters which may be resolved shortly, or whether the States have encountered any fundamental land management difficulties which might result in a much lengthier period before State legislation is fully operational.[9]

The uncertainty of the future legal position — and, indeed, the present legal position — has its own implications for those who are currently in the process of seeking to obtain mining tenements. But it is proposed to deal with the legal position on the basis that the *Native Title Act* 1993 (Cth) is the only relevant legislation in force in Queensland (which is the current position), and on the assumption that that legislation is constitutionally valid.

2. Native Title Act 1993

Regarding the *Native Title Act* 1993 (Cth), which is arguably the most notable and controversial legislation enacted by the

Commonwealth, there is one point upon which particular controversy has not arisen and that is that the Act does not represent the pinnacle of plain English drafting. It may be that the reasons for some of the obscurities and ambiguities in the Act include the pressure under which it was drafted,[10] the complexity of the political instructions and the fact that there were more than one hundred amendments to the Bill made in the Senate. But whatever are the reasons for the lack of clarity in some aspects of the Act, it is a feature of it which is of significance to those, such as miners, who must use the Act as a working document.

Another feature of the Act which may prove to be of practical significance to the mining industry is the shift of power from the States to the Commonwealth in relation to grants in respect of which native title exists, or is claimed to exist. So far as past grants are concerned, this transfer of power is evidenced by the Commonwealth's imposition of conditions upon which the States may legislate to provide that any past grants which are invalid because of the existence of native title may be taken to be valid.[11] Coupled with this is the imposition of an obligation upon the States to pay compensation to native title holders if the States do not validate past invalid grants.[12] It may also be observed that the Commonwealth retains the power, by regulation, to negate entirely or in part so much of the legislation of any State or Territory which, by complying with the Act, validates past grants.[13]

So far as the future is concerned, the shift of power to the Commonwealth is apparent in Part 2, Division 3, Subdivisions A and B which state the conditions under which any future titles which might affect native title may be granted by the States. An important feature of these provisions, is that even if a State is permitted by the Commonwealth to take over the 'right to negotiate' provisions in section 26 by appointing a State body (such as a Wardens Court) to become the 'recognised State body',[14] the Commonwealth minister will retain a discretion to revoke the authority of that State body.[15] The Commonwealth minister is also given the power to exclude any particular act (which would include any particular mining grant) from the 'right to negotiate' provisions,[16] and, conversely, the power to render any future grant of any kind subject to the 'right to negotiate' provisions.[17] Thus real and significant power in respect of mining tenements which may affect native title is vested in the Commonwealth, and will remain there even if State schemes for future grants are approved and implemented.

Another general feature of the legislation is that it does not seek to refine the principles regarding native title, nor to resolve the apparent differences in approach adopted with respect to particular issues in the three different majority judgments delivered in *Mabo*. A much discussed example of those differences is the approach adopted, or tentatively adopted, to leases containing provisions protective of indigenous inhabitants, by Brennan J. on the one hand[18] and by Deane and Gaudron JJ. on the other.[19] Questions of this and a related kind, such as whether the valid grant of pastoral leases in common form extinguished native title, have been left for resolution to the National Native Title Tribunal and the courts.

Finally on this topic, the impression given by the sheer size of the Act and the extent of public comment which has accompanied its enactment and implementation may have been that it is anticipated that native title will be found to exist extensively throughout Australia. A rather different impression is conveyed by the reasons for judgment of Brennan J.[20] and the joint reasons of Deane and Gaudron JJ.[21] Which impression turns out to be accurate may be influenced by the outcome of extensive and protracted litigation of a kind which seems to have become a permanent feature in Canada.

3. Validation of Invalid Titles (if any)

Assuming that the Act is valid, that appropriate legislation[22] is proclaimed to commence in the States and Territories and that the Commonwealth does not regulate under section 228(10)(b), the validity of titles granted before 1 January 1994 should be regarded as unaffected by the existence of native title when the grants were made.[23] If, as some commentators have suggested, no titles were invalidated by the unacknowledged existence of native title when the grants were made, this section of the *Native Title Act* 1993 (Cth) will have no substantive operation.

The provisions of the *Native Title Act* 1993 (Cth) (and therefore of complying State and Territory legislation) provide for compensation payable upon validation to be paid by governments, not by title holders. Accordingly, from the perspective of title holders, including miners, the question of whether any past mining titles were invalidated because of the unacknowledged existence of native title when the grants were made, generally should become a question of only academic interest, so far as the validity of titles is concerned. But that question will retain residual significance for other reasons. The question of validity of past titles will remain one of great significance for governments and for native title claimants. Upon the answer to that question will hinge the existence of rights of compensation against governments. If governments are required to pay compensation, the general community — no doubt including the miners — will be called upon to pay.

The question of validity may remain of significance for miners for another reason. The *Native Title Act* 1993 (Cth) provides that the validation of invalid leases, *except* invalid mining leases, will have the effect either of extinguishing native title or of extinguishing native title to the extent to which it is inconsistent with the lease.[24] Invalid mining leases are singled out for different treatment. If there are any invalid mining leases, the validation of them would 'suspend' native title only for the duration of the lease and renewals, so that native title might have to be taken into account for some future grants.

4. Future Mining Titles

Although the relevant provisions of the *Native Title Act* 1993 (Cth) include provisions for the registration of native title claimants on the basis of an opinion of an administrative body as to the '*prima facie*' validity of the claim,[25] and although provision is made both for such parties to be involved in negotiations before the grant of titles and for a determination by a tribunal that titles may not be granted,[26] it seems that a failure to comply with this statutory regime should ultimately have the consequence of invalidity of a new title only if native title in fact existed when the grant was made, and to that extent only.[27]

In short, if a government is correct in thinking that there is no native title even though native title is claimed and a claim is accepted by the Native Title Tribunal, then the government might validly grant a mining tenement though it did not comply with the notice and other provisions in the *Native Title Act* 1993 (Cth). If a native title claimant wished to prevent the grant occurring, or wished to prevent mining activity from taking place pursuant to the grant, the native title party would be left to legal remedies, the most obvious of which is a claim for an interlocutory injunction.

An application for an injunction was made but, on the particular facts of the case, was dismissed in a recent Western Australian case.[28] In Canada, where native title has been recognised for about twenty years,[29] interlocutory injunctions have been granted against mining companies and governments to prevent activities, including exploration activities, pending the final determination of a claim for native title.[30] Although litigation may prove unavoidable in particular cases, it is not generally regarded as a desirable method of securing grants of land. In the ordinary case, the viability of a project would be assessed having regard to the effect of the provisions of the *Native Title Act* 1993 (Cth) relating to future grants, even if a miner considered that it was probable that native title did not in fact exist despite a claim to the contrary.

The relevant provisions of the *Native Title Act* 1993 (Cth) have been summarised and explained in other papers.[31] For that reason the effect of the Act is examined here in a more general way. When a miner first seeks a tenement for the relevant area of land, the miner would ordinarily assess the time frame within which a grant might be expected. For the purpose of planning future activities, a miner will not be able to assume that any satisfactory or speedy resolution of all native title claims will occur by agreement. It is therefore convenient to illustrate the potential effect of the *Native Title Act* 1993 (Cth) by assuming a hypothetical case in which claimants for native title fully exercise their legal rights to oppose a grant, whilst accepting, of course, that the reality in particular cases may be different.

The miner may not have any certain knowledge as to the identity of any native title claimant, the nature of any potential native title, or whether it exists at all. The *Native Title Act* 1993 (Cth) does contain provisions permitting persons claiming to hold native title to apply for native title determinations[32] and provisions for a register recording determinations of native title by the National Native Title Tribunal, the Federal Court, the High Court, recognised State or Territory bodies and other courts or tribunals.[33] But the Act contains no particular incentive to encourage native title claimants to procure registration before a mining tenement is about to be granted, nor does it contain any 'sunset' provision requiring claims to be registered within any particular period. So the absence of any entry in the register has no meaning so far as the presence or absence of native title is concerned.

In an article written before the enactment of the *Native Title Act* 1993 (Cth), Frank Brennan S.J. suggested that it will be necessary that each jurisdiction provide a system for notification and registration of traditional title and that 'otherwise, uncertainty and delay will plague any attempts to negotiate joint land use between miners and pastoralists and those claiming to be traditional owners'.[34] In a similar context, Frank Brennan S.J. said, 'not until a register is complete can a developer be guaranteed immediate certainty about whom to notify and consult'.[35] If the Act remains in its current form, there is no reason to think that the National Native Title Register will ever be complete.

It may also be observed that even if there is an entry on the register identifying details of native title and native title holders, the entry may not be conclusive. Even what is called an 'approved determination of native title' (the consequences of which are not defined in the *Native Title Act* 1993 (Cth)),[36] may be varied or revoked in a case in which events have taken place that have caused the determination no longer to be correct, or in which 'the interests of justice require the variation or revocation of the determination'.[37] The breadth of this discretion renders it impossible now safely to predict its practical effect upon the reliability of approved determinations of native title.

5. The 'Right to Negotiate'

In the context of full opposition to the exploration permit and a mining lease, the effect of the *Native Title Act* 1993 (Cth) is to add at least two years to the time required to obtain the mining lease. Under the *Native Title Act* 1993 (Cth), if the miner successfully obtained the exploration permit and then applied and obtained a determination by the National Native Title Tribunal that the mining lease might be granted, the last event in the two year period might be a decision by the Commonwealth minister that the minister considered it to be in 'the national interest' or in 'the interest of the State' to overrule that determination of the Tribunal, with the consequence that the mining lease could not be granted. This assumes, as has been mentioned, that appropriate State provisions have not been approved and implemented, or if they have, that approval has subsequently been revoked. In the case of a complying State scheme, it would be the State minister who, in the interests of the State, could overrule the determination of the recognised State body.[38]

In referring to the period of two years delay, it is assumed that the exploration permit would not be treated as an 'act attracting the expedited procedure'. There are significant disincentives to the adoption of that procedure. It may be adopted only if the grant of the exploration permit 'does not directly interfere with the community life of the persons who are the holders ... of native title'.[39] Where that requirement, and the other requirements in the definition section (that is non-interference with areas of particular significance and no major disturbance to land or waters) are satisfied, nevertheless the procedure remains unattractive. If the procedure is adopted, native title parties are given a right to object to the procedure being adopted, and no time limit is provided for the determination of that objection. If the objection succeeds, the consequence of having invoked the procedure will be to increase the two year delay period. Furthermore, the adoption of the 'expedited' process for exploration permits prevents the possibility of a determination at the exploration permit stage which might bind the parties at a future stage.[40]

The two year estimate may be derived easily enough from the express provisions of Part 2, Division 3, Subdivision B. In essence it comprises the minimum negotiation periods of four months for the exploration permit, and six months for the mining lease,[41] a 'maximum' period for the inquiry[42] and determination of four months for the exploration permit and six months for the mining lease,[43] and two further periods of two months each for the exploration permit and the mining lease as the time within which the minister is empowered to overrule the determinations of the Tribunal.[44] The two year period does not involve the further time which must be taken in preparing and serving the notices required by section 29 of the *Native Title Act 1993* (Cth).

Although it is conceivable that some of these periods could be shortened even in the case of hard fought applications for the permit and the lease, it is also obvious enough that there is considerable scope for the periods to be much longer. The inquiry and determination stage, in particular, might easily occupy more than four months and six months respectively, given the obligation upon the Tribunal to take into account matters such as the effect of the proposed permit and lease upon the native title rights and interests, the way of life and cultural traditions of the native title parties, the development of the social, cultural and economic structures of any of those parties, the natural environment of the land or waters concerned, the wishes of the native title parties in relation to management, public interest and other matters which the Tribunal considers relevant.[45] The 'maximum' periods of four months and six months for exploration permit and mining lease respectively which apply at this stage are, of course, in no sense enforceable maximums. The obligation upon the arbitral body is to 'take all reasonable steps' to make a determination within those time periods.[46] With the utmost diligence, the Tribunal might find it impossible to meet those periods in particular cases. If it can not, its obligation is merely to notify the Commonwealth minister of its reason for not so doing.[47]

The possibility that the cumulative periods involved in obtaining the exploration permit and a mining lease might be shortened by binding decisions upon issues decided at the exploration permit stage is reduced by the provisions of section 40. That section prevents new issues being raised at the lease stage only in cases in which an issue was 'decided' during the earlier inquiry. There is no express restriction upon a party raising a new issue at the later stage. Furthermore, even if an issue is decided at the exploration permit inquiry, the same issue may be re-opened with leave of the Tribunal at the mining lease inquiry.

These potential delays and uncertainties now exist in relation to the future grants of exploration permits and mining leases. It is not intended to comment upon the arguments as to the desirability of provisions in this form. It is, however, appropriate to refer to two rather odd features of the provisions. The first is that these significant 'right to negotiate' provisions apply in their full rigour to the grant of any future mining tenement if it is granted over land or water at any place in Australia down to the low water mark. Once one steps into 'Commonwealth territory' (that is, below the low water mark, putting aside the question of internal waters and the like) the 'right to negotiate' provisions, and other restrictions in the *Native Title Act* 1993 (Cth), have no application.[48] A second oddity, perhaps arising from a drafting quirk, is that it appears that most re-grants of *invalid* mining tenements (if there are any) which take place after 1 January 1994 are exempt from the 'right to negotiate' provisions because, being 'past acts',[49] they are not 'future acts',[50] and therefore they are not 'permissible future acts',[51] and are thus not within section 26. But in some cases, similar re-grants of past, *valid* mining tenements may be subject to 'the right to negotiate' provisions[52] because they will not fall within the considerably narrower 'definitions' of renewals in section 25(1) and section 26(2)(c).

Notes

1. *Mabo v. Queensland (No. 2)* (1992) 175 C.L.R. 1.
2. *Attorney General (NSW) v. Brown* (1847) 1 Legge 312; *Cooper v. Stuart* (1889) 14 App. Cas. 286; *Williams v. Attorney General (NSW)* (1913) 16 C.L.R. 404 and *Randwick Corporation v. Rutledge* (1959) 102 C.L.R. 54.
3. 175 C.L.R. 1, 104, with reference to the propositions mentioned 102, 103.
4. *Id.* 109.
5. *Id.* 57-58.

6. J.R.S. Forbes, 'Mabo and the Miners' in M.A. Stephenson and S. Ratnapala (eds.), *Mabo: A Judicial Revolution* (Brisbane: University of Queensland Press, 1993), 206, 207: 'The question is not so much whether Mabo is judicial legislation but whether it is workable legislation ...'.
7. In the Northern Territory, the *Validation of Titles and Actions Act* 1994 was assented to on 10 March 1994, but it deals only with validation and preservation of existing reservations, and confirmation of certain existing rights pursuant to s.212 of the *Native Title Act* 1993 (Cth) (hereinafter referred to as the *N.T.A.*) The position in other parts of Australia, is as follows:

   QLD: *Native Title (Queensland) Act* 1993 was assented to on 17 December 1993 and Parts 1, 2, 3, 11 and elements of Part 13 commenced operation in November 1994. This Act generally conforms with the *N.T.A.*

   NSW: *Native Title (New South Wales) Act* 1994. Parts 1, 2, 3, 10 and 11 commenced operation in November 1994.

   TAS: *Native Title (Tasmania) Bill* 1994, so far as I am aware this Bill has not yet passed into law.

   ACT: *Native Title Act* 1994 (ACT) commenced operation in November 1994.

   VIC: *Land Titles Validation Act* 1993 (Vic). This is non-complying legislation.

8. *Native Title (Queensland) Act* 1993 ss.25, 26(1), 26(3), 27(1); *N.T.A.* ss.26(1), 26(2), 27(1), 28, 38(1), 42(1), 42(3).
9. One recent paper seems to assume the inevitable commencement of the State legislation: F. Brennan S.J., 'Forum on Native Title', National Property Lawyers' Conference, 24 August 1994, 22 - 23. Another writer has speculated that there is more than the compensation issue preventing the States going forward and implementing complementary legislation: G. Ewing, Assistant Director, Australian Mining Industry Council, 'The Australian Mining Industry and the Native Title Act 1993', paper delivered at the General Practice Section, Law Council of Australia Conference, 24 August 1994, 7.
10. Final drafting instructions could not have been given before late October 1993, when the government resolved upon the essential form of the legislation: See Dr J. Gardiner - Garden, 'The Mabo Debate - A Chronology', D.P.L., 'Mabo Papers - Parliamentary Research Service Subject Collection No. 1'. The Commonwealth had released an outline of proposed legislation on native title at the beginning of September 1993, but its 'final compromise position' was not reached until 20 October 1993. For one perspective on the development of the legislation, see B. Hocking, 'Human Rights and Racial Discrimination After the Mabo Cases: No More Racist Theft?' in *Essays on the Mabo Decision* (Sydney: Law Book Co., 1993), 178, 281 - 204
11. *N.T.A.* s.19(1).
12. *Id.* s.19(2), although the basis and measure of compensation 'for' a past grant which, by definition, is invalid and which would therefore not itself have affected native title remains unclear.
13. *Id.* s.228(10)(b). Note however that the Act does not purport to prevent States and Territories from validating past grants on their own terms (see s.233(2)), and the Prime Minister's second reading speech (2880) makes it plain that the Act was not intended to prevent such validation.

14. *Id.* ss.27(1), 251.
15. *Id.* s.251(4). Note also that the Commonwealth may control the composition and procedure of the State body, at least indirectly, by conditions included in a written agreement for provision of financial assistance under s.200, and by being required to be consulted on non-judicial appointments to the body under s.251(2)(g).
16. *Id.* s.26(3)(b), although the minister ought not to do so unless the minister considers the Act will have minimal effect on the native title concerned and has consulted with relevant Aboriginal/Torres Strait Islander bodies under s.26(4).
17. *Id.* s.26(2)(e).
18. *Mabo v. Queensland (No. 2)* (1992) 175 C.L.R. 1, 72-73.
19. *Id.* 116-117.
20. *Id.* especially 68-69.
21. *Id.* especially 109.
22. By appropriate legislation, I include legislation in a form which complies with the requirements of Part 2, Div.2 of the Act, but I do not exclude the possibility of legislation in a different form having a similar 'validating' effect. See also note 13 and related text. So far as I am aware no regulation has been made under *N.T.A.* s.228(10)(b).
23. See K. McDonald, 'Mabo and Native Title - The Final Implications: Past and Future Titles - Their Validity and Effect' (1994) 13(2) *A.M.P.L.A. Bulletin* 1, and H. Fraser Q.C., 'The Effect of Native Title Legislation Upon the Validity of Title to Land', C.L.E. Conference, 23 August 1994.
24. *N.T.A.* ss.15(1), 19(1), 229, 230-232; mining leases: ss.15(1)(d), 231, 238(8).
25. *Id.* ss.63, 64, 66(1).
26. *Id.* s.31, 38(1).
27. This follows because the provisions which purport to 'invalidate' future grants operate only in relation to 'future acts' as defined: see *N.T.A.* ss.22, 26(1) and 28. 'Future acts' comprehend only those acts which, apart from the *N.T.A.*, would affect native title: *N.T.A.* s.233(1). Native title exists only if it is in fact recognised by the common law as existing: *N.T.A.* s.233(1).
28. *Djaigween v. The State of Western Australia*, unreported, No. 2109 of 1993, 18 January 1994, Owen J.
29. This is since *Calder v. Attorney General (British Columbia)* [1973] S.C.R. 313; 34 D.L.R. (3d) 145.
30. For an example, see *Hamlet of Baker Lake v. Minister of Indian Affairs and Northern Development* (1978) 87 D.L.R. (3d) 342.
31. For example Justice R.S. French, 'The Role of the National Native Title Tribunal' (1994) 5(3) *Australian Dispute Resolution Journal* 164.
32. *N.T.A.* Part 3, Div. 1.
33. *Id.* Part 8.
34. F Brennan S.J., '*Mabo* and Its Implications for Aborigines and Torres Strait Islanders' in M.A. Stephenson and S. Ratnapala (eds.), *Mabo: A Judicial Revolution* (Brisbane: University of Queensland Press, 1993), 45.
35. See Brennan, *supra* note 9, in the context of a reference to the practical difficulties which will be encountered by miners in a 'two year interim' period for the ongoing operation of existing State mining legislation which the Queensland Act contemplates might occur before 'definitive registration of claimants and determination of native title holders'.
36. See *N.T.A.* s.13.

37. *Id.* s.13(5).
38. *Id.* s.42.
39. *Id.* s.237(a).
40. *Id.* s.40; see below.
41. *Id.* ss.31, 33, 34 and 35.
42. *Id.* s.142 which must permit submissions etc.
43. *Id.* ss.36(1)(a) and (b), 75(1), 77, 139(b).
44. *Id.* s 42.
45. *Id.* s.39.
46. *Id.* s.36.
47. *Id.* s.36(2).
48. *Id.* s.26(1) is restricted to acts done at 'onshore places', which is defined to mean land or waters within the limits of a State or Territory: *Id.* s.253. Note also that any future act done in relation to 'offshore' places is not invalidated by the provisions of the *N.T.A.* See ss.23(1), 235(8)(a).
49. *Id.* s.228(3), 228(8)(1).
50. *Id.* s.233(1).
51. *Id.* s.235, all of the sub-sections of which refer to 'future acts'.
52. That is if the grant of the tenement or activities under it did not extinguish native title.

Applications for a Determination of Native Title to the National Native Title Tribunal:

Basic Procedures and Some Problems of Proof

B.A. Keon-Cohen[*]

These are early days to be discussing evidential problems arising in the implementation of the *Native Title Act* 1993 (Cth).[1] As with one predecessor of equivalent magnitude, the *Aboriginal Land Rights (Northern Territory) Act* 1976 (Cth), the real strengths and weaknesses of the statutory scheme will take time and practical experience to assess. Despite various problems, unnecessarily complex drafting being just one, the *Native Title Act* 1993 (Cth) is a worthwhile initiative. At least from the applicants' perspective the scheme established for determination of native title and compensation is much preferred to the alternative, being actions at common law. Equally, however, much was lost in the negotiation process. Final acceptance of the compromise reflected by the Act must await further developments. These are in particular, first, the funding and administration of the land acquisition fund since only then will those Aboriginal communities most affected by colonisation and least able to access the *Native Title Act* 1993 (Cth) processes be able to assess the final product.[2] The second is the result of Western Australia's constitutional challenge, since if that succeeds in whole or in part the utility of the entire scheme may be affected.[3] The third is the delivery of results by the Tribunal

---

[*] Barrister, Victorian Bar.

process itself, and acceptance of those results by all parties as fair and reasonable.

Having said that, there remain many imponderables associated with the claims process in the National Native Title Tribunal (hereinafter referred to as N.N.T.T.) that are worthy of discussion. Here the claim procedures in the N.N.T.T. will be described and some pressing issues which have emerged thus far and which concern proving native title will be dealt with.

Claims Filed to Date

At the date of writing (mid September 1994), a number of claims of various types have been filed in the N.N.T.T. None has completed the mediation stage, let alone been referred to the Federal Court for trial.[4] Nevertheless, as at late August 1994, fifty-nine claims had been filed. These involved land located in all the States and Territories except Tasmania and the Australian Capital Territory. Twenty were for a determination of native title;[5] two for compensation;[6] and thirty-seven were filed by non-claimants ('non-claimant native title determination application').[7] Forty-one were accepted by the Registrar.[8] The first mediation conference was convened at Wellington, New South Wales in May 1994, by the President of the N.N.N.T., French J.[9] According to the *Australian*, as at 31 August 1994, these claims totalled about 100,000 sq km or 1.5% of Australia's continental land mass.[10]

The Act, Regulations and Notices Determinations

The *Native Title Act* was finally passed by the Commonwealth Parliament,[11] after 'the longest debate on any Bill in the history of the Australian Parliament' on 22 December 1993, and came into force on 1 January 1994.

A set of regulations have been promulgated[12] and amended.[13] Significantly, the amendments excluded a requirement of 'physical' connection with the land when providing details of native title rights and interests possessed under traditional laws and customs.[14] Further, on 24 December 1993, the responsible Minister[15] made a determination under the Act being *Native Title (Notices) Determination No. 1* 1993, gazetted on 30 December 1993.[16] This determination details notification requirements concerning proposed future acts,[17] rights to negotiate for permissible future acts,[18] notice to the public of a native title determination application[19] and procedures concerning special inquiries.[20]

Again, on 27 December 1993, the responsible Minister[21] issued a 'Determination of Representative Aboriginal/Torres Strait Islander Bodies'[22] which sets out the functions of such bodies. These are essentially to assist Aboriginal groups to make claims, and to negotiate regarding use of the land by governments or others, and compensation. A number of legal services and land councils have been nominated but more will be required. No body is nominated for Tasmania, and vast areas of Queensland are lacking such an office, since only the Cape York Land Council has been nominated with responsibilities limited to an area on the western Cape.

Practice Directions

Practice directions were issued by the N.N.T.T. President, French J., operative as of 16 May 1994. These are issued pursuant to the *Native Title Act* 1993 (Cth) section 123(1)(e). They apply to three kinds of applications: first, for a determination of native title;[23] secondly, for the revocation or variation of an approved determination of native title;[24] and thirdly for a determination of compensation.[25] They are stated as 'guidelines for the lodgement and processing of applications, the conduct of mediation conferences and inquiries in relation to applications and the making of determinations'.

As to assisting claimants to understand what has to be proved and how, these Practice Directions deal only with detailed procedural matters under the headings 'Lodgement of Applications', 'The Acceptance Process', 'Acceptance and Registration', 'Parties', 'Inquiries' and 'Conferences and Inquiries in Relation to Opposed Applications'.[26]

Regulations *Ultra Vires*?

An issue relevant to evidentiary burdens is lurking, but quietly, as to whether the regulations (or some of them) are within 'power', that is within the scope intended by various enabling sections of the Act.[27] The main head of power would appear to be the *Native Title Act* 1993 (Cth) section 215, which is couched in wide language. However, a comparison between the requirements of the Act section 62(1), which sets out the required material to accompany a native title claim, and the requirements as set out in the relevant Regulations[28] raises questions as to whether the regulations seek information far in excess of that required by the Act.[29] This point, to my knowledge has not yet been agitated at the stage of filing information with an application, and answering the Tribunal's letters seeking further information prior to the Registrar's deciding whether to accept the claim under section 63.

Complementary State Legislation

Several months after the passage of the *Native Title Act* 1993 (Cth) the States and Territories appear undecided about being in complete agreement with the Commonwealth, or are, in some cases, flatly refusing to enact complimentary schemes.[30] For the purpose of this paper such schemes, and the claims procedures and evidential burdens involved, may present significant choices of jurisdiction for future claimants.

To date, Western Australia has passed legislation clearly inconsistent with the *Native Title Act* 1993 (Cth)[31] and has launched an action in the High Court alleging essentially that the Act is either beyond the powers of the Commonwealth Parliament for a variety of reasons, and thus is inoperative; or has no operation in any event in Western Australia since native title was extinguished at the extension of sovereignty in 1829, or at a variety of stated later dates.

In 1993, the Northern Territory passed an Act concerning McArthur River which is referred to in the *Native Title Act* 1993 (Cth) but has nothing to do with the Commonwealth *Native Title Act* 1993.[32] The Territory Parliament has also enacted the *Confirmation of Titles to Land (Request) Act* 1993, being 'an Act requesting the Parliament of the Commonwealth to enact legislation relating to certain rights of Aboriginal inhabitants of Australia in or in relation to land in the Territory'. The

Commonwealth has declined to respond. Thus the Territory passed the *Validation of Titles and Actions Act* 1994[33] being legislation envisaged by the *Native Title Act* 1993 (Cth) in section 19 to validate past acts of the Territory. Queensland passed the *Native Title (Queensland) Act* 1993,[34] as complementary legislation, before the Commonwealth Act completed its journey through the Federal Parliament. The Queensland Act has annexed the *Native Title Bill* as it then stood, and not as it was finally passed. Not surprisingly, except for section 1, commencement of operation of the Queensland Act was not proclaimed until November 1994, since a number of amendments were required.

The Victorian Parliament similarly passed an Act before the Commonwealth *Native Title Act* 1993 was passed,[35] but, save for formal sections, the Victorian Act is not yet proclaimed and is not yet in operation. That Act would also appear to be inconsistent with the Commonwealth *Native Title Act* 1993. On 12 May 1994 the New South Wales Parliament passed complementary legislation being the *Native Title (New South Wales) Act* 1994. This Act adapts the Commonwealth *Native Title Act* scheme, and validates 'past acts' of the New South Wales Government.[36] The New South Wales Land and Environment Court and the Wardens Courts, established under the *Mining Act* 1922 (NSW), are to exercise similar functions to the N.N.T.T. South Australia's response has been to pass amendments to the relevant legislation, rather than to enact a special native title law.[37]

Another lurking issue with procedural and evidential implications is the relationship between the Commonwealth *Native Title Act* 1993, State complementary schemes as and when they become operative, and pre-existing State or Territory land-rights legislative schemes especially those that create Tribunal claims processes.[38] Doubtless the current Western Australian challenge will enlighten us on inconsistency issues which may arise in this general field, under section 109 of the Constitution, with reference particularly to the *Native Title Act* 1993 (Cth), and sections 9 and 10 of the *Racial Discrimination Act* 1975 (Cth). A variation of this issue, now resolved in the Full Federal Court, is the impact of a grant of title by the Federal minister to successful claimants under the *Aboriginal Land Rights (Northern Territory) Act* 1976 (Cth) upon *Mabo* traditional native title allegedly held at common law by a separate Aboriginal group in the same land. The Full Federal Court has held that such a grant does not extinguish traditional native title; the two interests are not mutually exclusive.[39]

Claim Procedures

Obviously, procedures will differ depending upon the application made. Four basic types of application appear to be contemplated:

(a) *native title determination* — one presumes usually by applicants or 'non-applicants';[40]

(b) *revised native title determination application* — usually by the title holding 'registered native title body corporate';[41]

(c) *compensation application by title holders*;[42]

(d) *right to negotiate* — applications concerning a proposed permissible future act by a government over claimed land,[43] for example to grant an exploration licence;[44] these applications subdivide into a 'future acts' determination application[45] and an objection to the use of expedited procedures application.[46]

'Special inquiries' may also be requested by the Commonwealth minister into a particular matter or issue relating to native title[47] leading to a report.[48]

Native Title Application Procedures

The basic procedural steps currently required by the *Native Title Act* 1993 (Cth) and Regulations are summarised below. For convenience, a useful flowchart, extracted from a publication by the Commonwealth Attorney-General's Department, is attached.[49] The flowchart indicates two stages being first, the Tribunal, and secondly, the Federal Court.

Research, Preparation and Acceptance of Claim

Subject to the issue of whether the regulations are *ultra vires*, the claimants must gather together sufficient information to satisfy the Registrar that the claim is not 'frivolous or vexatious'.[50] A further basis to reject a claim is that *'prima facie*, the claim cannot be made out'.[51] Real issues arise here,[52] including the role of representative bodies and their funding,[53] what level of detail is required regarding, for example the identity of the claimants, the boundaries of claimed land, the content of customs and tradition, and (with a compensation claim) the identity of 'first acts' alleged to found a claim to compensation (usually) against a State government. One commentator has suggested that a 'minimalist' approach in preparing claims is a mistake.[54] It is suggested that section 62(1) of the Act should prevail over the more demanding regulations. Section 61 certainly does not require the claimants to prove their claim twice!

The onus is on the Registrar to accept the claim, but, as indicated, it may be rejected by reference to two criteria.[55] A rejection by the Registrar may be overridden by a presidential member. If the President confirms the Registrar's rejection, a right of appeal lies to the Federal Court on a question of fact or law.[56] This aspect is discussed further below.

Registration

The claim, once accepted, is registered on a public register, the Tribunal Register of Native Title Claims.[57] This may be searched by the public, and is one indicator of the '*in rem*' nature of the entire claims process.

Notice and Interveners

The Registrar is required to give notice, as prescribed, of the claim 'to all persons whose interests may be affected by a determination [of] the application'.[58] As to the requirements of public notice, see section 66(2)(b) and *Native Title (Notices) Determination No.1* 1993.[59] During two months following the giving of the above notices, any person wishing to be a party to the action may notify the Registrar.[60] That person thereupon becomes a party to the application if he or she has a proprietary interest in the land under claim[61] or if his or her 'interests may be affected'[62] and if notification is given to the Tribunal within the two months deadline.[63] The width of this standing provision remains unclear. Such interests do include a person with a proprietary interest in land, registered in a Torrens or other register.[64] Does the definition of 'interest' in section 253 embrace wider interests, for example rights to royalties? The question will doubtless be agitated, since a person whose interests may be affected is entitled to oppose the application.[65] This issue, if raised, is to be resolved by a presidential member,[66] and such a decision is said to be 'conclusive'.[67] As at mid-September 1994, the Yorta Yorta claim to areas of State forests on both sides of the Murray River in the Echuca–Deniliquin area had attracted expressions of interest communicated to the N.N.N.T. from about one thousand parties.

Processing the Claim

At this stage, procedurally, a native title claim determination falls in three principal classes:
- opposed applications;
- unopposed applications; and
- consent applications.

The Tribunal deals with unopposed applications[68] and consent applications, that is applications initially opposed but thereafter settled on terms agreed to by all parties.[69] When determining unopposed applications, the Tribunal must be satisfied that there is a *prima facie* case, and that it is just and equitable in all the circumstances to make the determination.[70]

'Consent' applications arise in two circumstances. First, at the conclusion of the two months public notification period[71] if the parties are agreed they may advise the Tribunal accordingly,[72] and the Tribunal may make a determination in accordance with the terms of the agreement, provided those terms are within the Tribunal's powers, and are 'appropriate in the circumstances'. It is presumed that such agreement could not be achieved until after the notice period had expired, since only then would all 'interested' parties be known. It is further presumed that 'sweetheart' deals outside the Tribunal's powers (for example royalty arrangements) whilst not expressly barred, are to be revealed, since they would be part of the relevant 'circumstances'. Secondly 'consent' applications arise where, after a compulsory mediation conference in an opposed matter[73] the parties resolve their differences and agree. The Tribunal may then make a determination pursuant to those agreed terms, as indicated above.[74]

As to opposed applications, a mediation conference before a member must be held.[75] The conference is on a without-prejudice basis[76] and specific provision is made for involvement by television, phone or 'other means of communication'.[77] If the matter is not resolved, the Registrar must refer the claim to the Federal Court for resolution.[78] How mediation procedures will work remains to be seen but this compulsory procedure is certainly preferable to the often entrenched positions encountered by litigants in the courts. This is an area where practice directions are required to ensure the *bona fides* of, and to maximise the potential of face-to-face sensible discussions. Preparatory documentation, provision for private sessions, presence of the real decision-makers, tabling of 'shopping lists' of issues and the role of legal or other advisers might all be given attention.

A matter of current controversy is whether, at any time during the processing of 'an inquiry', the Tribunal may, on its own initiative or at the request of a party, refer a question of law to the Federal Court for a decision.[79] The presiding member must agree to such referral before the reference is made[80] and the Tribunal must not make any determination in which the question of law is relevant while that reference is pending.[81] 'Inquiry' is, however, defined restrictively, in the *Native Title Act* 1993 (Cth) section 139, to deal with 'unopposed applications'[82] a 'right to negotiate application'[83] or a 'special matter'.[84] Reference of a question of law at the initial application stage (for example to assist the Registrar to decide whether to accept a claim)[85] or at the mediation stage is not allowed under the Act. French J. has suggested amendments to enable, *inter alia*, a question of law to be referred to the Federal Court earlier in the process.[86] This would seem a useful reform. Such a procedure could break a mediation deadlock involving a question of law, which would then allow negotiations to be concluded successfully.

Federal Court Proceedings

Once seized of an opposed matter, the Federal Court 'must pursue the objective of providing a mechanism of determination that is fair, just, economical, informal and prompt'.[87] Except perhaps for 'informal' hearings, is the Parliament suggesting that Federal Court judges do not pursue these objectives in their other jurisdictions? In 'informal' hearings the judges are directed that in this jurisdiction, they are not bound by 'technicalities, legal forms or rules of evidence'.[88] Is it a 'technicality' to object to jurisdiction[89] or to determine whether, and if so, what onus of proof applies? Doubtless the judges will tell us. Nevertheless, the parties to the Federal Court proceedings are the parties to the original application to the Tribunal, identified in accordance with section 68.[90] The Federal Court has power to join other parties if their interests are affected by the matter, or may be affected by a determination in the Federal Court proceedings.[91] The Federal Court Rules will apply — including New Rules (interim) introduced already for this jurisdiction.[92]

Accepting a Claim — Section 62

One issue which has already arisen concerns the procedures to be followed, and the weight of material to be provided to enable the Registrar to decide whether to accept or reject a claim under sections 62 or 63. Section 62(1) enumerates the material to accompany applications by native title claimants, and provides that the application must:

> Contain all information known to the applicant about interests in relation to any of the land or waters concerned that are held by persons other than as native title holders.

Section 63 states:

> If the requirements of s.62 are complied with, in relation to the application, the Registrar must accept it, unless he or she is of the opinion:
> (a)   that the application is frivolous or vexatious; or
> (b)   that *prima facie* the claim cannot be made out.

The Registrar has rejected the *Carpenteria* claim, being a claim to 247 hectares near Burketown, Queensland. The

Registrar, as required by the *Native Title Act* 1993 (Cth), has referred the matter to the Tribunal President for review of this rejection.[93] French J. heard submissions from the claimants in late August 1994 as to why the claim should be accepted.[94] His decision is pending at the time of writing. The Registrar, it seemed, was determined to refuse to accept the application because the claim embraced an area which was the subject of a pastoral lease. The Registrar reasoned that *prima facie* the claim could not be made out.[95] He took the view that a pastoral lease extinguishes, not just impairs, all native title, whatever the content of that title might ultimately be proven to be, and whatever actual use of that land was made by the pastoralist. This view was taken despite public statements by French J. suggesting that the issue was unclear. In a paper delivered on 16 June 1994 French J., after analysing *dicta* in *Mabo (No. 2)* concerning leases, concluded that it was 'arguable' that leasehold interests did not extinguish native title.[96] His Honour also noted that in June 1993, the Commonwealth Attorney-General's Department publicly recognised 'uncertainty at common law with respect to leasehold interests'.[97] Further, in an interview at that time, French J. stated:

> So far as freehold grants are concerned, we will reject an application which seeks to establish native title over freehold land, but anything else which hasn't yet been the subject of statutory validation and is at all arguable, having regard to what was said in *Mabo*, will probably get through the screening.[98]

This 'acceptance' procedure thus raises the very contentious issue of the impact at common law, of the grant of a pastoral lease in regard to native title rights over the same land. A number of significant procedural issues are raised. First, what type of supporting material or 'evidence', in particular how much detail about interests in the claimed land both historically and currently, should be presented in order for the Registrar to determine whether *prima facie* the claim could be made out?[99] The practice directions state:

(11) An application is not required to establish a *prima facie* case in order to have an application accepted.

(12) The acceptance phase of the application is to be treated as a screening process so that the time and resources of the Tribunal are not taken up with patently hopeless applications, or applications which have not met the requirements of s.62 of the *Native Title Act* 1993 (Cth).

Prior to the rejection of the *Carpenteria* claim, the practice of the Registrar was to seek information from the claimants about other interests, but not to reject a claim merely because of the presence of a leasehold interest. Thus, in the *Ngaluma Ingibundi* claim in the Pilbarra and the *Muduwongga* claim to an area including the Kalgoorlie goldfields, the Registrar had requested the applicants to specify freehold, leasehold and Crown Reserve lands within the claimed areas.[100] There appears to be no clear answer as to what is required; each decision under sections 62 and 63 will be made in the context of each particular case.

A second issue emerging concerning the acceptance process is who has the onus of researching and detailing the title history of any particular area of land, often a large and expensive task. Section 62(1)(b) mentioned above, requires that the application 'contain all information known to the applicant of interests in relation to any of the land or matters concerned that are held by persons other than as native title holders'. The current practice is to insist that *the claimant* conduct title searches of an exhaustive type, and present the results to the Registrar as part of the acceptance process.

It is suggested that this requirement is difficult to describe as a mere 'screening test'. It is also beyond the capacities of most claimants except those with significant funding. Further, as suggested above, the regulations and N.N.T.T. application forms which support this interpretation are arguably beyond the scope of the *Native Title Act* 1993 (Cth) and to that extent, invalid. The section 63 'screening test' originally appeared in clause 57 of the *Native Title Bill* 1993. Clause 57 as it then stood was onerous: it required the applicant to search all official title registers in relation to the land claimed. That requirement was deleted by amendment in the Senate.[101] The Registrar's current insistence, that applicants bear the onus of conducting all relevant searches to ascertain if any freehold, leasehold or other titles exist or previously existed in the claimed area, would seem to contravene not only the spirit of the Senate amendment, but the letter of section 62(1)(b) of the *Native Title Act* 1993 (Cth). 'Information known to the applicant' in that sub-section, should surely not be interpreted as equivalent to 'all the evidence as to other interests to be ultimately relied upon'.

The Registrar's interpretation may, however, have been influenced by *dicta* emanating from the Chief Justice, Sir Anthony Mason, in *Coe v. The Commonwealth*.[102] There, Mason C.J. was dealing with an interlocutory application to strike out a so-called ambit claim to large areas of central New South Wales. In addition to alleging sovereignty and genocide, the statement of claim sought a declaration, *inter alia*, that 'the Wiradjuri people are entitled as against the whole world to possession, occupation, use and enjoyment of those Wiradjuri lands where native title has not been extinguished'.[103]

The Chief Justice struck out the statement of claim, but granted leave to file and serve an amended statement of claim. His Honour stated that if the action was to proceed the plaintiff 'should identify correctly the lands claimed'.[104] In relation to the claim that native title had not been extinguished, Mason C.J. said:

> This is a *Mabo (No. 2)* style native title claim to the Wiradjuri lands *to the extent that such a title has not been extinguished*. The qualification to which I have given emphasis means that the actual lands which are the subject of the claim remain unidentified by the plaintiff except to the extent that they are lands which fall within the lands described in the particulars ... Subject to four qualifications which I shall mention, this is a tenable claim. The first qualification is that not only should the Wiradjuri lands be described precisely but also that the lands which are the subject of the *Mabo (No. 2)* style claim to native title should be described precisely so that it is possible to identify the lands which are the subject of that claim. The second qualification is that the Court will only determine a question of title to land in proceedings which all those persons who have a possible interest in opposing the declaration of title sought by the plaintiff are joined as defendants. As I remarked earlier, having regard to the many parcels of land which appear to be affected by the declarations of titles sought by the plaintiff, proceedings will become unwieldy if steps are taken to join all interested parties .... The

third qualification is that, as Brennan J. pointed out in *Mabo (No. 2)* [(1992) 175 C.L.R. 1,6.]

> ... [i]f a lease be granted, the lessee acquires possession and the Crown acquires the reversion expectant on the expiry of the term. The Crown's title is thus expanded from a mere radical title and, on the expiry of that term, becomes a plenum dominium.

The plaintiff's claim to the [particular] land [leased by the NSW Crown] therefore meets a formidable obstacle.

The fourth qualification is that the plaintiff is evidently proceeding on the footing that it is for the second defendant to prove extinguishment, that is, the defendant bears the onus of proving that matter.... I do not consider that the defendant bears the onus. It seems to me, that, if the plaintiff asserts native title to land, then the plaintiff must establish the conditions according to which native title subsists. Those conditions include (a) that the title has not been extinguished by inconsistent Crown grant; and (b) that it has not been extinguished by the Aboriginal occupiers ceasing to have a requisite physical connection with the land in question.[105]

The *Native Title Act* 1993 (Cth) now prevails over these statements to the extent that section 62 speaks about these issues. French J.'s decision in the *Carpenteria* claim will be studied with interest. Meanwhile, it seems, claimants bear a heavy and expensive burden of title searching when seeking to have their claims accepted by the Registrar.

Pastoral Leases and Native Title

The above events raise squarely the substantive question of the impact of a pastoral lease upon native title.[106] When the lease contains an Aboriginal access clause, as occurs, for example in pastoral leases in Western Australia,[107] South Australia[108] and the Northern Territory,[109] can it be confidently said that all native title rights and interests are nevertheless extinguished? This precise issue is raised by a number of claims now before the N.N.T.T. and was the subject of discussion before Drummond J. in the *Wik* claim in October 1994. It is suggested that despite the *dictum* of Brennan J. quoted by Mason C.J. above, the grant of a pastoral lease does not, of itself, thereby extinguish all native title. Each situation must be examined as to the supporting legislation, the terms of the lease instrument and the actual use made of the lease area, before concluding that the claim '*prima facie* cannot be made out'. It is suggested that a pastoral lease at common law will impair, but not extinguish native title in the same land. The point is particularly important in circumstances where the lease has been issued and terminated prior to the claim being made. The *Native Title Act* 1993 (Cth) states that such a past lease, not now current, becomes a Category D past act, which does not extinguish title.[110] As a matter of practical reality it seems ridiculous that vast stretches of otherwise vacant Crown land which may have been the subject, for a short period of years, of a leasehold or freehold title which was then terminated or surrendered to the Crown[111] and which may not have been actively utilised during its existence should nevertheless extinguish all native title in that area for all time.[112]

It is worth noting that in Canada recently, four judges of the British Columbia Court of Appeal, in a major native title case, stated that the grant of a fee-simple title (let alone a lease) may not extinguish common law native title. In *Delgamuukw v. British Columbia*[113] Macfarlane J.A. stated (and three other Judges of Appeal expressly agreed):

> A fee simple grant of land does not necessarily exclude Aboriginal use. Uncultivated, unfenced, vacant land held in fee simple does not necessarily preclude the exercise of hunting rights: *R v. Bartleman* (1984) 12 D.L.R. (4th) 73. On the other hand, the building of a school on land usually occupied for Aboriginal purposes will impair or suspend a right of occupation.[114]

Lambert J.A.[115] expressly disagreed with Brennan J.'s more conservative approach to extinguishment by issue of a fee simple title. Lambert J.A. takes the view that the actual factual use of the land can be determinative; it 'depends, perhaps, on the use that the holder of the fee simple title is making of the land'.[116] *Delgamuukw*, a Canadian decision, is the only major land rights case to date to discuss these issues in the light of *Mabo (No. 2)*. Whatever the decision of French J. on the procedural question, it seems certain that we have not heard the last of this vexed question of the relationship of pastoral leases and native title.

Notes

1. For a useful discussion see J. Fingleton, M. Edmunds and P. McRandle, *Proof and Management of Native Title: Summary of Proceedings of a Workshop* (Canberra: A.I.A.T.S.I.S., 1994).
2. See *Native Title Act* 1993 (Cth) (hereinafter referred to as *N.T.A.*) s.201. The legislation establishing the Indigenous Land Corporation had its Second Reading on 30 August 1994, amidst much political controversy. See the *Age*, 31 August 1994, 1, 6. The Government has committed $1.1 billion to the fund over the next decade.
3. Three actions are being heard together: *Western Australia v. The Commonwealth* P4 of 1994; *Wororra and Yawuru v. Western Australia* M147 of 1993; and *Martu v. Western Australia* P45 of 1993. The hearing of a number of questions before the full High Court was set down for nine days in September 1994.
4. *N.T.A.* s.74.
5. *Id.* ss.13(1), 61(1).
6. *Ibid.*
7. *Id.* ss.13(1), 61(1) and 67.
8. *Id.* ss.62, 63.
9. *Id.* s.72(1).
10. For a description of the first eighteen claims received, see The *Australian*, 31 August 1994, 3.
11. Senator G. Evans, Senate, 16 December 1993, *Hansard* 5500. He calculated a total of 51 hours 45 minutes.
12. See *National Native Title Tribunal Regulations*: SR 1993, No. 380, Commonwealth Gazette, 30 December 1993.
13. See *National Native Title Tribunal Regulations (Amendment)* SR 1994 No.6, Commonwealth Gazette, 4 February 1994.
14. See for example *National Native Tribunal Regulations*, *supra* note 12, Schedule I, Form 1, 3.
15. F. Walker, Special Minister of State, acting under s.4 *Acts Interpretation Act* 1901 (Cth).
16. See *Commonwealth Gazette*, 30 December 1993, Special No. 402.
17. *N.T.A.* s.23(7).
18. *Id.* ss.26(b)(i), 29(3).
19. *Id.* s.66(2)(b).
20. *Id.* s.138.
21. R. Tickner, Minister for Aboriginal Affairs, acting under s.202(1) *N.T.A.* and s.4 *Acts Interpretation Act* 1901 (Cth).
22. *Id.* s.202(4). See *Commonwealth Gazette*, 30 December 1993, Special No. 402.
23. *N.T.A.* s.13(1).
24. *Ibid.*
25. *Id.* s.50(2).
26. *Id.* ss.70 and 71.
27. See, for Regulation-making powers, *N.T.A.*, ss.58, 201(3), 215, 226(4), 251(5).
28. See Regulations, Schedule 1 Form 1, especially Items A8–A11.

29. See *N.T.A.* s.62(1)(a)-(d). As to the principles concerning regulations being struck down as beyond the scope of the parent Act, see *Australian Boat Trade Employees Federation v. Whybrow* (1910) 11 C.L.R. 311, 324 per Barton J.; *Footscray Corporation Pty. Ltd. v. Maize Products* (1943) 67 C.L.R. 301; *Question Life Assurance Society v. Bishop* [1902] A.C. 287, 290-292 per Earl of Halsbury L.C.; *Paull v. Munday* (1976) 9 A.L.R. 245.
30. See *N.T.A.* s.19.
31. See *Land (Titles and Traditional Usage) Act* 1993 (WA), assented to and operative 2 December 1993.
32. See *N.T.A.* s.46 and *McArthur River Project Agreement Ratification Amendment Act* 1993 (NT).
33. Assented to 10 March 1994.
34. Assented to 17 December 1993.
35. See *Land Titles Validation Act* 1993 (Vic) assented to 17 August 1993.
36. *N.T.A.* s.8.
37. For example see *Mining Act* 1971 (SA); *Environment Resources Development Court Act* 1993 (SA); *Lands Acquisition for Public Purposes Act* 1914 (SA).
38. See for example *Aboriginal Land Rights (Northern Territory) Act* 1976 (Cth); *Aboriginal Land Act* 1991 (Qld); *Torres Strait Islander Land Act* 1991 (Qld); *Land Titles (Validation) Act* 1993 (Vic) and *Aboriginal Land Rights Act* 1983 (NSW).
39. *Pareroultja v. Tickner* (1993) 117 A.L.R 206.
40. *N.T.A.* ss.67-74, 160.
41. *Ibid.*
42. *Id.* ss.61, 65, 161.
43. *Id.* s.26(1).
44. *Id.* ss.26–42.
45. *Id.* ss.35, 71(1).
46. *Id.* ss.32(3), 75(1). See also s.162.
47. *Id.* ss.137-138.
48. *Id.* s.162.
49. See *Native Title: Legislation and Commentary* (Canberra: A.G.P.S., 1993) Commentary C21.
50. *N.T.A.* s.63(1).
51. *Ibid.*
52. See generally, Fingleton, *supra* note 1.
53. *N.T.A.* ss.202–203. These bodies are to be distinguished from prescribed bodies corporate: see *N.T.A.* ss.55-60.
54. See M. Maurice, 'Practice Directions' in Fingleton, *supra* note 1, 19.
55. *N.T.A.* s.63.
56. *Id.* s.169(2).
57. *Id.* s.66(1)(b).
58. *Id.* ss.66(1)(a), 66(2)(a)(i)–(vi).
59. See *Commonwealth Gazette*, 30 December 1993, Special No. 402.
60. *N.T.A.* s.66(3)(b).
61. *Id.* s.68(2)(a).
62. *Ibid.*
63. *Id.* s.68(2)(b).
64. *Id.* s.66(2)(a)(v).
65. *Id.* s.68(2).
66. *Id.* s.69(2).

67. *Id.* s.69(1).
68. *Id.* s.70.
69. *Id.* ss.71, 73.
70. *Id.* s.70(1).
71. *Id.* ss.66, 71(a).
72. *Id.* s.71(a).
73. *Id.* s.72.
74. *Id.* s.73.
75. *Id.* s.72(1).
76. *Id.* s.72(3).
77. *Id.* s.72(5).
78. *Id.* s.74.
79. *Id.* s.145(1).
80. *Id.* s.145(2).
81. *Id.* s.145(4).
82. *Id.* ss.70, 71 or 73.
83. *Id.* s.75.
84. *Id.* s.137.
85. *Id.* s.63.
86. See The *Australian*, 1 August 1994, 1; *West Australian*, 5 August 1994, 4.
87. *N.T.A.*, s.82(1).
88. *Id.* s.82(2).
89. See below re injunctions.
90. See *N.T.A.* ss.80, 84(1).
91. *Id.* s.84(2).
92. Federal Court Rules, O 75.
93. *Id.* s.63(2).
94. *Id.* s.63(3).
95. *Id.* s.63(1).
96. See Justice R.S. French, 'The Role of the National Native Title Tribunal' in R. Bartlett and G. Meyers (eds.), *Native Title Legislation in Australia* (Perth: Centre for Commercial and Resources Law, University of Western Australia and Murdoch University, 1994).
97. *Ibid*, citing a Discussion Paper *Mabo — the High Court Decision on Native Title* (Canberra: A.G.P.S., 1993), para. 2.10.
98. See (1994) 21(5) Law Society for Western Australia *Brief* 16.
99. *N.T.A.* s.63(1).
100. See G. McIntyre, 'Running a Native Title Case', paper delivered to the Environment and Planning Law Association (NSW) Annual Conference, Potts Point, August 1994, 11.
101. See *Hansard*, Senate, 16 December 1993, 5308–5310.
102. (1993) 118 A.L.R. 193.
103. *Id.* 198.
104. *Id.* 194.
105. *Coe v. Commonwealth* (1993) 118 C.L.R. 193, 205–206.
106. See H. Reynolds, 'Native Title and Pastoral Leases' in M. Stephenson and S. Ratnapala (eds.), *Mabo: A Judicial Revolution* (Brisbane: University of Queensland Press, 1993), 119-131; *Mabo v. Queensland (No. 2)* (1992) 175 C.L.R. 1, 68 per Brennan J.

107. The Western Australian Land Regulations in the 19th Century, and the *Land Act Amendment Act* 1934 s.106(2) contained such provisions. Section 106(2) still reads: 'Aboriginal natives may at all times enter upon any unenclosed and unimproved parts of the land, the subject of the pastoral lease, to seek their sustenance in their accustomed manner'.
108. See *Pastoral Land Management and Conservation Act* 1989 (SA), s.47(1).
109. See *Pastoral Land Act* 1992 (NT) s.38.
110. See *N.T.A.* s.229(2)(a)(i), 229(3)(a)(c)(i).
111. See, regarding the sardine factory lease on Dawar Island, *Mabo v. Queensland (No. 2)* (1992) 175 C.L.R. 1, 71–73 per Brennan J.
112. See *Id.* 64–65, 67–68, 69–73 per Brennan J.; 88–90, 104–109, 110–112, 116–120 per Deane and Gaudron JJ.; 192–196 per Toohey J. and 145–146, 158–159 per Dawson J.
113. (1993) 104 D.L.R. (4th) 470. It was held in *Delgamuukw* that the plaintiffs held unextinguished non-exclusive Aboriginal rights, other than a right of ownership or a property right.
114. *Id.* 532.
115. *Id.* 670–671.
116. *Id.* 670.

Determination by NNTT and Federal Court of Applications by Persons Claiming to Hold Native Title

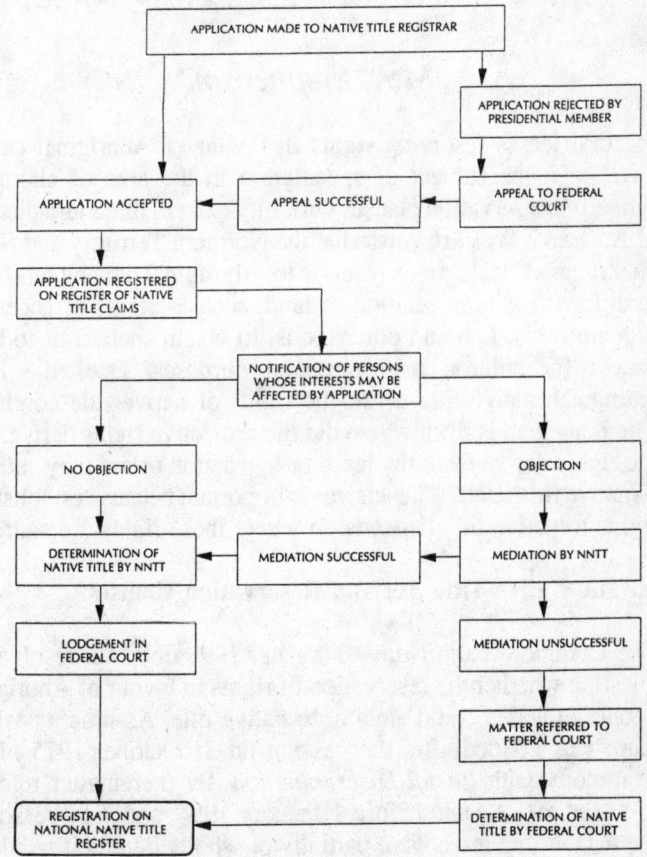

* *Native Title* (Canberra, A.G.P.S., 1994), C21.

Pastoral Leases and Reservation Clauses

M.A. Stephenson[*]

Pastoral leases reserving rights in favour of Aboriginal people have been the subject of speculation in the area of claimable property. Reservation clauses currently exist in three jurisdictions in Australia: Western Australia, the Northern Territory and South Australia. A lease may reserve to Aboriginal inhabitants their traditional rights in relation to land, such as rights of access to procure birds, fish and other foods, to obtain shelter, or to have access for cultural or ceremonial purposes. Does the lease extinguish native title or do the rights of native title continue? The issue here is from where did the protective rights derive. Did the rights derive from the lease or legislation or are they sourced in native title itself? The answer is important because establishing rights to native title depends on where these rights are sourced.

A. The Native Title Act and Reservation Clauses

The Commonwealth *Native Title Act* 1993 does not resolve the question whether the reservation of rights in favour of Aboriginal people in leases could amount to native title. Assume a pastoral lease was granted after the passing on 31 October 1975 of the Commonwealth *Racial Discrimination Act* (hereinafter referred to as the *R.D.A.*) and before 1 January 1994, and if by reason of the *R.D.A.* that lease were partially or wholly invalid it would be validated by the *Native Title Act* 1993 (Cth) as a Category A 'past act'.[1] If any aspect of native title was impaired by the lease then the whole lease would come within the definition of a 'past act', although aspects of native title may have survived.[2] On the

---

[*] Lecturer in Law, University of Queensland.

validation of a 'past act' attributable to the Commonwealth *all* native title rights would be extinguished.[3] Despite a reservation clause preserving native title rights, it is difficult to envisage a situation where some native title rights would not be impaired by the grant of a pastoral lease, even if this were only in relation to the homestead living area.

Thus consideration should be given to the question: does a lease with a reservation clause preserve *all* native title interests? Consideration should also be given to whether a lease with a reservation clause could be deemed to be partially invalid, that is invalid in that part of the lease, or to the extent that native title rights have been extinguished. Is partial validation of a lease under the Native Title legislation possible?[4] The Commonwealth *Native Title Act* 1993 makes no mention of partial validation. Under section 15 of that Act any statutory validation would totally extinguish native title. As most pastoral leases are granted by the States much will depend on the precise drafting of State validation legislation. Section 19 of the Act provides that if a law of a State has the same effect as the Commonwealth legislation, in sections 15 and 16, then State 'past acts' will be valid.[5]

Reservation clauses in leases subject to the Commonwealth *Native Title Act* 1993 or complementary State legislation will rarely be an issue. Only a small number of leases would have been granted between October 1975 and January 1994 over land where no previous government dealings had taken place.

B. Reservation Clauses at Common Law

The effect of reservation clauses in pastoral leases will generally arise in leases granted prior to the Commonwealth *Racial Discrimination Act*, 31 October 1975. Any native title rights and interests that were inconsistent with the pastoral lease would be extinguished by the lease unless expressly preserved by the reservation. Does a lease automatically extinguish native title rights in a factual sense? Traditional native title rights and pastoral leases can and have co-existed successfully for many years. This is evidenced by the current reservation clauses in pastoral leases granted in the three jurisdictions of South Australia, Western Australia and the Northern Territory. Is extinguishment of native title to be determined on a theoretical legal analysis or on a factual case by case basis?

1. Mabo and Pastoral Leases

The High Court in *Mabo v. Queensland (No. 2)*[6] found that native title would be extinguished by the grant of a lease, accepting that a lease granting exclusive possession is inconsistent with the continuance of native title. Brennan J. stated that if a lease is granted, the tenant acquires possession and the Crown acquires the reversion at the expiration of the term. Thus the Crown's title is expanded from a mere radical title and on the expiry of the lease, becomes a *plenum dominium* (full ownership).[7] Deane and Gaudron JJ. also found that native title is extinguished by an unqualified grant of a lease (or a fee simple estate) conferring the right to exclusive possession.[8] Both Brennan J. and Deane and Gaudron JJ. analysed the impact a lease has on native title rights under the *legal* and not factual tests.

But this approach is to be contrasted with Brennan J.'s framework of reference in dealing with other types of grant. Where the Crown has granted land in trust or reserves, and dedicated land for public purposes, 'the question whether the Crown has revealed a clear and plain intention to extinguish native title will sometimes be a question of fact, sometimes a question of law and sometimes a mixed question of fact and law'.[9] In these circumstances Brennan J. found that native title will be lost to the extent that it is factually inconsistent with the interest granted.[10]

In a recent Canadian case, *Delgamuukw v. British Columbia*,[11] the British Columbia Court of Appeal decided that a fee simple grant of land does not necessarily exclude Aboriginal use of vacant, uncultivated and unfenced land for hunting rights. However, the plaintiffs' interest in that case was not a property right of ownership but rather an unextinguished and non-exclusive Aboriginal right.

It appears that a distinction has been made by the High Court between grants of estates that are inconsistent at law and grants that may only be factually inconsistent. It would appear that native title rights would be extinguished on the grant of the lease by the Crown even if the grant was made over a century ago, and although the tenant under that lease may never have entered into possession of the land or used the leased land in any way, and although Aboriginal people may have continued to use the land in their traditional ways.

2. Mabo and Reservation Clauses

In *Mabo v. Queensland (No. 2)*[12] it was clear that a grant of a lease would extinguish native title.[13] However, it was not entirely clear whether a lease containing a reservation of rights in favour of Aboriginal people would completely extinguish native title or whether those rights would be extinguished only to the extent of inconsistency.

In *Mabo*, a sardine factory was granted a lease over two islands for twenty years. This lease included a reservation that the tenant was not to obstruct or interfere with the use by the Murray Island natives of their traditional gardens and plantations on the land that was leased. Brennan J., with whom Mason C.J. and McHugh J. agreed,[14] considered that the lease extinguished native title although it contained this special condition. He stated that:

> [T]he limited reservations in the special conditions are not sufficient to avoid the consequence that the traditional rights and interests of the Miriam People were extinguished. By granting the lease, the Crown purported to confer possessory rights on the lessee and to acquire for itself the reversion expected on the termination of the lease. The sum of those rights would have left no room for the continued existence of rights and interests derived from Meriam laws and customs.[15]

On this view reservations do not preserve native title. Applying this reasoning, it is difficult to envisage any reservation which could preserve native title rights. Could pastoral leases be categorised differently? Deane and Gaudron JJ. were undecided on the question of reservations, but considered there may be *no* extinguishment of native title. They noted that:

> This lease recognised and protected usufructuary rights of the Murray Islanders...It would seem likely that, if it was valid, it neither extinguished nor had any continuing adverse effect upon any rights of Murray Islanders under common law native title. It is, however, appropriate to leave the question of the validity and the possible effect of that lease until another day.[16]

There was, however, an unresolved question in *Mabo* as to whether the sardine factory lease had in fact been validly granted under the *Land Act* 1910 (Qld). It was submitted that the Crown had no power under the *Lands Acts* to grant such a lease; however, as the question was not raised in argument it was not finally determined by the High Court. Thus all observations made by the Court in *Mabo* were strictly *obiter*.

It can therefore be seen that the question is not finally settled. While the majority in *Mabo* agreed that when the Crown grants a lease, that grant is inconsistent with the continued right of native title and does extinguish native title, there is no clear answer concerning reservation clauses.

National Native Title Tribunal Guidelines

The National Native Title Tribunal's guidelines regarding the Tribunal's dealings with claims over pastoral leases indicate that the Tribunal Registrar will not accept native title claims over land that has been subject to a lease where the lease confers exclusive possession.[17] However, claims will be accepted over pastoral leases if the lease is invalid to the extent that it is inconsistent with native title, or if the lease is not validated pursuant to the Commonwealth *Native Title Act* 1993 or by equivalent provisions of a State or Territory law. Claims will also be accepted where there is a reservation within that lease which grants rights to Aboriginal peoples. These guidelines also indicate that the Tribunal will not accept claims that seek rights that are wider than the terms of any reservation.

3. The Various Arguments for Dealing with Reservation Clauses in Leases

(i) Exclusive Possession and Reservation Clauses

Consideration should be given to the legal nature of the lease itself. An essential element in the creation of a lease is the legal right to exclusive possession. If this is not present, a true lease cannot be created despite the interest being called a lease. All that is given is a licence to use the land for certain purposes. The leading case in Australia advocating exclusive possession as the test to establish a lease is *Radaich v. Smith*.[18] In that case Windeyer J. stated:

> What then is the fundamental right which a tenant has that distinguishes his position from that of a licensee? It is an interest in land as distinct from a personal permission to enter the land and use it for some stipulated purpose or purposes. And how is it to be ascertained whether such an interest in land has been given? By seeing whether the grantee was given a legal right of exclusive possession of the land for a term or from year to year or for a life or lives. If he was he is a tenant.[19]

While the intention of the parties to grant a lease may be relevant in some circumstances, there can be no lease without a legal grant of exclusive possession.[20]

Exclusive possession means that the tenant has the right to exclude from the leased premises everyone including the landlord. This right allows the tenant to sue for trespass, to protect rights of possession granted by the lease and (subject to statutory exceptions) to bring actions for the recovery of the land. Is there exclusive possession if a leaseholder cannot remove people from the leased land? The granting of limited access rights to others, for example the landlord, the public or even by way of easement, would not necessarily destroy the character of a lease nor destroy the exclusive possession.

In *Mabo* the majority of the Court agreed that native title is extinguished by a grant of a lease conferring the right to exclusive possession of the land. The Court differed on whether reservation of rights made any difference.

It is arguable that the theoretical nature of a lease conferring exclusive possession extinguishes native title, native title rights being greater than limited rights of access; native title then would be inconsistent with a grant of exclusive possession. The result would be that Aboriginal rights reserved in a lease are effective because of the lease and not because the reservation recognises native title. If this is the correct view then no claim can be made for native title despite a reservation in favour of Aboriginal people in a lease.

(ii) Native Title — Rights of User
An alternative argument is that native title rights, being usufructuary and having some proprietary characteristics, constitute rights that are consistent with a grant of exclusive possession conferred under a pastoral lease. Native title rights in most cases consist of rights of access for traditional purposes such as hunting, gathering, fishing, access to water and for shelter. In some instances this also includes rights of access for cultural and ceremonial purposes.

These rights could, rather like an easement or a profit à prendre, remain a burden on the leased land. Rights of native title may not be such as to deprive a tenant of a legal right of exclusive possession to the land. In such case the reserved rights are native title rights and continue alongside the lease. If this view is correct then a claim under the native title legislation is available.

(iii) Lease or Licence
A less plausible argument is that the tenant under a pastoral lease does not enjoy a legal right of exclusive possession because native title rights are so extensive that despite the terminology used (pastoral lease), all that has been granted is an irrevocable licence and not a lease. In this case again native title rights would be sourced in native title itself and would not be extinguished by the lease. The reservation recognises the existing native title and has the effect of limiting the grant to a mere licence.[21]

(iv) Statutory Reservations

It is further arguable that if a statutory reservation is contained in legislation then such reservation preserves native title. This is contrasted with the position of a reservation in a lease which extinguishes native title. The reason for this can be found in the statements of Brennan J. in *Mabo*. Brennan J. found that if a lease is granted, the tenant acquires possession and the Crown acquires the reversion at the expiration of the term. Here, the Crown's radical title becomes full ownership. The statutory reservation would clearly indicate that the Crown's interest was not intended to be expanded to give absolute and beneficial ownership at the expiry of the lease.[22] Thus there would be no 'clear and plain intention' by government to extinguish native title.

On this view of a statutory reservation, the Crown is in no better position than it would have been if the lease had not been granted. This is because, as the argument runs, a statutory reservation confirms and protects the native title and negates extinguishment. Thus native title would not be extinguished under a statutory reservation. On this view, a native title claim would be available.

(v) 'The Invalidity Argument'

Henry Reynolds questions whether Aboriginal native title in land held under pastoral leases has been validly extinguished.[23] The arguments raised involve complex constitutional questions concerning States' rights to legislate in land management.

The Colonial Office policy in the 1840s was that pastoral occupation was consistent with, and could co-exist with a continuing enjoyment by Aboriginal peoples of their traditional rights of use and occupancy. An Order in Council in 1849 was designed to implement that policy.[24] The Order in Council provided:

> And whereas it is expedient that all such pastoral leases should contain such conditions, clauses of forfeiture, exceptions, and reservations, as may be necessary for securing the peaceful and effectual occupation of the land comprised in such leases, and for preventing abuses and inconveniences incident thereto.

However, while such an Order in Council conferred power on government to include a reservation in leases, it contained no legal obligation to do so and afforded no legal protection to Aboriginal rights. No statutory obligation to include reservations of Aboriginal rights in leases was enacted by the Queensland Government. Although reservation clauses have been inserted in pastoral leases in Queensland, few, if any, remain today.[25] It may have been questionable whether action by the government in granting a pastoral lease showed 'a clear and plain intention' to extinguish native title when a reservation was included in a lease. However, as each renewal of a lease is a new lease, unless there was a legal obligation to insert a reservation clause in pastoral leases this argument becomes irrelevant.

Henry Reynolds further contends that the Australian Government was bound to legislate to protect Aboriginal rights including rights over pastoral leased land because of certain Imperial legislation.[26] This argument is, in effect, that New South Wales and Queensland lacked the constitutional power to grant leases affecting Aboriginal rights to land.

The enactment of an Act entitled *An Act to Repeal the Acts of Parliament now in Force Respecting the Disposal of the Waste Lands of the Crown in Her Majesty's Australian Colonies and to make other Provision in Lieu Thereof*[27] while giving the colonies powers to legislate for the disposal of Crown lands, subjected this power to the 'preservation and fulfilment of contracts, promises and engagements made by, or on behalf of Her Majesty with respect to land'.[28] For this argument to be upheld it will be necessary to show evidence of such a 'contract, promise or engagement' made by the government for the protection of Aboriginal rights. As there were no statutory provisions recognising Aboriginal rights to land in Queensland and New South Wales, and as the Order in Council 1849 was no more than a conferral of executive power to permit and not to compel the inclusion of reservation clauses in leases, proof of such a 'contract, promise or engagement' may be difficult. With the passage of the *Australia Acts* 1986 when the repugnancy limitation arising under section 2 of the *Colonial Laws Validity Act* 1865 (Imp) was abolished, it became possible for the States to enact legislation to clarify the position. Any such legislation would be subject to the *R.D.A.*

C. Examples of Reservation Clauses

Western Australia

The laws of Western Australia have comprised a series of Land Regulations, the originals of which were issued in the form of Colonial Office circulars in 1828 and 1829 to regulate the allocation of Crown land.[29] Pastoral leases and licenses were provided for and issued under varying terms and conditions as laid down in regulations promulgated from time to time. In December 1850 an Order in Council (22 March 1850) published in the Perth Government Gazette stated that 'from and after the proclamation of that Order in Council in Western Australia, rules and regulations comprised in the following chapters of the Order in Council shall in Western Australia be observed and have the force and effect of law'. The Regulations forming part of the Order in Council included the provision that:

> Nothing contained in any pastoral lease shall prevent the Aboriginal natives of this colony from entering upon the lands comprised therein and seeking their sustenance therefrom in their accustomed manner.

A slightly amended reservation was contained in the August 1884 regulations: the right to enter upon any *unenclosed* lands comprised within the limits of any pastoral or tillage lease. Rights reserved were greatly extended by the 1865 Regulations: Clause 25 provided that suitable sites should be reserved for the exclusive use of Aboriginal natives so as to afford them free access to wood and water. The Land Regulations of 1882 provided the reservation: 'full right to the Aboriginal natives of the said colony at all times to enter upon any unenclosed or enclosed but otherwise unimproved part of the said premises for the purpose of seeking their sustenance therefrom in their accustomed manner'.

The *Land Act* 1898 (WA) repealed all former land regulations and purported to set out in full regulations for the leasing of Crown Lands. The previously existing form of reservation in the 1882 regulations was contained in that Act. This form of regulation was continued until the *Land Act Amendment Act* 1932

(WA) omitted the reservation in the standard form of pastoral lease. No reference to the reservation was made in legislation until the *Land Act Amendment Act* 1934 (WA) added a new section 106(2) which set out the statutory conditions to be contained in all pastoral leases.[30] This has remained unchanged. The current reservation clause provides:

> Aboriginal natives may at all times enter upon any unenclosed and unimproved parts of the land, the subject of a pastoral lease, to seek their sustenance in their accustomed manner.[31]

While native title rights may arguably continue over much of the leased land, it appears that native title would be extinguished over enclosed and improved parts of the land such as the areas used in relation to the homestead or in relation to cattle or sheep yards and working areas on the pastoral property.

Northern Territory

Section 38 of the *Pastoral Land Act* 1992 (NT) requires all pastoral leases to be subject to reservations in favour of Aboriginal people. This reservation applies not only to Aboriginal people who traditionally are entitled to use or occupy the leased land but also to those who ordinarily reside on the leased land. The reservation allows Aboriginal people:

(i) to enter and to be on the leased land;
(ii) to take and use the water from the natural waters and springs on the leased land; and
(iii) to take or kill for food or for ceremonial purposes animals *ferai naturai* and to take for food or for ceremonial purposes vegetable matter growing naturally on the leased land.

This reservation is stated not to apply to that part of the leased land within two kilometres of a homestead. The Act further provides that the Aboriginal people are not to erect or to use a structure on the leased land that would serve as a permanent shelter for human occupation, other than in a place on the leased land where they ordinarily reside. Rights of native title may arguably exist over most of the pastoral lease; however, native title would certainly be extinguished within two kilometres of the homestead.

South Australia

In South Australia the *Pastoral Land Management and Conservation Act* 1989[32] guarantees that Aboriginal people may enter, travel across or stay on the pastoral land for the purposes of their traditional pursuits. No camping is permitted within one kilometre of any house or building or within five hundred metres of a dam. Leases generally contain a standard form of reservation which allows Aboriginal people the following rights:

(i) full and free access into, upon, over and from the land except such parts as improvements have been erected upon, and full access to the springs and surface waters thereon; and

(ii) to make and erect wurlies and other native dwellings; and

(iii) to take and use for food, birds and animals *ferai naturae* as if the lease had not been made.

Such reservation would arguably allow rights of native title to continue except in those areas specifically excepted or where improvements have been erected upon the leased land.[33]

D. The Significance of the Preservation of Native Title

Reservations contained in leases or mandated by Statute preserve certain Aboriginal rights. Why then is it important to determine whether the reserved rights are native title rights? One reason is that if mining is to be conducted over pastoral lease land in the future then the native title holders would have the 'right to negotiate' concerning the granting of mining interests. That right would not be available to native title holders if they simply held rights that were sourced in the lease itself or in statutory provisions. Similarly, if a mining company wished to renew a lease over a pastoral property, where no legally enforceable right to renew existed, native title holders would have a 'right to negotiate' with government concerning the renewal.[34]

Another reason may be because section 47 of the *Native Title Act* 1993 (Cth) allows Aboriginal people who hold a pastoral lease to obtain native title under the Act. The Act provides that it is still necessary to prove any connection required by common law to establish native title rights. There is also the question of what happens to the reserved rights if the lease expires or is surrendered. If the rights are classified as native title they would continue independently of the lease.

E. Occupation Rights or Native Title?

The validation of a lease and the subsequent extinguishment of native title does not confer rights to remove Aboriginal people who reside on, or have access over a pastoral lease. This is guaranteed in section 15(2) of *the Native Title Act* 1993 (Cth). Section 15(2) does not, however, state the legal nature of the 'right' that is provided to Aboriginal people. Is this a licence, or simply a right of occupation recognised by the *Native Title Act*? Could it be argued that the right is a right of native title? 'Native title' is defined in section 223 of the Act by reference to the rights and interests that were possessed under the traditional laws and customs of the community. Rights of hunting, gathering and fishing are recognised as native title under section 223. Some or all of these rights may be encompassed under section 15(2) and could also be recognised as rights and interests at common law. So, does section 15(2) create native title? Native title is further defined in section 223 to include any replacement of common law rights by statutory rights. If section 15(2) confers statutory rights then does it also confer some limited form of native title? Is this an extinguishment where there is no extinguishment? Probably the section does no more than recognise and preserve rights to stay on the leased land but the position is not clear. Section 15(2) does not require the lease to contain any clause guaranteeing such rights. It will be a question of fact whether Aboriginal people actually reside on, or have access over the relevant land.

The validation of a leasehold title with the subsequent extinguishment of native title by a lease under section 15 of the *Native Title Act* 1993 (Cth) does not affect the rights that Aboriginal people have under legislation, at common law or pursuant to a reservation. This is guaranteed under section 16(b) of the Act. These rights or interests are stated to be rights other than native title rights. What is the effect of section 16 rights? Is this a real extinguishment of native title rights under section 15 as native title holders can exercise substantively the same rights under Section 16?

These provisions apply to Commonwealth leases. However, section 19 allows States to have laws to the same effect that will validate 'past acts' and extinguish native title. Thus the same provision could apply in State legislation.

F. Renewals of Pastoral Leases

A renewal of a pastoral lease granted before 1 July 1993 may be deemed to be a 'past act' under section 228(3) of the *Native Title Act* 1993 (Cth) where any offer, commitment, arrangement or undertaking was made prior to that date. Subject to complying with certain restrictions (for example that similar activities are carried on under the renewed lease and that the renewed lease takes effect on the termination of the previous interest)[35] the renewal of existing pastoral leases appears to pose few problems.

The future renewal, regrant or extension of the term of a pastoral lease could also be classified as a 'permissible future act' under the *Native Title Act* 1993 (Cth).[36] Where a legally 'enforceable right', that is a right contained in the lease itself or in the legislation guaranteeing renewal, existed and was created before 1 January 1994, then such a right of renewal is protected.[37] This is subject to the renewed, regranted or extended lease containing the same reservations or conditions in favour of Aboriginal people and that the lease is subject to the same terms and conditions and does not create proprietary interests greater than were created by the initial lease.[38]

Where no rights to renew or regrant a pastoral lease exist or if the renewal did not comply with the limitations discussed above, then native title holders (where native title has not been extinguished) would have a right to negotiate with government concerning the renewal or regrant.

Conclusion

Of the varying views on the effect of reservations in pastoral leases the analysis by Brennan J. appears to be correct: the true legal nature of a lease as a grant of exclusive possession of land excludes native title rights. It is also possible, however, that even on the technical analysis of the true legal nature of a lease, native title rights could, in a similar way to an easement or profit à prendre, continue despite the grant of legal possession under a lease. There is at present no settled answer to the question whether a pastoral lease with reservations terminates native title. At the time of writing the matter is still being argued and pastoral leases are currently an issue in the *Wik* claim.[39]

The author thanks Carolyn Sappideen for her valuable assistance in the preparation of this article.

Notes

1. *Native Title Act* 1993 (Cth) (hereinafter referred to as *N.T.A.*) ss.15(1), 228(2), 229(4).
2. *Id.* s.228(1) defines 'past act' to include the situation where native title existed and the act was invalid to any extent but would have been valid to that extent if native title did exist. S.15(1) validates such 'past acts'.
3. *Id.* s.15(1).
4. French J. has raised this interesting question. Justice R.S. French, 'Pastoral Leases, Reservations, and Native Title' in M. Edmunds (ed.), *Land, Rights, Laws: Issues of Native Title* (Canberra: Native Title Research Unit, AIATSIS,1994), Issue Paper No.1. See also on the question of pastoral leases Justice R.S. French, 'The Role of the National Native Title Tribunal' in R. Bartlett and G. Meyers (eds.), *Native Title Legislation in Australia* (Perth: Centre for Commercial and Resource Law, University of Western Australia Murdoch University, 1994).
5. See Justice French, *supra* note 4.
6. *Mabo v. Queensland* (1992) 175 C.L.R. 1.
7. *Id.* 69–73.
8. *Id.* 110.
9. *Id.* 68.
10. *Ibid.*
11. (1993) 104 D.L.R. (4th) 470.
12. (1992) 175 C.L.R. 1, 69–73 per Brennan J., 110 per Deane and Gaudron JJ.
13. In *Waanyi* French J., President, National Native Title Tribunal considered that *Mabo* (No. 2) establishes that the grant of a leasehold unqualified by any right of access in favour of Aboriginal people extinguishes native title. However, this general proposition is subject to the terms and conditions of particular leases which, for one reason or another, may negative the characterisation of the grant as intending extinguishment. (*In the Matter of the Native Title Act 1993 and in the Matter of the Waanyi* Application No. QN94/9) 75.
14. Dawson J. agreed with Brennan J. and considered that the lease was inconsistent with the preservation of native title although the lease was subject to conditions. *Id.* 158.
15. *Id.* 72–73.
16. *Id.* 117.
17. National Native Title Tribunal Guidelines in Relation to Claims over Freehold land and Certain Leaseholds, revised September 1994. Consistent with the Tribunal's Guidelines an application has been refused on the ground that a pastoral lease granted by the Queensland Government prior to 1975 extinguished native title. (See In the *Matter of the Native Title Act 1993 and in the Matter of the Waanyi* Application No. QN94/9.)
18. (1959) 101 C.L.R. 209.
19. *Id.* 222.
20. See for example *Wood v. Browne* [1984] 2 Qd.R. 593. Campbell C.J. (Kelly J. concurring) said '...the arrangement must be looked at as a whole in order to ascertain the intention of the parties and although exclusive possession is essential for there to be a lease, it does not necessarily establish tenancy' (596). See *Street v. Mountford* [1985] A.C. 809. Lord Templeman found that a lease will be created where the legal requirements

are satisfied and the parties cannot alter the status of their agreement by referring to it as a license. However, he further noted (826-827) that an occupier who enjoys exclusive possession is not necessarily a tenant under a lease.
21. At least one commentator has taken this view – See Dr. H.A. Amankwah, 'Extinguishment of Native Title and Pastoral Leases Revisited' (1993) 3 *Aboriginal Legal Bulletin* 13. See also R. Bartlett, 'The Aboriginal Land Which may be Claimed at Common Law: Implications of *Mabo*' (1992) 22 *Western Australian Law Review* 272, 287-288. However, it is considered that leases must be distinguished from occupational licences.
22. See Bartlett, *supra* note 20.
23. H. Reynolds, 'Native Title and Pastoral Leases' in M. A. Stephenson (ed.), *Mabo: A Judicial Revolution* (Brisbane: University of Queensland Press, 1993), 120. See also H. Reynolds, *Law of the Land* (2nd ed., Victoria: Penguin Books Australia Ltd., 1992), 146-148.
24. Professor Reynolds explains the imprecision of the Order in Council in a statement by Secretary of State, Earle Grey, that the Order would be sufficient if it was accompanied by an explanatory dispatch. So the true meaning was to be found less in the Order and more in the dispatch. In accompanying correspondence Earle Grey said there could be 'little doubt that the intention of the government was ... to give only the exclusive right of pasturage in the runs, not the exclusive occupation of the land, as against the Natives using it for ordinary purposes'. Reynolds, 'Native Title and Pastoral Leases', *supra* note 22, 127.
25. Clause reserving to the Aboriginals 'free access to the said parcel of land' which would 'enable them to procure the animals, birds, fish and other foods of which they subsist'.
26. Reynolds, 'Native Title and Pastoral Leases', *supra* note 22, 128-130.
27. 18 & 19 Vic. c.56 (1855). Section 1 of this Act repealed the Acts 6 Vic. c.36 *An Act for Regulating the Sale of Waste Land in the Australian Colonies* and 10 Vic C.104 *An Act to Amend an Act for Regulating the Sale of Waste Land belonging to the Crown in the Australian Colonies*.
28. In s.30 of the *Constitution Act* 1876 (Qld), the same restraint was placed on Queensland after its separation from New South Wales.
29. The author acknowledges the assistance of the Pastoral Board of Western Australia in obtaining this information.
30. If a lease were issued between 1932–1934 (when the reservation clause was omitted) then native title would be extinguished on the *Mabo* test, despite a reservation clause subsequently being inserted in the pastoral lease.
31. *Land Act* 1889 (WA) as amended s.106(2).
32. *N.T.A.* s.47.
33. For a discussion of such clauses: see F. Brennan S.J., 'Pastoral Leases, *Mabo* and the *Native Title Act* 1993 in M. Edmunds (ed.), *Land, Rights, Laws: Issues of Native Title* (Canberra: Native Titles Research Unit AIATSIS, 1994), Issues Paper No. 1, 3.
34. Brennan, *supra* note 32.
35. *N.T.A.* s.228(4).
36. *Id.* s.235(7).
37. *Id.* ss.25, 235(7).
38. *Id.* s.235(7).
39. A claim raised in current proceedings in the Federal Court of Australia known as the *Wik* claim.

The Commonwealth Native Title Act 1993: A Critique

Hon. P.D. Connolly, Q.C.*

The main thrust of this legislation is two fold. First, it prescribes the extent to which acts of sovereign authority, legislative or otherwise, extinguish or otherwise affect native title as discovered by the High Court in *Mabo v. State of Queensland (No. 2)*.[1] Secondly, it prescribes the compensation recoverable for loss or diminution of the rights enjoyed under native title. The task of reviewing this legislation is not an easy one. Its subject matter is title to the land comprised in the Australian continent, and that subject is not within any of the enumerated grants of power in section 51 of the Constitution. Again, the native title, the existence of which was declared by the High Court, is something the nature and incidents of which are at present unknown. And thirdly, the Commonwealth has not been prepared to accept (or so it would appear) all that the High Court has laid down with respect to acts of sovereignty and their effect upon this new form of title.

Effect of Acts of Sovereignty

It will be convenient first to examine the provisions of the Act on this subject, bearing in mind that the law as laid down by the High Court includes the proposition that, where the Crown has validly alienated land by granting an interest that is wholly or partially inconsistent with a continuing right to enjoy native title, that title is extinguished to the extent of the inconsistency, and that where the Crown has validly and effectively appropriated

---

* Former Justice of the Supreme Court of Queensland and currently President of the Court of Appeal of Solomon Islands and a Judge of the Court of Appeal of Kiribati.

land to itself and the appropriation is wholly or partially inconsistent with a continuing right to enjoy native title, the title is extinguished, again to the extent of the inconsistency.

The effect of acts of sovereignty on native title is governed, in relation to the Commonwealth, by sections 14 and 18 and in relation to a State or Territory by sections 19 and 20. The sovereign act which is calculated to affect native title is described in the legislation as simply an 'act'. It is elaborately defined in section 226, but for present purposes it is sufficient to say that it includes both legislation and grants under legislation or other authority. A provision of questionable validity was clause 211(4) which provided that 'an act is not to be taken into account if it is declared by the regulations to be excluded'. If a sovereign act which would have the effect recognised by the statement of the new common law is to be denied that effect by a law of the Commonwealth the source of that law must obviously be identified so far as the States are concerned. The provision has been deleted from what is now section 226.

Past Acts of the Commonwealth

By section 14 such acts are taken always to have been valid. Section 15 classifies past acts into four categories: *Category A past acts* being freehold grants before 1 January 1994 and subsisting on that date; freehold grants made after 1 January 1994 by reason of rights acquired in the past; and acts pursuant to arrangements entered into prior to 1 July 1993.[2] Grants to a Crown agency, or to or for the benefit of Aborigines or Torres Strait Islanders are excluded. The first mentioned exclusion is plainly inconsistent with the common law as formulated by the Court, while the second reflects the decision of the Court in *Mabo v. State of Queensland (No. 1)*[3] subject to similar qualifications. Grants of commercial leases, agricultural leases, pastoral leases and residential leases are also classified as Category A past acts, as are residential developments on mining leases.[4] With similar qualifications the construction of a public work is a Category A past act; *Category B past acts* being leases other than those within Category A and mining leases, subject to qualifications similar to those set out in relation to Category A;[5]

Category C past acts being mining leases[6] and *Category D past acts* being any other past acts.[7]

Turning to the effect of the various past acts of the Commonwealth, it has been seen that section 14 declares them always to have been valid. The question which arises is why this provision was enacted at all, for, as has been said above, the High Court so declared in *Mabo (No. 2)*.[8] Section 15 provides that Category A acts extinguish native title, there being special provisions in relation to the construction of public works.[9] Category B acts extinguish native title to the extent to which they are inconsistent with it,[10] and Categories C and D in effect suspend native title rights during their currency to the extent of their inconsistency with them.[11] Section 16 entitles the native title holders to compensation from the Commonwealth for any of these acts according to their effect. This is, of course, a major departure from the common law rights declared by *Mabo (No. 2)*.[12] The Court, of course, said nothing in relation to compensation, for there cannot be compensation for an act of sovereignty except as a matter of grace. Past acts are defined by section 228(2) as legislative acts before 1 July 1993 and any other types of act which occurred before 1 January 1994 which were invalid to any extent (by reason of the existence of native title). The High Court judgment does not suggest that past acts, at least prior to the enactment of the *Racial Discrimination Act* 1975 (Cth) (herinafter referred to as the *R.D.A.*), were invalid by reason of the existence of native title. The acts in question were those of the Crown in right of the colonies (or the States as they subsequently became) or, since Federation, of the Commonwealth or the Territories. The only acts of the Crown therefore which might call for validation are those which occurred after the passing of that Act in 1975. Before leaving the position of the Commonwealth, some attention should be directed to section 18 which is a rather mysterious provision. It is headed 'Where "just terms" invalidity'. It applies 'if the *invalidity* (disregarding section 14) of a past (Commonwealth) act results from a paragraph 51(xxxi) acquisition ... otherwise than on ... just terms'. It thus assumes the invalidity of past acts of acquisition otherwise than on just terms. This assumption is of course correct if it was in truth an acquisition under section 51(xxxi).[13] The effect of section 18 would seem to be to sanction the acquisition allegedly made under section 51(xxxi) although not made on just terms, once just terms were provided, something the Commonwealth just could not do.

Compare section 53(1) which calls for the same comment. The provisions will perhaps be read by the courts as providing for fresh statutory acquisitions under section 51(xxxi) where just terms are ultimately provided. If so their effect will not be momentous. However, their place in the scheme of this Act is unclear. Is section 53(1) intended to apply to the past grants of the Commonwealth? Such grants were, of course, like those of the colonies or States, not seen as acquisitions under section 51(xxxi) or under resumption and compensation legislation but as acts of sovereignty, the title being in the Crown. *Mabo (No. 2)*[14] decided that the beneficial title was not in the Crown but affirmed the unchallengeable sovereign right of the Crown to make such grants.

The provisions relating to the past acts of the Commonwealth call for a number of other comments, all of them being fairly obvious. The Commonwealth assertion of the validity of its past acts is not surprising, it really accords with *Mabo (No. 2)*.[15] Any of its acts pursuant to a statute since it enacted the *R.D.A.* would probably have been regarded as overriding that Act. Be that as it may, the main innovation is in the creation of a right to compensation for the past sovereign and statutory acts of the Commonwealth which did not previously exist.

Past Acts of the States/Territories

An examination will now be made of the provisions relating to the past grants of the States and Territories. They are sections 19 and 20 of the *Native Title Act* 1993 (Cth).[16] Section 19 empowers the States and Territories to provide that past acts attributable to them are valid and taken always to have been valid if the law by which this is done contains provisions to the same effect as sections 15 and 16, the provisions of which categorise the past acts as set out above in relation to the Commonwealth, and preserve beneficial reservations and conditions in favour of Aboriginal peoples and Torres Strait

Islanders. Two questions arise. First, what need is there to
validate the past acts of States and Territories? The decision in
Mabo (No. 2)[17] does not suggest any. The legislation of
Queensland struck down by *Mabo (No. 1)*[18] was thought by the
majority to be inconsistent with the R.D.A. which had come into
force in 1975. The validity of the anterior grants by the colony
and later by the State of Queensland were not in doubt. It may
be that there has been concern over other grants since 1975,
although made in good faith and in total ignorance of native title
which was not created by the High Court until June 1992. If so,
validation may be called for but why with the permission of the
Parliament of the Commonwealth? Native title, according to
Mabo (No. 2)[19] is recognised by the common law as a type of
title which may be extinguished by sovereign grants or
legislation. The problem is posed of course by the R.D.A. which,
as has been seen in *Mabo (No. 1)*,[20] may result, depending on
the view of the courts, in the invalidity of validating legislation
unless it provides for compensation. The thinking therefore may
be that section 19 is intended to be read as necessarily implying
that acts of States or Territorial validation under section 19 are
to be treated as exceptions to the R.D.A. In other words, for
political reasons, the party in government does not wish overtly
to displace the R.D.A. but rather to achieve this result without
saying so.

It would seem obvious that the Commonwealth can repeal the
R.D.A. and therefore can obviously limit its operation as it thinks
fit. However, if this is not the intention and effect, what other
legislative power sustains section 19? It is not the function of the
Commonwealth to give permission to the States to pass
legislation. The answer can only be that it is hoped to sustain it
under section (xxvi) as a special law for the descendants of the
original inhabitants. This may be regarded as questionable. Of
itself section 19 gives nothing to such descendants. Indeed its
purpose is to give the States and Territories authority to take title
away from them. In fact it gives a State no authority it does not
already possess.

On the other hand, the provisions of sections 15 and 16 which
must be incorporated in the State legislation for the States to
acquire power under section 19 of this Act, are by no means of

minor importance. The effect of past sovereign acts under this legislation is distinctly more limited than under the common law as stated by the High Court. It is only grants of freehold and of some leaseholds which continue to have the full effect of extinguishing native title. At common law grants of all leaseholds extinguished native title,[21] doubtlessly because they carried the right to exclusive possession and were wholly inconsistent with the notion of continuing native title. The common law as declared by the Court involved no notion of revival of native title when the term in question came to an end. Again Category C past acts, namely the grant of mining leases, could obviously have the same result. A lease of a parcel of land for whatever purpose, an incident of which is the right to exclusive possession, is wholly inconsistent with the continued existence of native title over the same land. The notion of suspension of native title rights and their re-emergence at the end of mining operations is wholly a creature of this Act. As to Category D past acts, one would need, under the common law, to examine the nature and incidents of the act in question before expressing an opinion, but by section 15(1)(d) the Commonwealth's non-extinguishment principle is to apply. It would seem obvious therefore that the legal authority of the States and Territories at common law is considerably more extensive than it would be if they subjected themselves to sections 15 and 16 regimes.

Section 10 of the Commonwealth *Native Title Act* 1993 provides for the recognition and protection of native title and section 11 provides that native title may not be extinguished contrary to the Act. Section 12 provides that subject to the Act the common law of Australia in respect of native title has, after 30 June 1993, the force of a law of the Commonwealth. This, of course, is designed to bring into operation section 109 of the Constitution. This last mentioned provision is, however, a curious one for the reason that the content of this particular law of the Commonwealth is at present unknowable. The High Court has not affected to state the precise nature or incidents of native title. For this, one must search the laws and customs of the indigenous people who, by those laws and customs, have a connexion with the land. As those laws and customs seem to vary greatly and would seem to be capable of being different for every parcel of land involved, this is an impossible task until the laws and customs in question have been identified by evidence, for they are not of course recorded in writing. The only other comment which should be made about section 11 is that it appears to be prospective. One would not naturally read it as intending to invalidate the past acts of sovereignty on which most of the land-holding of Australia is based.

It is tolerably clear from the legislation that the Commonwealth is not unaware that the constitutional validity of this legislation may be challenged and is, at least in some respects, open to question. The last two paragraphs of the preamble plainly invoke the *Racial Discrimination Convention Article* 1(4) via section 51(xxix) and section 51(xxvi) for the Parliament intends that the Act be 'a special law for the descendants of the original inhabitants of Australia'. Moreover, the preamble supports the view expressed above that the capacity of the States to limit the effect of native title is intended to be cut down, for it recites that the rights and interests of native title holders under the common law of Australia—obviously meaning the body of law as modified and stated by *Mabo (No. 2)*[22]—need to be significantly supplemented.

This may well be the reason why Subdivision B of Division 2 of Part 2 of the *Native Title Act* 1993 (Cth) (sections 19 and 20) holds out to the States the inducement of being able to 'validate' their past acts provided that they enact provisions to the same effect as sections 15 and 16. As already pointed out, this assumes that the States need to 'validate' their past acts and that, in any case, in so doing they need the assistance of the Commonwealth. The suggestion has already been made that there is no reason to suppose that in fact they do. It may be that all of this is no more than a carrot to induce the donkey to come into the parlour of the spider - if I may mix the metaphors. Section 20(1) provides that on validation in accordance with section 19 the native title holders are entitled to compensation. Moreover, section 20 is intended to face the States with a dilemma for section 20(2) provides that the native title holders are entitled to compensation for acts which have *not* been validated by the States in accordance with section 19.

A minor curiosity of the provisions which confer the right to compensation is that the claim is given to native title *holders*. Section 224 defines 'native title holder' as the body corporate so registered, or in any other case the person or persons who 'hold the native title'. The whole gravamen of the right to claim compensation is that the title has been taken away. No doubt the language will be construed in accordance with principles of 'simple English' to mean the exact opposite of what it says.

Compensation for past acts attributable to a State or Territory is payable by the State or Territory.[23] Section 239 provides that an act is 'attributable' to the Commonwealth, a State or a Territory if the act is done by the Crown in right of the Commonwealth, the State or Territory or the Parliament thereof or any person under a law thereof. Presumably this definition refers to the past as well as the present, but what of acts done by the constituent colonies before Federation? It may be that Covering Clause 6 of the *Commonwealth of Australia Constitution Act* 1900 establishes legal identity of the States with the antecedent colonies. One asks oneself where the legislative power of the Commonwealth to impose an obligation to pay compensation on a State by virtue of an act of sovereignty by the antecedent colony is to be found. It seems likely that section (xxvi) is to be the lynch pin of the Commonwealth case in this regard. Before turning to section (xxvi) an entertaining feature of all of this is that if descendants of the Aboriginal people of the late eighteenth and early nineteenth centuries should emerge with claims against the areas now occupied by the cities of Sydney, Melbourne and Hobart as well indeed as Brisbane, the act in question is likely to be that of the colony of New South Wales, and the compensation therefore is likely to be payable, if the above analysis should be correct, by the State of New South Wales!

It seems to be the view of the Attorney-General, Mr Lavarch, that the central power available to the Commonwealth is indeed section (xxvi).[24] Understandably, he drew attention to the *Tasmanian Dam* case[25] in which a majority of the Court held that the Commonwealth legislation which subjected a vast area of Tasmania to an international regime under the *Convention for the Protection of the World Cultural and Natural Heritage* of

1972 was sustained by the consideration that this would prevent the inundation of certain Aboriginal sacred sites so as to be justly regarded as within section (xxvi).

Future Acquisitions and Grants

The legislation also makes elaborate provision with respect to future acquisitions. Part 2 Division 3 (sections 21 to 44) deals with future acts affecting native title. Section 21 provides for the extinction or modification of native title rights by agreement. Critical to non-consensual acquisitions and grants of land affected by native title is the definition of permissible future acts. Section 226 defines an 'act' in reference to native title in wide terms so that it includes both legislation and the making of grants under any authority of the Crown. A future act, by section 233, is a legislative act affecting native title after 1 July 1993 and any other act after 1 January 1994. Permissible future acts are defined by section 235 as legislation and other acts which apply to native title holders and place them in the same legal position as if they held 'ordinary' title to the land in question. 'Ordinary title' is defined by section 253 as freehold or, in the Australian Capital Territory or Jervis Bay, as leasehold, with the exception of grants to the indigenous people. Future legislation which does not answer this description will be impermissible[26] and is to be invalid to the extent to which it affects native title.[27]

The extinguishment of native title is dependent upon its being the subject of acquisition under a Compulsory Acquisition Act and on just terms.[28] Clearly enough, a State cannot grant a clear title to unalienated Crown land in future without resuming the native title at a cost which cannot be predicted and which will, of course, reduce the value, perhaps substantially, of the nation's land reserves.

Compensation for Past State/Territory Acts

Assuming that the State chooses not to 'validate' in accordance with section 19, the native title holders are entitled to compensation.[29] Such compensation is payable only in accordance with Division 5 of Part 2.[30] The criteria for determining compensation are contained in section 51. By section

51(1) it is an entitlement 'on just terms to compensate the native title holders for any loss, diminution, impairment or other effect of the act on their native title rights and interests'. This seems to leave the basis on which quantum is to be assessed at large. It is instructive to examine this aspect of the legislation on the assumption that the act will not be an acquisition under a Compulsory Acquisition Act. On that assumption the 'similar compensable interest' test will not be satisfied in terms of section 240 for compensation would not be payable under any law on the assumption that the native title holders held 'ordinary title'. The reason for this is that freehold or leasehold grants of unalienated Crown land were made long ago; there never was any provision for compensation for the loss of native title interests which did not then exist; and the acquisition did not occur under any Act which provided for compensation. This in turn means that section 51(3) will not operate in relation to the act in question. Section 51(4) will not operate unless there is a Compulsory Acquisition Act for the State or Territory in question and there will be no specific provision of the *Commonwealth Act* which governs the assessment of compensation, except that section 51(1) identifies the subject matter to be valued and requires the terms be just. This will leave it to the courts to decide such critical questions as the relevant date for determining the value of the lost or diminished interest. There is, of course, no provision for limitation of the period in which applications for compensation are to be made.

Mabo (No. 2)[31] did not contemplate the possibility of anything like the economic nightmare which this *Native Title Act* 1993 (Cth) could produce, which is, at the worst, claims for the current value of every square metre of Australian soil granted by the Crown since 1788. The High Court formulated, somewhat vaguely, a test which claimants must satisfy, which is that they continue to have 'a connexion with the land' in question according to 'the laws and customs' of the Aboriginal people in question. This will be decided by assessors, either of Aboriginal descent or sympathetic sociologists, on evidence which is not to be subject to cross examination except by leave. The court which will play the biggest part in this will be the Federal Court, an impressive body of judges for the most part. Much will depend on who in fact constitutes the Federal Court for the purposes of the legislation. This cannot be predicted.

On the judicial side, one bright spot is that the older claims, the claims for the acts of the mother colony in what are now the eastern States other than New South Wales, may well be within the original jurisdiction of the High Court as being claims against that State by residents of other States which may well be the reason for the reference to the High Court in section 50(3)(b).

Delay and Frustration of Government Policies

It is important that the validity of even permissible future acts is to be subject to Subdivision B of Division 3, which deals with the right of native title holders to make submissions to government about certain proposed future acts and imposes on the government the obligation to negotiate in good faith with a view to obtaining the agreement of those native title holders to the doing of the act and the conditions if any to be complied with. The subdivision applies to government proposals in relation to mining rights and the acquisition of native title for the benefit of others. The category may be extended by the Commonwealth minister who may also exclude an act.[32] The requirements for such an exclusion are set out in section 26(4). The machinery for negotiation is initiated by notice of intention to do the act by the government in question.[33] An arbitral body is provided to mediate the negotiations[34] and provision is made for an expedited procedure[35] when the government in question considers it appropriate.[36]

The arbitral body is to be the National Native Title Tribunal (hereinafter referred to as the N.N.T.T.) for both the Commonwealth and States and in addition an arbitral body can be recognised for the State in question. Recognition of the State arbitral body is recognition by the Commonwealth minister and the criteria to be satisfied before a State body receives the accolade of recognition by the Commonwealth minister are elaborately described in section 251(2). The arbitral bodies will, in default of agreement, make determinations as to whether the future acts may or may not be done and the conditions to be complied with,[37] the criteria for the making of such determinations being set out in section 39. These, however described, seem clearly to be judicial functions. As such a State body would exercise invested federal jurisdiction it is required to satisfy section 77(iii) of the Constitution that it be a court of a State, and section 48(4) of the *Native Title Bill* so required. This provision seems to have been deleted in the *Native Title Act* 1993 (Cth). Section 251(4) effectively places the State body in question under the control of the minister who, if he or she is not satisfied with it at any time, advises the State minister to that effect. If the recalcitrant body does not mend its ways in ninety days it is derecognised by the Commonwealth minister.[38] Moreover, section 42(1) empowers the State minister to overrule its determinations or overrule them subject to condition.[39] Similarly the N.N.T.T. may be overruled by the Commonwealth minister although its President is a judge of the Federal Court and its Deputy President a former judge. These provisions are quite anomalous, violating as they do the principle of the separation of powers in what most people will see as an unacceptable fashion. It may well be that judges will decline to constitute such a body.

If there is no agreement in relation to an authority to prospect or explore within four months of the notice under section 29, any party may apply to the arbitral body for a determination, and in other cases after six months.[40] The arbitral body must take reasonable steps to give a determination within a further four months and six months respectively from the date of the application.[41] The arbitral body has a very wide discretion. It may approve, disapprove or approve subject to conditions.[42] Although it may not award royalties as a condition of consent,[43] it is required to take a wide range of environmental and cultural considerations into account.[44] The constitutional power to impose this last mentioned requirement is open to question. It would not appear to be supported by section 51(xxvi). This may well explain the inclusion in this subdivision of section 42 which sets up the corporations power section 51(xx) wherever the proposed grantee is a corporation.

Two comments are called for at this stage. The legislation quite plainly goes far beyond giving a right of compensation to native title holders. It empowers the arbitral body to frustrate the government proposal altogether. Resumption statutes are commonly confined to the former. Now on any fair view, native title is a far more limited interest than freehold or leasehold, involving, at the most, intermittent use by a nomadic people. It may reasonably be questioned whether justice to the indigenous peoples really needs to go as far as this. The second comment which may fairly be made is that this subdivision cannot be rested upon anything done or said by the High Court in *Mabo (No. 2)*.[45]

Jurisdictional and Procedural Matters

A determination of native title, by section 225 is a determination of the following:

(a) whether native title exists in relation to a particular area of land or waters;
(b) if it exists:
   (i) who holds it; and
   (ii) whether the native title rights and interests confer possession, occupation, use and enjoyment of the land or waters on its holders to the exclusion of all others; and
   (iii) if not, the nature and extent of the native title rights and interests; and
   (iv) in any case—the nature and extent of any other interest in relation to the land or waters that may affect the native title rights and interests.

Section 3(1) provides for an application to be made to the Native Title Registrar for a determination of native title or to revoke or vary such a determination. An application for compensation seems to be made under section 50(2), again to the Registrar. On acceptance by the Registrar the matter is dealt with by the N.N.T.T. the main function of which seems to be the mediation of opposed claims. If the application is opposed and agreement is not reached, it then goes to the Federal Court.[46]

There is little point in examining all of the procedural provisions. The Federal Court, however, must take account of the cultural and customary concerns of Aboriginal peoples and Torres Strait Islanders and is not to be bound by technicalities, legal forms or rules of evidence.[47] An assessor is to be assigned to the court but is not to exercise judicial power, being subject to the control and direction of the court.[48] An unusual provision, which may prove dangerous in this area, is section 86 which empowers the Federal Court to accept as evidence the transcript of evidence in other cases and to adopt recommendations and findings, decisions or judgments of other tribunals. The reason it may be dangerous is, of course, that the relevant events have occurred up to two hundred years ago and that the evidence of the claimants is likely to include hearsay upon hearsay, little of which can be tested, or supported by alleged experts in the fields of anthropology, ethnology, sociology and the like, whose evidence will most likely be based on largely unverifiable hypotheses. It is clear from section 184 that a claim to native title may be made not only to the Registrar but to a 'recognised State/Territory body'.[49] Section 61 contains no reference to the State/Territory body but section 186(1) makes it clear that if the application is made to that body it may be initiated there, and by section 191 the Registrar may delegate his or her functions to that body, a truly extraordinary provision if the body in question is a court of a State.

Some of the procedural provisions are unusual and somewhat disturbing. By section 89 a party has a right to appear at a conference which is held with a view to resolving matters in dispute. However, by section 91(3) an assessor may direct that a conference be held in private and give directions as to the persons who may be present. By section 92(1) the Federal Court may direct that evidence given before an assessor or the contents of any document produced to an assessor must not be disclosed. Section 93 provides for the taking of evidence by an assessor and his leave is required for cross-examination or re-examination.[50] It should be noted that similar provisions apply in relation to the N.N.T.T.[51]

Notes

1. (1992) 175 C.L.R. 1.
2. *Native Title Act* 1993 (Cth) (hereinafter referred to as *N.T.A.*) s.229(2)(a).
3. (1988) 166 C.L.R. 186.
4. See *N.T.A.* s.229(3) read in relation to mining leases with s.245(3).
5. *Id.* s.230.

6. *Id.* s.231.
7. *Id.* s.232.
8. (1992) 175 C.L.R. 1.
9. *N.T.A.* s.15(1)(b).
10. *Id.* s.15(1)(c).
11. *Id.* s.15(1)(d) and s.238.
12. (1992) 175 C.L.R. 1.
13. See *Grace Bros. Pty. Ltd. v. Commonwealth* (1945) 72 C.L.R. 269, 290 per Dixon J.
14. (1992) 175 C.L.R. 1.
15. *Ibid.*
16. Subdivision B of Division 2 of Part 2.
17. (1992) 175 C.L.R. 1.
18. (1988) 166 C.L.R. 186.
19. (1992) 175 C.L.R. 1.
20. (1988) 166 C.L.R. 186.
21. See *Mabo (No. 2)* (1992) 175 C.L.R. 1, 69.
22. *Ibid.*
23. *N.T.A.* s.20(3).
24. See the Attorney-General's second reading speech on 24 November 1993 (Hansard 3583).
25. *Commonwealth v. Tasmania* (1983) 158 C.L.R. 1.
26. *N.T.A.* s.236.
27. *Id.* s.22.
28. *Id.* s.23(3).
29. *Id.* s.20(2) (which is part of Division 2 of Part 2).
30. *Id.* s.48.
31. (1992) 175 C.L.R. 1.
32. *N.T.A.* s.26(2) and (3).
33. *Id.* s.29.
34. *Id.* ss.27 and 31(2).
35. *Id.* ss.29(4) and 32.
36. *Id.* s.32(1).
37. *Id.* s.38.
38. *Id.* s.251(4)(b).
39. *Id.* s.42(3).
40. *Id.* s.35.
41. *Id.* s.36(1).
42. *Id.* s.38(1).
43. *Id.* s.38(2).
44. *Id.* s.39.
45. (1992) 175 C.L.R. 1.
46. *N.T.A.* s.74.
47. *Id.* s.82.
48. *Id.* s.83.
49. *Id.* Cf. the Explanatory Memorandum Part A, page 6.
50. *Id.* s.93(5).
51. *Id.* ss.152, 154(3), 155 and 156(5).

Compensation and Valuation of Native Title

M.A. Stephenson[*]

PART A. Compensation at Common Law — *Mabo*

The High Court in *Mabo v. Queensland*[1] was divided on the question of payment of compensation for extinguishment or impairment of native title.[2] A majority considered that no compensation claim would be available on the extinguishment of native title. Deane and Gaudron JJ. found that compensatory damages would be payable where native title was extinguished without legislative authority and where the intention to extinguish native title was not indicated in clear and unambiguous words.[3]

On this question of compensation Toohey J. in *Mabo* took a very different approach and found that governments were in the position of a trustee in relation to native titleholders.[4] His Honour found that the Crown's power to extinguish native title was subject to a fiduciary or trust duty to ensure native title was not dealt with contrary to the native titleholders' interests. Accordingly, he considered that compensation might be payable for this breach of fiduciary or trust duty.[5] In the Canadian case, *Guerin v. R.*,[6] damages were held to result for breach of such a fiduciary duty in relation to the Canadian Indian title.

Where the Commonwealth Government took action to extinguish native title then such action would be subject to the Commonwealth Constitution section 51(xxxi) which requires that the laws regarding the acquisition of property must be on 'just terms'. In the case of extinguishment by States, State laws inconsistent with Commonwealth laws would be invalid

---

[*] Lecturer in Law, University of Queensland.

to the extent of any inconsistency (Commonwealth Constitution section 109). Inconsistency may arise out of the *Racial Discrimination Act* 1975 (Cth) (hereinafter referred to as the *R.D.A.*). Section 9 of the *R.D.A.* makes it unlawful for a person to do any act (involving a distinction based on race) which has the effect of impairing the enjoyment of any 'human right or fundamental freedom'. Section 10 provides that where by reason of any law, persons of a particular race do not enjoy a right to the same extent as persons of another race, then by force of that section the first mentioned persons enjoy that right to the same extent.

In *Mabo (No. 1)*[7] the High Court considered the impact of the *R.D.A.* In 1985 the Queensland Parliament passed the *Queensland Coast Islands Declaratory Act* to remove any doubt about the annexation of the Murray Islands to Queensland and to extinguish native title at the time of their annexation. The High Court declared this Act to be inconsistent with section 10 of the *R.D.A.* therefore invalid by reason of section 109 of the Constitution. The Court found that this Act which extinguished native title without compensation deprived the Murray Islanders of a right that was enjoyed by people of other races, that is a right not to be arbitrarily deprived of property (presumably without compensation). It is arguable that the discriminatory aspect was the taking without compensation and not the taking itself. Extinguishment of native title after 1975 would be subject to compensation to avoid infringement of the *R.D.A.*

Valuation questions and calculation of damages were not issues in *Mabo*. The High Court decision in *Mabo*, which was that no compensation would be payable on the extinguishment of native title meant that native title rights could be extinguished by governments without compensation prior to the *R.D.A.* but would be subject to the *R.D.A.* after 1975.

PART B. Compensation after Enactment of *Native Title Act* 1993 (Cth)

(1) Circumstances when Valuation and Compensation Issues Arise

Valuation of native title

The first issue to consider is in what circumstances native title would have to be valued. Native title will be required to be valued when the issue of compensation for the past or future extinguishment or impairment of native title is raised or when native title is acquired under the Compulsory Acquisition legislation of a State, Territory or the Commonwealth. Generally this will occur after 1975. The question of valuation of native title for the purposes of sale or transfer of native title would probably not be necessary, as native title is generally regarded as inalienable. It cannot be sold or leased. The reason for this is that the customs and traditions of most native communities have traditionally forbidden alienation. While native title may not be transferred, native title can, under the *Native Title Act* 1993 (Cth),[8] be surrendered to the Crown and exchanged for alienable or inalienable freehold, for leasehold land, or for other interests in land. Accordingly, native title might need to be valued in order to ascertain that any conversion or 'swapping' of land was fair and just.[9]

Valuation of land subject to a native title claim

Freehold and leasehold titles are not subject to native title claims and therefore valuation is unaffected. Valuations of Crown land that the government is about to alienate or grant for the first time, for example as a development lease, a tourism lease, a pastoral lease or as freehold land, would raise the potential for a native title claim. The potential for a native title claim of such an area should be recognised in the valuation and the valuation should be completed only after legal advice has been sought. Government policy will probably dictate that a 'non-claimant' application be made under the *Native Title Act* 1993 (Cth) for a determination of native title.[10] Applications to the National Native Title Tribunal for a determination of native title can be made not only by Aboriginal people claiming native title[11] but also by a 'non-claimant' — either a holder of an interest in land or by a government.[12] Could the unimproved capital value of property actually be higher where a court or tribunal has determined that no native title exists? Possibly different markets will develop for land that is judged not to be subject to native title and for land where no determination has been made that native title does not exist.[13]

(2) The *Native Title Act* 1993 (Cth) Provisions

Consideration will be given to the circumstances in which compensation is payable and the method of determining the compensation.

(A) Compensation for 'past acts'

Compensation is available for 'past acts' under the *Native Title Act*.[14] The *Native Title Act* 1993 (Cth) validates titles that were granted prior to 31 December 1993 or relevant conduct, 'past acts', occuring before that date that might have been invalid because of the existence of native title and which were granted by, or undertaken by the Commonwealth Government.[15] 'Past acts' are designated into categories for the purposes of validation and the consequences thereof.[16]

(a) Compensation for Extinguishment of Native Title
Compensation must be on 'just terms' to allow for the 'loss, diminution or impairment or other effect of the act' on native title.[17] Native title holders may claim compensation in respect of Category A[18] and Category B[19] 'past acts' or grants for the extinguishment of native title. In the case of Category B 'past acts' native title may be partially or totally extinguished.[20]

(b) Compensation for Impairment of Native Title
Where the 'past act' affects native title, that is impairs but does not actually extinguish the native title, compensation may also be claimed. Under the non-extinguishment principle native

title is suspended or impaired during the period of the interest granted and revives and has full effect on the expiry of that interest.[21] Native title holders are unable to enjoy or perform all rights of native title. For example native title rights are impaired during the term of a mining lease and can be exercised only after the mining lease comes to an end. This will be the situation in relation to Category C[22] and Category D[23] 'past acts' or grants.

(i) Compensation will be on *just terms* if that act or grant could not have been done over 'ordinary title'[24] (that is freehold title or, in the Australian Capital Territory, leasehold land) or if the act was in relation to an *offshore place*[25] (the area below the low water mark).[26]

(ii) Compensation will be assessed on the basis of the *similar compensable interest* test[27] if the native title relates to an *onshore place*[28] (the area above the low water mark) and the grant or act could have been made over 'ordinary title' land. Under the 'similar compensable interest' test, compensation will be paid in the same circumstances and assessed on the same grounds as it is for the holders of 'ordinary title'.[29] For example, if a mining interest is granted over native title land then the native title interest must be accompanied by 'full' compensation, even though only a right of hunting is lost. The effect is that native title is valued as if it were freehold land under the compensation provisions of the legislation: an extension of the High Court's interpretation of native title.

(c) Compensation under the Racial Discrimination Act 1975 (Cth)

Section 45 provides that if the effect of the *R.D.A.* is to give native title holders a right to compensation rather than to invalidate any grant or act such compensation can be pursued under the *Native Title Act* 1993 (Cth). It would have been helpful if the legislature had stipulated the effect of the *R.D.A.* It is suggested that the combined effect of the High Court decisions in *Mabo (No. 1)* and *(No. 2)* and section 10 of the *R.D.A.* is to entitle native title holders to a right to compensation for extinguishment of native title.[30] Alternatively, the combined effect of section 10 of the *R.D.A.* and the *Mabo* decisions might be that any legislation or grant of an interest in land that deprives native title holders of a right that was enjoyed by people of other races (that is the right not to be arbitarily deprived of property) could be inconsistent with the *R.D.A.* and would be invalid by reason of section 109 of the Constitution. Thus the invalid grant would be ineffective to pass title.

(d) Who is Liable to Pay Compensation?
If the title being validated by the *Native Title Act* 1993 (Cth) was issued by the Commonwealth, or if the 'past act' by the Commonwealth amounted to an 'acquisition of property under section 51(xxxi) of the Commonwealth Constitution'[31] then compensation is payable by the Commonwealth.[32] States are liable for compensation where the State granted the past title or where the State 'validates' its 'past acts'.[33]

The *Native Title Act* 1993 (Cth) is silent on the question of whether States can require grantees of interests to be responsible, or liable for compensation for 'past acts'. Presumably, as no authorisation is provided for States to share the cost, the States will bear the total costs themselves. However, provision is included in the Act for the Commonwealth to enter a written agreement with States and Territories for the provision of financial assistance in relation to any liability to pay compensation.[34] It is likely that the Federal Government would have limited liability for compensation as most grants and acts would have been made by the States.

(e) Time for Compensation
The Commonwealth *Native Title Act* 1993 provides that native title holders are entitled to compensation for the 'past acts' attributable to a State or Territory which have *not* been validated in accordance with section 19 of the *Native Title Act* 1993 (Cth).[35] Therefore it is not necessary that a grant be validated before compensation can be claimed.

No time period or cut off date has been specified in the legislation which restricts the period during which compensation may be claimed for 'past acts' or grants. Arguably every extinguishment or impairment of native title since 1788 will be subject to compensation because such titles could be regarded as invalidly granted as the interests of the native title holders were not considered. The better view, however, is that the only grants that are invalid because of the existence of native title are those which are made after the *R.D.A.* was passed in 1975.[36] Therefore compensation will be paid only for extinguishment or impairment of native title after 1975 when the *R.D.A.* was enacted.

(f) Date on Which Land Should be Valued
Would the value of native title be assessed at the date of the taking of the land, that is on the extinguishment of native title? This could occur at any time since the *R.D.A.* 1975. Alternatively, should the time for considering the value be the date of the assessment of the compensation? If the valuation is to be at the date of the taking of the land, then the question arises whether native title holders would be entitled to the payment of interest. The better view is that valuation should be determined at the time of extinguishment, and that since native title holders have not been compensated as required, interest should be payable.[37]

(g) Nature of Compensation
Usually compensation will be calculated as a monetary payment.[38] Compensation may also comprise the transfer of property or the provision of goods or services if requested by the native title holders.[39]

(B) Compensation for Future Dealings

Compensation is guaranteed under the *Native Title Act* 1993 (Cth) to native title holders in relation to any 'future acts' that affect the rights and interests of their native title.[40]

(a) Compensation for Extinguishment of Native Title
If native title is extinguished by a 'future act' then compensation must be assessed on 'just terms' to provide for any 'loss, diminution, impairment or other effect of the act' on native title.[41] Extinguishment of native title could occur by

the agreement of native title holders, for example the surrender of native title to the government.[42] Extinguishment would also take place through compulsory acquisition together with a subsequent grant of an interest.[43] The native title holders are entitled to compensation on 'just terms' even though the State legislation provides for assessment on a different basis.[44] Any compensation payable by the States to native title holders for a compulsory acquisition is to be on constitutional 'just terms' although other 'ordinary' title holders may not be entitled to such compensation. 'Just terms' will, in effect, be a top up measure where the compensation under State or Territory legislation is less than 'just terms'. Perhaps this has been done because the spiritual connection with the land is valued as well. Where the future act is an acquisition under a Compulsory Acquisition Act then in assessing 'just terms' the criteria in the relevant State or Territory Compulsory Acquisition Act for determining compensation must also be considered.[45]

(b) Compensation for Impairment
Where impairment rather than extinguishment is involved native title holders will be entitled to compensation as follows:
  (i) Compensation will be assessed on the basis of the *similar compensable interest* test. This provides compensation on the same basis as it is for ordinary title holders where *onshore* native title is impaired.[46] If no State right to compensation exists for impairment of title, then a Commonwealth right to compensation is provided.[47]
  (ii) Compensation will be on the basis of *just terms* for the impairment of *offshore* native title by acts other than low impact acts.[48] Here the Commonwealth would pay the compensation.[49]

(c) Compensation after an Unopposed Determination of Native Title
Applications for a determination of native title can be made by Aboriginal people or by a non-claimant applicant, either the holder of an interest in land or a government, State, Territory or Commonwealth.[50] If on a non-claimant application no

claimant appears within two months of notice being given then the application is deemed to be unopposed[51] and after the Tribunal conducts an inquiry into the existence of native title rights a determination can be made in relation to native title. Special provision is made where there is an unopposed application for a determination of native title and no native title was found to exist. Where at a later date it was proved that the land was subject to native title then native title holders may have claims for compensation if native title was extinguished or impaired.[52] Future acts that occur after an unopposed determination are valid. Compensation for impairment of native title rights is on the basis of what an 'ordinary title' holder would receive under the test in section 17(2) *Native Title Act* 1993 (Cth).[53] Compensation on the 'just terms' standard is payable for the extinguishment of native title.[54]

Similar rights of compensation are provided to native title holders in relation to the renewal of an interest pursuant to a legally enforceable right of renewal. Compensation is the same as for impairment of native title.[55]

(d) Who is Liable to Pay Compensation for Future Dealings?
Compensation is recoverable from the government to which the act is attributable.[56] However, the Commonwealth, States or Territories may pass laws imposing a liability to pay compensation on the person who requested that the future act be done.[57] If the Commonwealth acquires native title rights, the Commonwealth laws could amount to an acquisition of property. The Commonwealth is obliged by the Constitution (section 51(xxxi)) to pay compensation on 'just terms'.

(e) Compensation Generally
Compensation payable for 'past acts', 'future acts', or in relation to other provisions in the *Native Title Act* 1993 (Cth),[58] is payable only in accordance with Division 4.[59] In assessing compensation consideration must be given to compensation payable under a State law as no multiple compensation will be paid.[60] Application may be made to the Native Title Registrar for a determination of compensation.[61] Jurisdiction vested in other courts to hear appeals or review a

determination of compensation is not affected by the *Native Title Act* 1993 (Cth).[62] Jurisdiction to hear a compensation claim is vested in the Tribunal, and also in the Federal Court, the High Court or State assessment bodies, if so established by States.[63]

PART C. The Valuation of Native Title and Just Terms

A claim for compensation contains two requirements. The first is the detailed nature of the interest in land which has been acquired. It would be impossible to value a native title interest until the full quantum of rights that comprise native title is known and ascertained. Native title is not always the equivalent of freehold. Rights to use the land may be shared by other groups. The native title interest might amount to a freehold equivalent of ownership of land where the native title holders have exclusive possession and control of the land and where they exercise the same types of rights in relation to the land that freehold title holders enjoy. Here compensation should be determined on a fee simple basis. In many cases, however, native title, in the nature of usufructuary rights, will be more like an easement or a profit à prendre. In such cases the value would have to be assessed accordingly. Such valuation can be achieved through the 'similar compensable interest' test in the *Native Title Act* 1993 (Cth).[64] In considering valuation, it should be remembered that a critical feature giving rise to recognition of native rights was the need to uphold the traditional culture of the native title holders. Accordingly, compensation should relate to the value of those traditional rights.

The second requirement is to ascertain the value of the interest in the land. The 'value' of land is the monetary worth that the land or the interest in land possesses. The main criteria for assessing compensation under the *Native Title Act* 1993 (Cth) are:

(i) *just terms*,[65] and in ascertaining *just terms* reference to the principles established in any Compulsory Acquisition Act,[66] or

(ii) the *similar compensable interest* test — that is in accordance with the law relating to compensation in respect of 'ordinary title'.

If one of the criteria in the determination of 'just terms' is reference to the State or Territory Compulsory Acquisition Acts, then is there a distinction without quality between 'just terms' and the 'similar compensable interest' test? The criteria in the Commonwealth Compulsory Acquisition legislation are not so very different from the those used to assess resumptions under the State and Territory laws. While the principles of compensation and valuation in the Compulsory Acquisition legislation are what the community has considered 'just terms', they offer little in the way of compensation for special attachment by Aboriginal people. 'Just terms' should refer not only to existing principles of valuation but also to what is fair and reasonable in the circumstances. Here both the interests of the dispossessed owner and the general community must be considered.[67]

(1) Just Terms

The valuation of native title and the assessment of the quantum of compensation on the basis of 'just terms' is not precisely defined or determined under the legislation and will be left to the courts to decide. The principles of 'just terms' can be summarised as follows:

(a) The concept of 'just terms' is not always equivalent to 'just compensation'. 'Just compensation' generally refers to the full monetary equivalent of the land. 'Just terms', however, focuses on what is fair and reasonable in the particular circumstances. This may not be a full monetary equivalent.[68]

(b) 'Just terms' should refer not only to the interests of the person whose rights are acquired but also to general community interests.[69]

(c) Standards of what is just will vary and the courts have some discretion in assessing 'just terms'.[70]

(d) Terms will not be considered unjust merely because they differ from ordinary and established principles of compensation law.[71]

2. Current Valuation Criteria

To assist in assessing 'just terms', reference can be made to existing principles set out in the Compulsory Acquisition Acts.[72]

Market Value: In ordinary circumstances the value of land acquired is its market value.[73] The test of market value is what price will the willing buyer pay and what sum will the willing seller accept.[74] Market value is difficult to apply to a title that is inalienable, non-transferable, and not able to be sold or leased, and where the content of native title may vary from group to group.[75]

Highest and Best Use: Another concept of valuation is to consider the 'highest and best use' of the land. This concept allows the land to be valued for its most advantageous purpose. It is a concept that is relevant where the value of the land may alter if the land was put to a different use. In applying this concept to native title land the compensation for a right to hunt or fish may not be very high. However, if the land were available for commercial development the value could be increased.

Other factors: Other factors relevant to compensation are set out in the Commonwealth *Land Acquisition Act* 1989 in sections 52(2), 58 and 61. These include the following bases for compensation:
- *Special value* — In addition to the market value that land has, an additional special value to the owner which is incidental to the use of the land or is a particular attribute of the land is compensated. Usually this involves a financial advantage to the owner and must relate to the quality of the land. Could this take into account the spiritual and cultural significance that Aboriginal people feel for the land? A wide reading of special value suggests that this is possible. However, the

more usual case where special value is assessed is where land is adapted to a particular kind of use made by the claimant.[76]
- *Severance* — Where land is severed from the balance of the owner's land then compensation is allowed for the reduction in the market value of the land retained by the owner.[77]
- *Injurious affection* — Where part of a property is acquired compensation will be allowed for loss that is caused to the balance of the land because of the use which the acquiring body intends for the acquired land. Such use may well depreciate the market value of the retained land or may even prevent the owner's current use of the land.[78]
- *Reinstatement* — Where there is no general market value this could involve costs of reinstating the dispossessed owner on other land or it could refer to the total cost of buying comparable land. Also it could be a method of valuing acquired land, for example the market value of the improvements on the acquired land may be $10,000 but the cost of replacing them may be $20,000.[79]
- *Disturbance* — This is the loss or damage which has been suffered or any costs that have been incurred as a direct and reasonable consequence of the acquisition. It could include loss of profits or the cost of renting another property in the interim. Here, an element of personal loss is recognised.[80]
- *Other costs* — This would incorporate any legal or professional costs (such as obtaining legal advice) that were incurred because of the acquisition.[81]
- *Special compensation* — Here special compensation, involves the payment of *solatium* where the acquired land contained a dwelling which was the owner's principal place of residence.[82] Brown indicates that *solatium* can incorporate an additional amount of money in respect of the 'hardship, inconvenience or unspecified loss' caused by the compulsory acquisition and could be used to compensate for 'injured feelings' due to the acquisition of property.[83] In some statutes *solatium* is

assessed as a percentage of the compensation; in others no reference to a percentage is included. Section 61 of the *Land Acquisition Act* 1989 (Cth) provides for a lump sum payment by way of *solatium* to enable a dispossessed owner of a dwelling to obtain a 'reasonably equivalent dwelling'. Could *solatium* be used to compensate Aboriginal people for their special loss and attachment to the land where their 'abodes' were located? On one view awards of *solatium* may not be helpful in assessing loss of native title rights because they are not an alternative to the market value method of assessing compensation.[84]

The basis of assessment of compensation under the *Land Acquisition Act* 1989 (Cth) is essentially monetary value. The only non-monetary basis is in relation to *solatium* and this is restricted to dwelling houses.

In determining what amounts to 'just terms' compensation, the real issue is what considerations over and above the standard elements or methods of assessing compensation should be taken into consideration? Section 51(1) *Native Title Act* 1993 (Cth) provides that an entitlement to compensation is:

> An entitlement on just terms to compensate the native title holders for any loss, diminution, impairment or other effect of the act on their native title rights and interests.

The emphasis in this section is on the *loss* to the native title holders and not on the value of the land.[85] In meeting the 'just terms' principle of fair and reasonable compensation reference must be made to criteria in addition to those set out in the legislation, as it is difficult to account for the Aboriginal loss of spiritual connection with land under existing standards.

3. Special Attachment

In determining 'just terms' the special attachment that Aboriginal people have in relation to the land should be valued. The Prime Minister in his second reading speech stated that any special attachment to the land will be taken into account in determining 'just terms'.[86] This will be a new and additional basis for assessing compensation. One thing that seems clear about compensation in relation to Aboriginal groups is that they are not prepared to be 'bought out' by cash payments for their spiritual connection with the land. Perhaps innovative ways of handling this should be considered to recompense for spiritual loss. For example it may be that an Aboriginal community would prefer to acquire items of spiritual or cultural significance previously lost to the community. Perhaps a research fund could be set up to preserve ancient language and customs, or a buy back arrangement established to acquire elements of Aboriginal art that have been lost. It has also been suggested that broader concepts of non-economic loss should be addressed. These could include cultural, religious, environmental and other loss. The basis for assessment of these criteria is uncertain.[87]

In summary 'just terms' should consider the value of the land to the owner taking into account the different cultural response and the different relationship that Aboriginal people have to their land. Assessment of compensation will depend on what native title rights are and what special sites of significance are to be found on that native title parcel. Unlike freehold land native title land may not necessarily have a uniform value, as sacred sites would require a different basis for assessment. New strategies in valuation may need to be introduced as part of the standard valuation process. Consultation with the native title holders will be essential in determining the value of native title.

Compensation for Breach of Fiduciary Duty

The extent of any fiduciary duty or trust obligation owed by the Crown to native title holders has yet to be fully determined in Australia.[88] Where both a fiduciary duty and breach of that obligation can be established, a claim for damages on bases different from those under the *Native Title Act* 1993 (Cth) would arise. Remedies for equitable damages could include an account of profits or a constructive trust.[89] Subject to laches, delay or the relevant Statutes of Limitation, claims for breach of fiduciary duty (where that duty can be established) may also exist in the period prior to 1975 when the *R.D.A.* was passed.

Thus the claiming of equitable remedies for brach of fiduciary duty could have an effect on the choice of forum for claims for compensation.

Conclusion

The *Native Title Act* 1993 (Cth) has attempted to establish fair and just standards in its compensation provisions. No specific guidance or direction is provided, however, for valuing the special cultural and religious attachment which Aboriginal people experience in relation to the land. This has been left to the courts to determine on 'just terms'.

The author thanks Carolyn Sappideen for her valuable assistance in the preparation of this article.

Notes

1. *Mabo v. Queensland (No. 2)* (1992) 75 C.L.R. 1.
2. Deane, Gaudron and Toohey JJ. held that compensation would be payable: *contra* Mason C.J., Brennan, Dawson and McHugh JJ.
3. *Mabo v. Queensland (No. 2)* (1992) 75 C.L.R. 1, 112.
4. *Id.* 203.
5. *Id.* 199–207.
6. (1984) 13 D.L.R. (4th) 321.
7. (1988) 166 C.L.R. 188.
8. *Native Title Act* 1993 (Cth) (hereinafter referred to as the *N.T.A.*) s.21.
9. *Ibid.*
10. *Id.* s.61.
11. *Id.* s.13(1).
12. *Id.* s.61.
13. See G. Neate, 'Some Environmental Law and Valuation Issues', Conference paper, Queensland Environmental Law Association Conference, 1994.
14. *N.T.A.* s.17.
15. *Id.* ss.14, 228.
16. *Id.* s.15(1).
17. *Id.* s.51.
18. *Id.* s.229. Category A 'past acts' include freehold title, certain leases such as commercial, agricultural, pastoral and residential, certain public works on Crown lands.
19. *Id.* s.230. Category B 'past acts' include leases that are not in Category A or C, that is all other leases except mining leases, for example leases to non-commercial community groups such as girl guides.
20. *Id.* s.17(2) and (3).
21. *Id.* ss.15(1)(d) and 238.

22. *Id.* s.231. A category C 'past act' consists of a mining lease. Native title is extinguished where a mining lease forms part of a permanent city, town or private residence and associated residential infrastructure.
23. *Id.* s.232. Category D 'past acts' include any past act that is not in the prior categories and includes other governmental 'acts' such as licences for fishing, pearling, tourism and transport.
24. *Id.* s.253 (definition of 'ordinary title').
25. Under the *N.T.A.* 'acts' are categorised as occurring in onshore or offshore places, a distinction based on State boundaries. (See s.253) *Onshore* place is defined (*N.T.A.* s.253) to mean land and waters within the limits of a State to which the *N.T.A.* extends, other than an offshore place. State sovereignty does not extend beyond the low watermark, so onshore place would include the area to the low watermark. A possible exception exists in relation to waters which have traditionally or historically been included within the limits of a State. *Offshore* place is defined to mean land and waters to which the *N.T.A.* extends other than an onshore place. S.6 *N.T.A.* provides that the Act applies to the land and waters over which Australia asserts sovereign rights under the *Seas and Submerged Lands Act* 1973 (Cth). Commonwealth sovereignty extends from the low water mark to twelve nautical miles over the territorial sea.
26. *N.T.A.* s.17(2), 51.
27. *Id.* s.40 details when the 'similar compensable interest' test is satisfied.
28. An onshore place is defined in s.253 *N.T.A.* to mean land within the limits of the State or Territory and thus would include areas above the low water mark.
29. *Id.* ss.17(2), 51(3).
30. See however, G. Orr, 'Compensation for Loss of Native Title Rights' in R. Barlett and G. Meyers (eds.), *Native Title Legislation in Australia* (Perth: Centre for Commercial and Resources Law, University of Western Australia and Murdoch University, 1994).
31. *N.T.A.* s.18.
32. *Id.* s.17.
33. *Id.* s.20.
34. *Id.* s.200.
35. *Id.* s.20(2).
36. 'Past acts' are defined in s.228 *N.T.A.* to include acts which took place prior to 1 July 1993 in the case of legislation and prior to 31 December 1993 in the case of titles granted by the Crown and which are invalid in some way because of the existence of native title. The *N.T.A.* does not specify that the 'past acts' which are invalid, because of the existence of native title, are those which have taken place since the *R.D.A.* 31 October 1975. It will be in the interests of both native title holders who wish to claim native title and governments who must pay compensation to ascertain exactly which acts are invalid, as compensation is payable only for invalid 'past acts'. See H. Fraser, 'Native Title Legislation and Mining' in Stephenson, M.A., *Mabo: The Native Title Legislation* (Brisbane: University of Queensland Press, 1994).
37. This raises the question of whether 'just terms' compensation requires the payment of interest. The view generally taken by the High Court has been that interest is not essential for 'just terms' compensation. It was considered by Latham C.J., Dixon and McTiernan JJ. that interest was

not necessary for 'just terms' compensation in *Bank of New South Wales v. The Commonwealth* (1948) 76 C.L.R. 1. However, Starke, Rich and Williams JJ. thought that interest was necessary. See R.W. Baker, 'The Compulsory Acquisition Powers of the Commonwealth', in R. Else–Mitchell, *Essays on the Australian Constitution*, (2nd ed., Law Book Co., 1961).
38. *N.T.A.* s.51(5).
39. *Id.* s.51(6).
40. 'Future act' is defined in the *N.T.A.* s.233 as an act that takes place on or after 1 July 1993 in the case of legislation and after 1 January 1994 in the case of any other 'act'.
41. *Id.* s.51.
42. *Id.* s.21.
43. *Id.* ss.23(3) and 11. Acquisition under a Compulsory Acquisition Act (defined s.253) will not extinguish native title. An act done to give effect to the acquisition, for example by the grant of an interest in land that is inconsistent with native title, such as a development lease or the grant of a freehold estate, may extinguish native title. See *N.T.A.* s.23 (3) (b).
44. *Id.* s.23(3)(c).
45. *Id.* s.51(2). S.23(3)(c) provides that if the Compulsory Acquisition Act does not provide for 'just terms' where there has been a future acquisition then the *N.T.A.* does.
46. *Id.* s.23(4) and 51(3).
47. *Id.* see s.23(4)(b)(ii)(C).
48. Low impact acts are defined in *N.T.A.* s.234 and would probably include minor licences and permits for activities such as recreational fishing. These low impact acts must not involve a grant of a lease or freehold estate or a right of exclusive possession or permit the construction of any structure or fixture or the disposal of any garbage, poisonous, toxic or hazardous substance. Thus the construction of wharves, jetties or marinas would not be categorised as low impact acts.
49. *Id.* s.23(4)(b)(i) and s.51(1).
50. *Id.* s.61.
51. *Id.* s.67.
52. *Id.* s.24(1)(d)(e) and 17(2).
53. *Id.* s.24(1)(e).
54. *Id.* s.24(1)(d).
55. *Id.* s.25(1)(c).
56. *Id.* s.23(5).
57. *Ibid.*
58. *Id.* Divisions 2, 3 and 4.
59. *Id.* s.48.
60. *Id.* s.49(b).
61. *Id.* Part 3, s.50(2).
62. *Id.* s.50(3).
63. *Id.* s.43. This may include Mining Wardens Courts.
64. Compensation for the acquisition of interests less than a fee simple is recognised by the law. See generally R.E. Megarry and H.W.R. Wade, *The Law of Real Property* (5th ed., London: Stevens, 1984). Leasehold interests are compensated on the basis of what a willing purchaser would pay a willing vendor for the lease. (*Spencer v. The Commonwealth* (1907) 5 C.L.R. 418.) A party who has the benefit of an easement such

as for access rights will obtain compensation for its extinguishment. This will be assessed on the basis of what a willing purchaser would pay a willing vendor to obtain the easement. Compensation for loss of rights of access has been generously interpreted: see *Caledonian Railway Co. v. Walker's Trustees* (1882) 7 App.Cas. 259. Holders of a profit à prendre have also been recognised to be entitled to compensation for its loss. See *Unimin Pty. Ltd. v. The Commonwealth* (1974) 32 L.G.R.A. 324. See J. Gobbo, 'Compensation for the Extinguishment of Native Title' (1993) 67 (12) *Law Institute Journal* 1163, 1167, who notes that 'although the range of interests is broad, no real guidance emerges from the cases as to the method of determining compensation for these interests'.

65. *N.T.A.* s.51(1).
66. *Id.* s.51(2).
67. See P. Hanks, *Constitutional Law in Australia* (Sydney: Butterworths, 1991), 408.
68. See *Nelungaloo Pty. Ltd. v. The Commonwealth* (1948) 75 C.L.R. 495.
69. This is one of the consequences of 'just terms' focusing on fairness. See *Grace Brothers Pty. Ltd. v. The Commonwealth* (1946) 72 C.L.R. 269, 280 per Latham C.J., 285–286 per Starke J., 291 per Dixon J. See also P.H. Lane, *Commentary on the Australian Constitution* (Sydney: Law Book Co., 1986), 225. Baker, *supra* note 37, 295 explains that while the 'price to be paid for the public advantage should not be allowed to fall on the one individual, it should not give that individual a profit: the benefits and burdens are to be spread over the whole community'. In *Poulton v. The Commonwealth* (1953) 89 C.L.R. 540, the distinction between 'just terms' and 'just compensation' was relied on to support the validity of acquisitions of wool where the compensation did not include any allowance for profits on a future resale.
70. See *Grace Brothers Pty. Ltd. v. The Commonwealth* (1946) 72 C.L.R. 269, 295 per McTiernan J. This is a further consequence of 'just terms' relating to fairness. See L.C. Howard, *Australian Federal Constitutional Law* (3rd ed., Sydney: Law Book Co., 1985), 251. It is not necessary that exact justice be afforded to every dispossessed owner if the law provides general standards of just compensation.
71. See *Minister of State v. Dalziel* (1944) 68 C.L.R. 261, 291. Starke J. stated that '[t]he law must be so unreasonable as to terms that it cannot find justification in the minds of reasonable men'. In that case compensation would include loss of profits, if the business was destroyed.
72. *N.T.A.* s.51(2) and (4).
73. Under the Commonwealth *Lands Acquisition Act* (1989) s.55(2)(a)(i), the *Lands Acquisition and Compensation Act* 1986 (Vic) ss.40, 41(1)(a) and the *Land Acquisition (Just Terms Compensation) Act* 1991 (NSW) ss.5, 56 reference is made to the market value of the land. The *Acquisition of Land Act* 1967 (Qld) s.20 (1), the *Public Works Act* 1902 (WA) s.63(a) and the *Lands Resumption Act* 1957 (Tas) s.32(2), refer to the value of land. This expression has been interpreted to be generally market value.
74. *Spencer v. The Commonwealth* (1907) 5 C.L.R. 418.
75. *Lands Acquisition Act* 1989 (Cth) ss.55(2)(a)(i), 56 and 57. See D. Brown, *Land Acquisition* (3rd ed., Sydney: Butterworths, 1991).

76. *Lands Acquisition Act* 1989 (Cth) s.55(2)(a)(ii). See M.A. Stephenson, 'The High Court Decision in Mabo and Valuation of Native Title Issues' (1993) November *The Valuer and Land Economist* 605. See Brown, *supra* note 75.
77. *Lands Acquisition Act* 1989 (Cth). s.55(2)(a)(iii).
78. *Id.* s.55(2)(a)(iv). Brown, *supra* note 75, 129.
79. *Id.* s.58. See Brown, *supra* note 75, 120.
80. *Id.* s.55(2)(c). Brown, *supra* note 75, 112.
81. *Id.* s.55(2)(e). Brown, *supra* note 75.
82. *Id.* s.61(2)(b). Brown, *supra* note 75, 133.
83. Brown, *supra* note 75, 133.
84. This is the view taken by J. Gobbo, *supra* note 64, 1167.
85. See Orr, *supra* note 30.
86. 2nd Reading Speech Native Title Bill, H. of R., Hansard 2882, 16 November 1993.
87. See Orr, *supra* note 30.
88. Mason C.J. in *Coe v. Commonwealth* (1993) 118 A.L.R. 193 accepted that in some circumstances a fiduciary relationship might arise out of a representation, or an undertaking.
89. See K. Roach, "Remedies for Violations of Aboriginal Rights" (1992) 21 *Manitoba Law Journal* 498 and L. Di Marco, "A Critique and Analysis of the Fiduciary Concept in Mabo v. Queensland" (1994) *Melbourne University Law Journal.* In *Guerin v. R* (1984) 13 D.L.R. (4th) 321, the calculation of damages for repairing a breach of trust obligation was not confined to a contract or tort basis.

The Relationship Between the National Native Title Tribunal and the Queensland Native Title Tribunal

Dominic McGann*
David Yarrow**

The Bill that I have just introduced into this House, on the fourth anniversary of the election of this Government, provides a legislative framework for the recognition and treatment of ancient rights in lands that belong to Aboriginal and Torres Strait Islander people on an equal basis to all other land-holders. The need for this legislation results from the High Court's decision in the *Mabo* case and the consequential Commonwealth *Native Title Bill* 1993. There can be no doubt in the minds of all fair-minded Australians that the High Court's decision in the *Mabo* case has provided the basis for Australian Governments to tackle an issue that is fundamental to our national identity.[1]

The Premier, the Hourable Wayne Goss MLA, second reading speech for
Native Title (Queensland) Bill 1993

Introduction

The *Native Title Act* 1993 (Cth) introduced a comprehensive legislative framework which regulates many issues related to native title. Importantly, the *Native Title Act* 1993 (Cth):
- addresses the perceived uncertainties that arose from the High Court decision in *Mabo v. State of Queensland (No.*

---

* Former Program Director, Aboriginal and Torres Strait Islander Land Interests Program, Queensland Department of Lands.
** Program Officer, Aboriginal and Torres Strait Islander Land Interests Program, Queensland Department of Lands.

2)² by validating tenures which are invalid due to the existence of native title;³
- provides a mechanism by which the existence of native title can be established;⁴ and
- introduces a regime, stipulating the manner in which native title may be dealt with in future,⁵ which is aimed at recognising the existence of, and protecting native title.

The *Native Title (Queensland) Act* 1993 was enacted on 10 December 1993 and received the Royal Assent on 17 December 1993.⁶ Prior to its commencement, the *Native Title (Queensland) Act* 1993 was amended by the *Native Title (Queensland) Amendment Act* 1994. The *Native Title (Queensland) Act* 1993 establishes a mechanism for dealing with native title in a manner that is complementary to the approach of the *Native Title Act* 1993 (Cth).⁷ A mechanism of this kind is anticipated by section 8 of the *Native Title Act* 1993 (Cth).⁸

The Relationship Between Queensland and Commonwealth Native Title Legislation

The Prime Minister, the Honourable Paul Keating M.P., made it clear in his Second Reading Speech for the *Native Title Bill* 1993 (Cth) that the Commonwealth legislation is intended to operate alongside complementary legislation of the States and Territories:

> The Bill recognises that the bulk of dealings in land is done by the States and Territories. The Bill does not seek to change this situation — on the contrary it is properly sensitive to the prerogatives of the States. The Commonwealth is, however, playing its proper role in setting national standards and establishing a national framework for dealing with native title. The Bill will enable State and Territory governments to validate their past grants with certainty provided they adhere to the standards set out in the Bill.
>
> The Bill specifically provides for States and Territories to propose their own tribunals and arrangements for, firstly, determining native title claims and, secondly, deciding whether proposed grants affecting native title may be made.⁹

The *Native Title (Queensland) Act* 1993 represents a detailed legislative approach to implementing the *Native Title Act* 1993 (Cth) policy objectives that are applicable to Queensland while, at the same time, integrating the management of native title issues with other land management policies which are of particular relevance to Queensland. An issue of particular importance, which is beyond the scope of this paper, is the relationship between the *Native Title (Queensland) Act* 1993, the *Aboriginal Land Act* 1991 (Qld) and the *Torres Strait Islander Land Act* 1991 (Qld).[10] The interrelated nature of the *Native Title Act* 1993 (Cth) and the *Native Title (Queensland) Act* 1993 is clear from the terms of the Queensland Act. The preamble of the *Native Title (Queensland) Act* 1993 relevantly provides:

> (6) The Commonwealth Government has proposed legislation to provide a national scheme for the recognition and protection of native title and for its coexistence with the existing land management system.
>
> (7) It is the intention of the Parliament that Queensland should participate in the national scheme proposed by the Commonwealth Government.

The objects of the *Native Title (Queensland) Act* 1993 are stated in section 3 of the Act, which relevantly provides:

> (2) The main objects of this Act are:
> (a) in accordance with the Commonwealth Native Title Act, to validate past acts invalidated because of the existence of native title and to confirm certain rights; and
> (b) to ensure that Queensland law is consistent with standards set by the Commonwealth Native Title Act for future dealings affecting native title; and
> (c) to establish State-based mechanisms for deciding claims to native title that are complementary to, and consistent with the mechanisms established by the Commonwealth Native Title Act.

Despite the fact that the Queensland Act is, in some cases,[11] required to conform with the statutory language of the *Native Title Act* 1993 (Cth), it is clear that the *Native Title (Queensland) Act* 1993 does not operate to merely reproduce the provisions of the *Native Title Act* 1993 (Cth). As the Premier, the Honourable Wayne Goss M.L.A., observed in his Second Reading Speech for the *Native Title (Queensland) Bill* 1993:

The Queensland Bill that I have presented to this House today seeks ... to recognise the Commonwealth legislation, once enacted, in Queensland. It is important to note here that the Native Title (Queensland) Bill 1993 does not result in the enactment of the Commonwealth legislation. Rather, the Native Title (Queensland) Bill 1993 operates in conjunction with the Commonwealth Native Title Bill 1993.[12]

There are many significant connections between the *Native Title Act* 1993 (Cth) and the *Native Title (Queensland) Act* 1993, among them being:
- the validation of past acts;
- the confirmation of ownership of natural resources and access to beaches;
- the use of specialist tribunals to determine native title claims;
- the exchange of evidence between the National Native Title Tribunal and the Queensland Native Title Tribunal;
- the capacity for joint appointments to the Queensland Native Title Tribunal and the National Native Title Tribunal;
- the delegation of duties by the National Native Title Registrar to the Queensland Native Title Registrar;
- the relationship between the National Native Title Register and the Queensland Native Title Register; and
- the use in the *Native Title (Queensland) Act* 1993 of terms and definitions contained in the *Native Title Act* 1993 (Cth).

Some of these issues will be examined in turn as elements of the relationship between the National Native Title Tribunal and the Queensland Native Title Tribunal.

The Relationship Between the National Native Title Tribunal and the Queensland Native Title Tribunal

1. Structure, Functions and Powers of the Queensland Native Title Tribunal and the National Native Title Tribunal

The National Native Title Tribunal consists of presidential and non-presidential members, as will the Queensland Native Title Tribunal (when instituted).[13] The qualifications for appointment to the Queensland Native Title Tribunal appear in section 95 of the *Native Title (Queensland) Act* 1993, which provides:

(1) A person is eligible for appointment as a presidential member only if the person is —
    (a) a District Court Judge; or
    (b) the chairperson or a deputy chairperson of a Land Tribunal; or
    (c) a presidential member of the National Native Title Tribunal; or
    (d) a former Judge; or
    (e) a lawyer of at least 5 years standing.

(2) A person is eligible for appointment as a non-presidential member only if —
    (a) the person is —
        (i) a non-presiding member of a Land Tribunal; or
        (ii) a non-presidential member of the National Native Title Tribunal; or
        (iii) a member of a recognised State/Territory body; or
    (b) the person has, in the Governor in Council's opinion, special knowledge about —
        (i) Aboriginal or Torres Strait Islander societies; or
        (ii) land management; or
        (iii) dispute resolution; or
        (iv) anything else considered by the Governor in Council to have substantial relevance to the duties of a non-presidential member.

The qualifications for appointment to the National Native Title Tribunal are similar to those qualifications required for appointment to the Queensland Native Title Tribunal.[14]

The National Native Title Tribunal is established by section 107 of the *Native Title Act* 1993 (Cth). The purpose of the Tribunal is to hear and determine applications made under the *Native Title Act* 1993 (Cth) and to make such inquiries and determinations as the *Native Title Act* 1993 (Cth) requires.[15] The Queensland Native Title Tribunal is established by section 19 of the *Native Title (Queensland) Act* 1993. The clear policy intention is that the Queensland Native Title Tribunal should qualify as a 'recognised State/Territory body' under section 251 of the *Native Title Act* 1993 (Cth).[16] For this reason,[17] many of the procedural provisions for the *Native Title (Queensland) Act*

1993 and the *Native Title Act* 1993 (Cth) are similar. For example, section 21 of the *Native Title (Queensland) Act* 1993 provides:

(1) The Tribunal must pursue the objective of performing its functions in a fair, just, economical, informal and prompt way.
(2) In conducting inquiries, the Tribunal —
 (a) must take account of relevant cultural and customary concerns of Aboriginal peoples and Torres Strait Islanders; and
 (b) is not bound by technicalities, legal forms or rules of evidence.

The *Native Title Act* 1993 (Cth) contains similar provisions.[18]

The Queensland Native Title Tribunal and the National Native Title Tribunal are modelled on the policy and procedures developed in relation to the role of the Aboriginal Land Commissioner under the *Aboriginal Land Rights (Northern Territory) Act* 1976 (Cth) and the Land Tribunals established under the *Torres Strait Islander Land Act* 1991 (Qld) and the *Aboriginal Land Act* 1991 (Qld). The Commissioner or Tribunal hear claims to land that is available for claim.[19] A successful claim gives rise to a recommendation to the relevant minister. It is the relevant government which decides whether to grant title over any or all of the land recommended for grant.[20] In the case of a determination of native title, whether by the National Native Title Tribunal (but only in the case of an unopposed application or where the parties to the application reach agreement), the Federal Court or the Queensland Native Title Tribunal (if a 'recognised State/Territory body'), the determination is final.[21]

An important distinction between the Queensland Native Title Tribunal and the National Native Title Tribunal arises from the limitation imposed upon the exercise of Federal judicial power by the Commonwealth Constitution. Applications made to the National Native Title Tribunal which are not settled by mediation or which are opposed must be lodged with the Federal Court.[22] In the case of the Queensland Native Title Tribunal, a determination is final and conclusive of the matters decided therein (subject to appeal).[23] Appeals from the Federal Court are to the Full Federal Court whereas appeals from the Queensland Native Title Tribunal are to the Land Appeal Court.[24]

2. *Approved Determination of Native Title*

For an application for a determination of native title under Part 7 of the *Native Title (Queensland) Act* 1993, the following process applies:[25]

- the Registrar decides whether the application shall be accepted;[26]
- the Registrar must notify certain persons;[27]
- applications which are unopposed are then dealt with by the Queensland Native Title Tribunal;[28]
- where parties reach agreement, the Queensland Native Title Tribunal must make a determination consistent with the agreement if certain pre-conditions are met;[29]
- a mediation conference is held at which agreement may be reached;[30]
- applications which are not settled are dealt with by the Queensland Native Title Tribunal.[31]

If the Commonwealth minister makes a determination under section 251 of the *Native Title Act* 1993 (Cth) that the Queensland Native Title Tribunal is a 'recognised State/Territory body',[32] then the Queensland Native Title Tribunal will make determinations of native title in a manner complementary to the determinations of the National Native Title Tribunal. Section 13 of the *Native Title Act* 1993 (Cth) relevantly provides:

(1) An application may be made to the Registrar under Part 3:
  (a) for a determination of native title in relation to an area for which there is no approved determination of native title; or
  (b) to revoke or vary an approved determination of native title on the grounds set out in subsection (5).
(2) If:
  (a) the NNTT or the Federal Court is making a determination of compensation in accordance with Division 5; and
  (b) an approved determination of native title has not previously been made in relation to the whole or part of the area concerned;
the NNTT or Federal Court must also make a current determination of native title in relation to the whole or the part of the area, that is

to say, a determination of native title as at the time at which the determination of compensation is being made.

(3) Subject to subsection (4), each of the following is an **"approved determination of native title"**:

    (a) a determination of native title made on an application under paragraph (1)(a) or in accordance with subsection (2);

    (b) an order, judgement or other decision of a recognised State/Territory body that involves a determination of native title in relation to an area within the jurisdictional limits of the State or Territory.

(4) If an approved determination of native title is varied or revoked on the grounds set out in subsection (5) by:

    (a) the NNTT or Federal Court, in determining an application under Part 3; or

    (b) a recognised State/Territory body in an order, judgement or other decision;

then:

    (c) in the case of a variation — the determination becomes an **"approved determination of native title"** in place of the original; and

    (d) in the case of a revocation — the determination is no longer an approved determination of native title.

(5) For the purposes of subsection (4), the grounds for variation or revocation of an approved determination of native title are:

    (a) that events have taken place since the determination was made that have caused the determination no longer to be correct; or

    (b) that the interests of justice require the variation or revocation of the determination.

Accordingly, if the Queensland Native Title Tribunal is a 'recognised State/Territory body' then its determinations would be subject to variation by the National Native Title Tribunal only in the circumstances provided by section 13(5) of the *Native Title Act* 1993 (Cth).[33] Conversely, if the Queensland Native Title Tribunal were not a 'recognised State/Territory body' then its determinations would have no binding effect on the National Native Title Tribunal.

Drummond J. examined the effect of an 'approved determination of native title' in light of the legislative framework of the *Native Title Act* 1993 (Cth) and concluded that approved determinations of native title by the Tribunal, the Federal Court and recognised State and Territory bodies have the character of judgments *in rem*.[34] Therefore, in Drummond J.'s opinion, an 'approved determination of native title' has the effect of a public decision of the title to land.[35]

3. Evidence Before the Queensland Native Title Tribunal and the National Native Title Tribunal

Provisions of both the *Native Title Act* 1993 (Cth)[36] and the *Native Title (Queensland) Act* 1993[37] facilitate the exchange of evidence between the two tribunals. The provisions of both Acts are similar. Section 59 of the *Native Title (Queensland) Act* 1993 provides:

In an inquiry, the Tribunal may —
(a) receive into evidence the transcript of evidence in another proceeding before:
 (i) a court; or
 (ii) the Tribunal; or
 (iii) the National Native Title Tribunal; or
 (iv) a Land Tribunal; or
 (v) a recognised State/Territory body; or
 (vi) another entity;
 and draw conclusions of fact from the transcript; and
(b) receive into evidence a document or other thing introduced into evidence in other proceedings before a court, tribunal, body or other entity and draw conclusions from the document or thing; and
(c) adopt findings, reports, recommendations, decisions, determinations or judgements of a court, tribunal, body or other entity.

4. Joint Appointments to the Queensland Native Title Tribunal and the National Native Title Tribunal

The joint appointment of members to the National Native Title Tribunal and the Queensland Native Title Tribunal is clearly anticipated by both the *Native Title Act* 1993 (Cth)[38] and the *Native Title (Queensland) Act* 1993,[39] although a presidential member of the Queensland Native Title Tribunal is not qualified by virtue of presidential member status of a 'recognised State/Territory body', to be a presidential member of the National Native Title Tribunal, only a non-presidential member. However, by virtue of presidential member status, a presidential member of the National Native Title Tribunal is qualified to be a presidential member of the Queensland Native Title Tribunal. It may be that joint appointments will promote consistency in the approach of the Queensland Native Title Tribunal and the National Native Title Tribunal.

5. The Queensland Native Title Registrar and the National Native Title Registrar

In the same way that the National Native Title Tribunal and 'recognised State/Territory bodies' operate in a complementary manner, the duties of the Queensland Native Title Registrar and the National Native Title Registrar are significantly related. The Queensland Native Title Register will contain similar material to both the Register of Native Title Claims and the National Native Title Register.[40] Where there is a 'recognised State/Territory body', the National Native Title Registrar may delegate duties in respect of the Register of Native Title Claims and the National Native Title Register to the 'recognised State/Territory body'.[41] The Queensland Native Title Registrar is required to notify the National Native Title Registrar of applications made to, and determinations of the Queensland Native Title Tribunal.[42] This provision satisfies one of the criteria that the Commonwealth minister must believe is satisfied before the minister can make a determination that a body is a 'recognised State/Territory body'.[43]

Conclusion

The *Native Title (Queensland) Act* 1993 addresses native title issues in Queensland in a comprehensive manner, which recognises the national approach of the *Native Title Act* 1993 (Cth) and integrates this approach with other land management policies which are of particular relevance to Queensland. Given the capacity for a native title claimant to apply to the National Native Title Tribunal, or any court of competent jurisdiction, in addition to the Queensland Native Title Tribunal, the *Native Title (Queensland) Act* 1993 makes appropriate provision for the possibility of native title claims being made in a number of different forums. These provisions (including the use of evidence before another body, joint appointments to bodies and the maintenance of comprehensive State and Commonwealth registers of native title claims and determinations) are intended to mitigate against complexity and delay in the national system dealing with native title issues established by the *Native Title Act 1993* (Cth). Together, they represent the commitment of the Queensland Government to the recognition and protection of native title.

Notes

1. Queensland Government, Legislative Assembly, 'Debates', 2 December 1993, 6404.
2. (1992) 175 C.L.R. 1.
3. *Native Title Act 1993* (Cth) (hereinafter the *N.T.A.*) s.14.
4. *Id.* s.61 which, amongst other things, permits an application for a native title determination to be made.
5. See, for example, *id.* s.22 which provides: 'Subject to sections 24 and 25, if an act is an impermissible future act, the act is invalid to the extent that it affects native title'.
6. As of the date of preparation of this paper (2 December 1994), Parts 1, 2, 3, 11 and elements of Part 13 of the *Native Title (Queensland) Act 1993* had commenced operation (see Subordinate Legislation Nos. 408 and 421). Those Parts of the *Native Title (Queensland) Act 1993* which relate to the Queensland Native Title Tribunal had not commenced. References in this paper are to the sections as introduced; they may change on the reprint of the legislation.
7. The *Native Title (Queensland) Act 1993* also operates to address the effect of native title issues upon the *Mineral Resources Act 1989* (Qld), the *Petroleum Act 1923* (Qld), the *Acquisition of Land Act 1967* (Qld), the *State Development and Public Works Act 1971* (Qld), the *Aboriginal Land Act 1991* (Qld), and the *Torres Strait Islander Land Act 1991* (Qld).
8. *N.T.A.* s.8 which provides: 'This Act is not intended to affect the operation of any law of a State or Territory that is capable of operating concurrently with this Act'.
9. C. of A., House of Representatives, 'Debates', 16 November 1993, 2878–2879.
10. See D. McGann, 'A Brief Analysis of the Impact of Native Title Legislation Upon the *Aboriginal Land Act 1991* and the *Torres Strait Islander Land Act 1991*', paper delivered at the Native Title — Indigenous Rights Conference, Brisbane, 1–3 June 1994, and G. Neate, 'The Native Title (Queensland) Act 1993' in R. Barlett and G. Meyers (eds.), *Native Title Legislation in Australia* (Perth: Centre for Commercial and Resources Law, University of Western Australia and Murdoch University, 1994).

11. For example, s.19 of the *N.T.A.* relevantly provides: '**(1)** If a law of a State or Territory contains provisions to the same effect as sections 15 and 16, the law of a State or Territory may provide that past acts attributable to the State or Territory are valid, and are taken to always have been valid'.

    In order to conform with this provision, ss.10–14 of the *Native Title (Queensland) Act* 1993 are drafted so as to constitute 'provisions to the same effect as sections 15 and 16' of the *N.T.A.*
12. Queensland Government, Legislative Assembly, 'Debates', 2 December 1993, 6405.
13. *Native Title (Queensland) Act* 1993 ss. 92 and 93, *N.T.A.* s.110.
14. *N.T.A.* s.110.
15. *Id.* s.108.
16. *Native Title (Queensland) Act* 1993 ss.25 and 26.
17. *N.T.A.* s. 251 provides:

    (1) The Commonwealth Minister may, in writing, determine that a court, office, tribunal or body (which court, office, tribunal or body is called the **"body"**) established by or under a law of a State or Territory is a **"recognised State/Territory body"** if the State Minister for the State, or Territory Minister for the Territory, nominates the body to the Commonwealth Minister for the purposes of this section.

    (2) In order to ensure that there is a nationally consistent approach to the recognition and protection of native title, the Commonwealth Minister must not make the determination unless the Commonwealth Minister is satisfied that:

    (a) any procedures under the law of the State or Territory for:
    - (i) approved determinations of native title by the body; and
    - (ii) determinations of compensation for acts affecting native title; and
    - (iii) determinations whether acts affecting native title may be done;

    will be consistent with those set out in this Act; and ...
18. *Id.* s.109.
19. *Aboriginal Land Rights (Northern Territory) Act* 1976 (Cth) s.50, *Aboriginal Land Act* 1991 (Qld) s.4.16, *Torres Strait Islander Land Act* 1991 (Qld) s.4.16.
20. *Aboriginal Land Rights (Northern Territory) Act* 1976 (Cth) ss. 50 and 11 examined by the High Court in *The Queen v. Toohey; Ex parte Meneling Station Pty. Ltd.* (1982) 158 C.L.R. 327 and *Minister for Aboriginal Affairs v. Peko-Wallsend Ltd.* (1986) 162 C.L.R. 24. *Aboriginal Land Act* 1991 (Qld) s.4.16 examined by the Land Tribunal: Land Tribunal, 'Aboriginal Land Claims to Cape Melville National Park, Flinders Group National Park, Clack Island National Park and Nearby Islands', May 1994, para. 170–187.
21. However, the decision in *Brandy v. Human Rights and Equal Opportunity Commission and Others* FC 95/006 will probably render determinations of the National Native Title Tribunal on unopposed applications unenforceable.
22. *N.T.A.* s.74.
23. *Native Title (Queensland) Act* 1993 s.77.
24. *Id.* s.78.
25. A similar process applies under Part 3 *N.T.A.*
26. *Native Title (Queensland) Act* 1993 s.33.
27. *Id.* s.35.
28. *Id.* s.39.
29. *Id.* s.40.

30. *Id.* s.41.
31. *Id.* s.43.
32. This is the aim of the Queensland Government, see *Native Title (Queensland) Act* 1933 s.26(1).
33. The Queensland Native Title Tribunal is entitled to vary an order of the National Native Title Tribunal on the same grounds: see *Native Title (Queensland) Act* 1993 s.29 and the definition of 'revised native title determination application' in s.4 together with *N.T.A.* s.13(4). This revised determination will not be an 'approved determination of native title' unless the Queensland Native Title Tribunal is a 'recognised State/Territory body'.
34. *Wik Peoples v. State of Queensland* (1994) 120 A.L.R. 465.
35. Refer note 21.
36. *N.T.A.* ss. 86 and 146.
37. *Native Title (Queensland) Act* 1993 s.59.
38. *N.T.A.* s.110 provides that one qualification for appointment as a non-judicial member of the National Native Title Tribunal is a person who is a member of a recognised State/Territory body.
39. *Native Title (Queensland) Act* 1993 s.95 provides:
    (1) A person is eligible for appointment as a presidential member only if the person is — ...
    (c) a presidential member of the National Native Title Tribunal; ...
    (2) A person is eligible for appointment as a non-presidential member only if —
    (a) the person is — ...
    (ii) a non-presidential member of the National Native Title Tribunal; ...
40. *Native Title (Queensland) Act* 1993 s.137. *N.T.A.* ss.186 and 193.
41. *N.T.A.* ss.191 and 198.
42. *Native Title (Queensland) Act* 1993 s.143.
43. *N.T.A.* s. 251 relevantly provides:
    (2) In order to ensure that there is a nationally consistent approach to the recognition and protection of native title, the Commonwealth Minister must not make the determination unless the Commonwealth Minister is satisfied that: ...
    (i) the law of the State or Territory will require the Native Title Registrar to be informed of:
      (i) any application for decisions, orders or judgements of the body that involve an approved determination of native title; and
      (ii) the making of any such determination by the body; ... .

The Land (Titles and Traditional Usage) Act 1993 Western Australia

A Racist and Invalid Enactment

Richard H. Bartlett[*]

Our motto must be 'theft is theft is theft'.[1]

Aboriginal people have lived in Western Australia for at least fifty thousand years. Just over one hundred and sixty years ago, in 1829, British sovereignty was asserted over the territory. The Crown issued grants over the land pursuant to the Crown lands and mining legislation and ordinances irrespective and regardless of the Aboriginal relationship to the land. In 1975 the *Racial Discrimination Act* was passed by the Commonwealth. This Act mandated equality before the law for all races thereafter. But it was not until June 1992 that the significance of the Act to the protection of what remained of the Aboriginal relationship to the land was fully realised. In *Mabo (No. 2)*[2] the High Court declared that the Aboriginal relationship to the land is a right and title recognised and enforceable *at law*. It is *not* an interest held merely 'at the pleasure of the Crown'.[3] It entails a relationship to land which will sustain an action of trespass or ejectment against a trespasser on or interfering with native title land.[4]

Eighteen months after the decision in *Mabo (No. 2)*[5] the Governor of Western Australia gave royal assent to the *Land (Titles and Traditional Usage) Act* 1993 (WA). This Act purports to extinguish native title throughout the State and replace it by statutory 'rights' of traditional usage. The mining industry launched an advertising campaign attacking the High Court

---

[*] Professor of Law, University of Western Australia.

decision in *Mabo* concurrently with a State government campaign in support of its legislation. Both campaigns were disguised in the language of equality. The mining industry campaign rested on the unstated presumption that no-one should be recognised as having rights to land because of a relationship to land prior to British sovereignty. The Western Australian State campaign presumed that such rights should not be given any substance and must give way to *every* other interest. Such presumptions are at odds with the fundamental common law principle demanding respect for existing rights. Until 1975 such discrimination as to the application of the principle was permissible. Since the enactment of the *Racial Discrimination Act* 1975 (Cth) (hereinafter referred to as *R.D.A.*) it is not. That Act requires that an equal respect be accorded the interests of all races including Aboriginal people. The *Land (Titles and Traditional Usage) Act* 1993 (WA) does not; and accordingly, far from being in the 'true spirit of the High Court decisions' [in *Mabo*] as asserted by the Premier, Mr Court, is a racist enactment which the High Court may well find invalid.

1. The Pragmatic but 'Racist' Compromise of Native Title at Common Law

Native title is the common law recognition of the relationship of Aboriginal people to their traditional land. Apart from the *R.D.A.* it may be extinguished by the Crown without consideration or compensation. The especial vulnerability of native title is founded in the pragmatic compromise first declared by the United States Supreme Court in *Johnson v. McIntosh*.[6] It is a pragmatism that is fundamentally 'racist' and distinguishes between the rights of Aboriginal people and the rights of those that came after. The compromise was founded on the need to give effect to the facts of settlement. The especial vulnerability of native title at common law is accordingly the essence of the racist compromise that legitimised the dispossession of Aboriginal people by European settlers.

In Canada and the United States the compromise was moderated by the denial of jurisdiction to the Provinces and States to extinguish native title and the institution in policy of the requirement of the consent of the Aboriginal people to any extinguishment. In Canada the compromise was overturned in 1982 when surviving Aboriginal rights were entrenched in the Constitution.[7]

2. The *Racial Discrimination Act* 1975 and Equality Before the Law

In Australia the compromise, and its racist diminishment of native title, remained in place until 1975. The *R.D.A.* of that year overturned the racist element in the compromise. Native title is now accorded the same protection as the rights of others from extinguishment and impairment. Brennan J. thus declared a rationale of extending 'full respect' to the rights and interests of the indigenous inhabitants of a settled colony.[8] Native title is afforded such respect only when protected by the *R.D.A.* It is the *R.D.A.* that demands, as applied in *Mabo (No. 1)*,[9] that the common law recognition of Aboriginal people's traditional relationship to the land and any statutory regime afford 'equality before the law', that is, 'full respect'.

Any assessment of a statutory regime respecting or replacing native title must consider if the traditional relationship to land of Aboriginal people is accorded equal treatment and status to the treatment and status accorded relationships of other racial groups. It is suggested that the standard treatment accorded other interests is, in accord with the fundamental common law principle, demanding respect for existing rights. That principle requires such respect as accords with the tenor of the rights. Only where particular public works demand may such respect not be accorded, and only then provided the action taken is not arbitrary and compensation is provided. The assessment requires a determination of the true tenor of the Aboriginal relationship to land.

The true tenor of native title is unique. The source of native title is the traditional Aboriginal relationship to the land. Native title is not derived from Crown grants. The tenor of native title is determined by the traditional laws and customs of the community or society. 'It is not an institution of the common law.'[10] Under the traditional laws and customs native title was not alienable nor subordinate nor inferior to non-Aboriginal interests. Native title bears a fundamental relationship to Aboriginal society. The existence of native title presupposes the existence of an Aboriginal society. The relationship of an Aboriginal community to land according to the laws and customs of the group is the foundation of the title. Native title also encompasses the spiritual attachment of Aboriginal people to their traditional land. That attachment is, of course, a concomitant of the unique and fundamental nature of native title. Full respect for the unique tenor of native title, in accordance with the *R.D.A.*, negates any inferior or subordinate status.

3. Western Australian Opposition to Mabo

Western Australia is the principal jurisdiction in the common law world which has made no provision for rights of Aboriginal people to their traditional land. *Mabo* undoubtedly has the greatest impact on Western Australia but that is because successive State Governments have failed to provide any meaningful rights to land. It is with the intent to continue to deny rights to land that the present Western Australian State Government has rejected the *Mabo* decision. As early as October 1992, Bill Hassell urged its rejection in so far as it provided a basis for judicially generated Aboriginal land rights. That position was soon after endorsed by Richard Court, now Premier of the State. The *Land (Titles and Traditional Usage) Act* 1993 (WA) maintains that position and seeks to repeal *Mabo*. The effect of the legislation is to extinguish, subordinate and diminish Aboriginal rights to land. It does not provide anything resembling equality before the law. Such a conclusion requires an analysis of the entire Act in order to determine the place the State Government would accord the Aboriginal relationship to land in its land and resource regime.

4. The Arbitrary Extinguishment of Native Title

Section 7(1) of the *Land (Titles and Traditional Usage) Act* 1993 (WA) (hereafter 'the *Western Australian Act*') extinguishes any native title subsisting in Western Australia at the commencement of the *Western Australian Act*. No compensation is payable for extinguishment. The *Western Australian Act* provides for the replacement of native title with 'rights of traditional usage' of inferior and subordinate status. The general extinguishment is explained in the preamble as necessary to provide for 'a single system of land titles and land management'. But the *Western Australian Act* does not provide for such a system. The substituted rights are not integrated into an existing system of title registration and the State 'Office of Traditional Land Use', established in December 1993, operates separately from Departments issuing other titles. The perversity of the extinguishment is, of course, made manifest by the *substitution* of 'rights of traditional usage'. The Commonwealth *Native Title Act* 1993 provides a regime accommodating native title. It does not provide for a general extinguishment of native title. The extinguishment under the *Western Australian Act* is arbitrary insofar as it lacks any proper motive. The only motive appears to be to deny the unique source of native title and to denigrate it by a change of description to 'rights of traditional usage' rather than 'title'.

5. The Replacement by Inferior and Subordinate Rights

Section 7(2) of the *Western Australian Act* replaces native title with 'rights of traditional usage' which 'unless this Act provides otherwise, are equivalent in extent to the rights and entitlements that they replace'. The *Western Australian Act* does provide otherwise. The cumulative effect of the regime is to deny any substance to the rights of Aboriginal people with respect to their traditional relationship to the land. The relationship is made subordinate to the rights and interests of others, denied the rights of protection appropriate to the tenor of native title but extended to others, and diminished as to the content of the statutory 'rights of traditional usage'. The especial vulnerability of the traditional relationship to the land of Aboriginal people is affirmed rather than denied. The Crown's ability to grant and take any action with respect to land to which Aboriginal people maintain a traditional relationship without regard to the interests of the Aboriginal community is essentially maintained.

(a) Subordinate to the Rights of All Others

The exercise of statutory rights of traditional usage is expressly made subject to, and such as not to 'restrict or impair the exercise of' the rights of all other title-holders, whether proprietary or not.[11] Title to land is defined to include all interests in, or in respect of land *except* rights of traditional usage.[12] Upon the granting of any such interest by the Crown it overrides the rights of traditional usage. The Aboriginal relationship to land is subordinate to the interests of all others of whatever kind including mining and petroleum tenements.

(b) Inferior Rights of Protection to All Others

The statutory rights of traditional usage may be overridden by grants under the following Western Australian legislation including: *Mining Act* 1978, *Petroleum Act* 1967, *Petroleum (Submerged Lands) Act* 1982, *Petroleum Pipelines Act* 1969, *Land Act* 1933 and the *Pearling Act* 1990.[13] The protection extended to holders of rights of traditional usage is inferior to that extended to holders of other interests. The regime does not respect the traditional relationship of Aboriginal people to their land according to its tenor.

The most obvious examples are afforded by the *Mining Act* 1978 (WA) and the *Land Act* 1933 (WA). Under both Acts the minister is required to consult with an Aboriginal group which is considered to have a *bona fide* claim to rights of traditional usage. Such a group may lodge a notice of objection. After consultation the minister makes a non-reviewable recommendation to the Minister of Mines or Lands. But the minister is not bound to accept the recommendation and may grant or refuse the application irrespective of any interference with rights of traditional usage. The Minister of Mines or Lands can 'disapply' even these procedures with respect to a particular area or application. Under both Acts grants will override the rights of traditional usage.

By contrast holders of other interests are accorded much greater protection. For example freehold farmers in the south west of the State are accorded a veto over mineral development,[14] even though at common law according to the terms of their interest where minerals are reserved to the Crown the Crown has a *right* to mine those lands. According to the tenor of their interest there can be no veto, yet the State Government has conferred such a veto. Moreover, the *Western Australian Act* does not provide for any consideration by an independent officer, such as a warden in open court or a public forum, before the granting of rights of entry and of rights to mine over lands subject to rights of traditional usage.

The contrast with the *Land Act* 1993 (WA) is even more dramatic. No holders of interests in land, other than holders of rights of traditional usage, are subject to a grant being made under the *Land Act* 1993 (WA) which overrides and is inconsistent with that interest. Holders of interests under the *Land Act* 1993 (WA) are provided with no particular protection under that Act because they do not need it. As Brennan J. explained in Mabo (No. 2), 'the general rule of the common law was that ownership could not be acquired by occupying land that was already occupied by another'.[15]

6. Unenforceable 'Rights' of Traditional Usage

The Crown may issue any disposition, without any resumption, irrespective of the 'rights' of traditional usage. Neither the State, statutory body nor State officer may be restrained from making any grant or taking any action that may result in the extinguishment, suspension or impairment of the 'rights'.[16] Nor does the existence of any court proceedings afford a bar. The 'rights' do *not* empower the Aboriginal people to engage in any use of the land which is inconsistent with any State action or Crown grant, they merely confer a right of compensation.

7. The Limited Content of the 'Rights'

At common law the content of native title is determined by the traditional relationship of Aboriginal people to land. It is likely to include rights to use the land and waters for traditional hunting, gathering and fishing and for ceremonial purposes. At common law native title might be extinguished only by legislation which revealed a 'clear and plain intention' to do so. Such intention 'is not revealed by a law which merely regulates the enjoyment of native title or which creates a regime of control that is consistent with the continued enjoyment of native title'.[17]

The *Western Australian Act* entirely removes the common law protection appropriate to native title rights. Section 17 states that general laws apply to 'rights' of traditional usage unless there is express provision to the contrary. The requirement of a 'clear and plain intention' to extinguish is replaced by a presumption of extinguishment. The general laws respecting hunting, fishing and foraging rights in Western Australia will limit, if not nullify traditional rights. Further, section 164(2) of the *Land Act* 1993 (WA) declares a general prohibition on residence, erecting structures, or removing 'anything of whatever kind' from Crown lands or reserves, including Aboriginal reserves. Section 164(2), as applied pursuant to section 17, would nullify native title. No compensation is payable with respect to the extinguishment or impairment of native title by the operation of section 17.

8. Past Titles Override and Extinguish Native Title

The *R.D.A.* required that the Aboriginal relationship to the land be treated equally with other interests. Accordingly native title was not extinguished by Crown grants thereafter. The respect accorded property rights after 1975 extends to the Aboriginal relationship to land as well as other interests. The *Western Australian Act* seeks to overturn this result.

The *Western Australian Act* provides that all Crown dispositions issued from the date the *R.D.A.* came into effect, 31 October 1975, until the *Western Australian Act* comes into effect, have effect according to their tenor. They are not invalid on account of, or affected by, or subject to native title. They override, and, to the extent necessary, extinguish or impair native title. The provision distinguishes between the Aboriginal relationship to land which is *denied* and all other interests, whether proprietary or not, which are given effect according to their tenor. No regard is accorded the purpose for which a grant was made, whether in the public interest or not. Holders of native title are accorded merely a right of compensation.

Section 5 of the *Western Australian Act* affirms the importance of the proposition that property interests should be respected

according to their tenor, but applies it to all interests *other* than
native title. The provision itself appears to be modelled on
section 4 of the Queensland statute, the *Queensland Coast
Islands Declaratory Act* 1985, which was struck down in *Mabo
(No. 1)*.[18]

9. Inadequate, Inferior or No Compensation

(a) No Compensation
No compensation is payable for:
(i) the extinguishment or impairment of native title prior to 31 October 1975;
(ii) the general extinguishment of any surviving native title at the time the *Western Australian Act* came into effect; and
(iii) the negation of native title by the combined effect of the substitution of 'rights of traditional usage' and the application of general laws.

(b) When Compensation Payable
Compensation is payable for:
(i) extinguishment or impairment of native title from 31 October 1975 to the commencement of the *Western Australian Act*; and
(ii) extinguishment, impairment or suspension of 'rights' of traditional usage by legislative or executive action after the commencement of the *Western Australian Act*.

(c) Inadequate and Inferior Amount
The *Western Australian Act* provides for principles of
compensation which contemplate an inadequate amount having
regard to the nature of the extinguished interest. Moreover, it is
an inferior amount of compensation to that generally provided by
the *Public Works Act* 1902 (WA). In particular that Act provides
expressly for compensation for the 'special circumstances of the
case', such as the Aboriginal attachment to land.[19] The *Western
Australian Act*[20] declares that provision to be inapplicable in the
consideration of native title and rights of traditional usage. It
imposes instead an arbitrary limit allowing for loss or
interference with special attachment to the land or spiritual or

cultural connection of twenty percent of the value of the loss of the traditional rights. Other jurisdictions have determined that if a court is compelled to place a monetary value upon the special, spiritual or cultural connection of Aboriginal people to the land, the value must include all the resources of the land.[21] Aboriginal people may not have the right to use those resources, but they afford a minimal means of measuring the monetary value of that special connection in the circumstances of a compulsory taking.

(d) Inadequate Limitation Period

The *Western Australian Act* declares a limitation period of eighteen months with respect to native title and twelve months with respect to 'rights' of traditional usage for claims for compensation. The application of such limitation periods with respect to claims founded upon an interest of such a unique tenor, of such peculiar complexity, arising over a substantial period of the past, by a uniquely disadvantaged group, is unsupportable. It does not provide equality before the law. The State of Victoria enacted a fifteen year limitation period. The Commonwealth *Native Title Act* 1993 contains no limitation period.

(e) More Onerous Proof

The *Western Australian Act* imposes a more onerous burden of proof upon those asserting rights of traditional usage in a claim for compensation than that imposed upon those asserting native title at common law. In any proceedings to obtain compensation the claimants must prove by reference to Aboriginal traditions:

- the extent of rights of traditional usage;[22]
- the boundaries of the lands subject to those rights;[23]
- the continuance of observance of Aboriginal traditions;[24]
- the maintenance of traditional connection with the land;[25]
- the identity of members of the Aboriginal group;[26] and
- the non-extinguishment or impairment of native title, or statutory rights of traditional usage.[27]

The common law does not impose such requirements with such particularity and the onus of proof with respect to extinguishment and non-maintenance of traditional connection lies upon the party seeking to establish such assertion.[28]

(f) 'Negotiation'
The procedure following submission of a claim to the minister contemplates 'negotiation' to settle the issues with respect to which the claimants bear the statutory onus of proof and the amount and form of compensation. But the bargaining position afforded by the *Western Australian Act* is merely that of the right to limited compensation and the significance of 'negotiation' is correspondingly diminished.

10. The Re-Assertion and Enhancement of the Vulnerability of Native Title

At common law and *before* the *R.D.A.* the traditional relationship of Aboriginal people to the land was diminished, in the interests of pragmatism, to legitimise the settlement of Aboriginal lands throughout the common law world. The principal aspect of the diminishment was the especial vulnerability of native title to extinguishment without any regard to the standards providing for consideration, protection and compensation accorded non-Aboriginal interests. Sections 23 and 26 of the *Western Australian Act* seek to re-assert the especial vulnerability of native title and apply it to 'rights' of traditional usage. For example the Office of Traditional Land Use has taken the highly questionable position that all pastoral leases extinguished native title, irrespective of a reservation in the lease protecting rights of traditional use. It accordingly rejects all objections from claimants to lands held under pastoral leases. The *Western Australian Act* even seeks to *enhance* the vulnerability of native title. Section 26 empowers the minister to extinguish or suspend 'rights' of traditional usage 'for any purpose for which land could be taken or compulsorily resumed', by notice.

11. Limitation of Usual Access to the Courts

The statutory rights of traditional usage may be overridden by grants under the various statutes referred to above. Those Acts provide a procedure for raising objections with the minister responsible for the *Western Australian Act* and the tendering of advice and recommendations by that minister to the minister responsible for the grant. However, the *Western Australian Act* expressly provides that 'any advice or recommendation of the responsible minister is not liable to be challenged, reviewed or called in question by a court on account of anything which the responsible minister has done or failed to do'.[29] The privative clause seeks to eliminate judicial review of the manner in which the minister performs the statutory functions, for example in failing to take account of relevant considerations. There is *no* such clause in the procedures provided with respect to any other interests governed by those Acts. The so-called 'rights' of traditional usage are rendered even more illusory.

Questions relating to the existence of rights of traditional usage may arise in proceedings other than those under the *Western Australian Act*, for example prosecutions for violation of fishing or wildlife legislation. The *Western Australian Act* declares that any determination in a court other than the Supreme Court has effect only for the purpose of those proceedings, and, in any event, the minister may 'direct the court to adjourn the proceedings and refer the question to the Supreme Court'.[30]

12. Advancement and Paternalism

Part of the significance of the *Mabo* decision and native title at common law is that it recognised rights enforceable in law. In the manner of classic nineteenth century paternalism the minister is empowered, having extinguished the legal rights of Aboriginal people to land, to grant title to, and interests in land similar to rights of traditional usage 'for the purpose of advancing the interests of Aboriginal persons'.[31] The grants are a matter of the 'grace and favour' of the minister, not as of right.

13. A Violation of the *Racial Discrimination Act* 1975 (Cth)

The *R.D.A.* seeks to prohibit racial discrimination and bring about equality before the law. Native title, the relationship of Aboriginal people to such of their traditional land as remains to them, is protected by the *R.D.A.* Equality before the law requires that 'holders of traditional native title' be clothed 'with the same immunity from legislative interference with their enjoyment of their human right to *own and inherit property*' as it clothes other persons in the community.[32] The right cannot be limited or recognised to a lesser extent than it applies to the rest of the community.

In 1988 the High Court in *Mabo (No. 1)*[33] held that Queensland legislation which sought to extinguish native title at common law without compensation and to validate the interests of all others was rendered invalid by the *R.D.A.* Deane J. explained that the effect of that Act was to extinguish native title in a context where other proprietary rights would not be adversely affected but would be enhanced to the extent that their validity or efficiency would otherwise be impugned by surviving traditional proprietary rights and interests.[34] The violation of the *R.D.A.* consisted in the singling out of native title interests for impairment or extinction while leaving other interests unaffected or enhanced.[35] The *effect* of the *Western Australian Act* is little different from that of the Queensland legislation. It denies any substantial content or status to the 'rights' which replace native title. Native title itself is extinguished without compensation. The *Western Australian Act* denies genuine equality before the law with respect to the Aboriginal relationship to the land.

Two of the principal Aboriginal organisations in Western Australia, the Aboriginal Legal Service and the Kimberley Land Council acting on behalf of groups of native title holders, have filed statements of claim challenging the validity of the *Western Australian Act*. The claims were lodged in the High Court in December 1993. The High Court has accepted and expedited the claims in its original jurisdiction. The arguments asserting that the *Western Australian Act* is a violation of the *R.D.A.* were heard in September 1994. The action in which the State has challenged the validity of the *Native Title Act* 1993 of the Commonwealth was heard at the same time. A decision is expected early in 1995.

The defence of the State asserts, *inter alia*, that all native title was extinguished in Western Australia upon settlement or in any event that the *Western Australian Act* allows a 'balance to be struck in the interests of the whole community between the interests of any native title holders and competing public and private interests in the land'. It is not considered that the High Court will find that equality before the law entails a 'balance' which allows discrimination against a disadvantaged racial group.

The advice the Aboriginal Legal Service has tendered to its clients is that the *Western Australian Act* is probably invalid. Accordingly 'as little time as possible should be spent' being concerned with the procedures under the Act 'so that Aboriginal groups have enough time and resources to deal with the important process of registering a claim with the Federal Native Title Tribunal'.

14. Legal Uncertainty and Resource Insecurity

The *Western Australian Act* ushered in an era of great legal uncertainty and resource insecurity. It is suggested that the *Western Australian Act* will be declared invalid by the High Court, but until that decision is rendered it is presumed to be valid. The *Western Australian Act* cannot provide resource security for development and indeed will harm it. Land and resource management, the responsibility of the State, has been poorly served by the Western Australian legislation.

Notes

1. H.M. Morgan, 'The Same Wind that carries them back would bring us hither' (1992) 11 *A.M.P.L.A. Bulletin* 7, 12. Hugh Morgan urged this motto upon the South Australian Branch of the Australian Mining and Petroleum Law Association as the proper characterization of government constraints upon mineral development.
2. (1992) 175 C.L.R. 1.
3. *Id.* 138.
4. *Id.* 61 per Brennan J., 113 per Deane and Gaudron JJ. *Johnson v. McIntosh* (1823) 21 U.S. 240. Also see *Martin v. Queen in right of British Columbia* [1985] 2 C.N.L.R. 58 (B.C.C.A.).
5. (1992) 175 C.L.R. 1.
6. (1823) 21 U.S. 240.
7. R. Bartlett, 'Resource Development and the Extinguishment of Aboriginal Title in Canada and Australia' (1990) 20 *University of Western Australian Law Review* 453.
8. *Mabo (No. 2)* (1992) 175 C.L.R. 1, 54-58.
9. (1988) 166 C.L.R. 186.
10. *Mabo (No. 2)* (1992) 175 C.L.R. 1, 59 per Brennan J.
11. *Land (Titles and Traditional Usage) Act* 1993 (WA) s.20.
12. *Id.* s.3(1).
13. *Id.* Schedule 1.

14. *Mining Act* 1978 (WA) s.29.
15. *Mabo (No. 2)* (1992) 175 C.L.R. 1, 45.
16. *Land (Titles and Traditional Usage) Act* 1993 (WA) s.24.
17. *Mabo (No. 2)* (1992) 175 C.L.R. 1, 64 per Brennan J. citing *R v. Sparrow* [1990] S.C.R. 1075, 1097.
18. (1988) 166 C.L.R. 186.
19. *Public Works Act* 1902 (WA) s.63(c).
20. *Land (Titles and Traditional Usage) Act* 1993 (WA) s.38(1)(n).
21. *Amodu Tijani v. Secretary of Southern Nigeria* [1921] 2 A.C. 399, 411; *Geita Sebea v. Territory of Papua* (1941) 67 C.L.R. 544, 552; *Miami Tribe of Oklahoma v. United States* (1959) 175 F.Supp. 926, 942; *United States v. Shoshone* (1938) 304 U.S. 111; *Otoe and Missouri Tribe v. United States* (1955) 131 F. Supp. 265, cert. denied 350 U.S. 848.
22. *Land (Titles and Traditional Usage) Act* 1993 (WA) s.9(1).
23. *Ibid.*
24. *Id.* s.9(2).
25. *Id.* s.9(3).
26. *Ibid.*
27. *Id.* s.10. Refer also ss.33, 34, 36. Note that native title was extinguished by the *Land (Titles and Traditional Usage) Act* 1993 (WA) s.5(1), and replaced with a 'right of traditional usage' s.5(2).
28. See *Amodu Tijani v. Secretary of Southern Nigeria* [1921] 2 A.C. 399, 409-410; *Calder* [1973] S.C.R. 313, 402 (Hall J.); *Mabo (No. 2)* (1992) 175 C.L.R. 1, 184 per Toohey J., 64 per Brennan J.; 'serious consequences', *Delgamuukw v. R.* (B.C.C.A.) (1993) 104 D.L.R. 4th 470, 520 per Macfarlane J.A.; *United States v. Sante Fe Pacific* (1941) 314 U.S. 339. Compare Mason C.J. in *Coe v. Commonwealth* (the Wiradjuri Claim) (1993) 68 A.L.J.R. 110, 119.
29. *Land (Titles and Traditional Usage) Act* 1993 (WA) Schedule 1, s.32F(3).
30. *Id.* s.12.
31. *Id.* s.41.
32. *Mabo (No. 1)* (1988) 166 C.L.R. 186, 219 per Brennan, Toohey and Gaudron JJ.
33. (1988) 166 C.L.R. 186.
34. *Ibid.*
35. *Id.* 231-232 per Deane J., 218 per Brennan, Toohey and Gaudron JJ.

The Relationship between Native Title and Statutory Title under Land Rights Legislation

Garth Nettheim[*]

Land Rights Legislation: Assumptions and Patterns

There was a long-held assumption that the common law as received in Australia provided no recognition to the pre-existing rights of Aboriginal peoples and Torres Strait Islanders. This assumption was affirmed in *Milirrpum v. Nabalco* (hereinafter referred to as the *Gove Land Rights* case).[1] This was, surprisingly, the first Australian decision in which the question had been directly raised by Aboriginal plaintiffs.

Justice Blackburn's judgment, long and careful though it was, had no higher judicial status than as a decision of a single Justice of the Northern Territory. However, it was widely regarded as a correct statement of the law, partly because it affirmed *dicta* in previous cases and because it coincided with the general view of the law. The decision was not taken on appeal, and the issue of Aboriginal 'land rights' shifted into the political/legislative arena. Some (but not all) Australian Parliaments enacted land rights legislation of greatly varying character.[2] Proposals by the Hawke Government to enact national land rights legislation foundered on the politics of States' rights and the mining industry, especially in Western Australia.[3]

There were suggestions in the High Court from time to time that the old assumptions might be incorrect, and that the common law for Australia might well be found to accommodate indigenous land rights. Such an accommodation was well

---

[*] Professor of Law and Chair, Aboriginal Law Centre, University of New South Wales.

established in the common law as received in other former British colonies, particularly in the United States, Canada and New Zealand. As early as 1973, the High Court acknowledged the continuance of indigenous land rights in the then territory of Papua.[4] In 1979, in the ill-fated *Coe v. Commonwealth*[5] action, the Justices recognized that the survival of indigenous rights would be an 'arguable question if properly raised'.[6] In 1985 in *Gerhardy v. Brown*,[7] Deane J. expressed concern at the injustice if Australian law was as Blackburn J. had held it to be.[8] From the late 1970s, the reality of the Aboriginal attachment to land had been vividly demonstrated in a number of land claim determinations by the Aboriginal Land Commissioner under the *Aboriginal Land Rights (Northern Territory) Act* 1976 (Cth) (hereinafter referred to as the *Land Rights (NT) Act*) which came before the High Court through processes of judicial review. The *Mabo* litigation itself was initiated in the original jurisdiction of the High Court as early as May 1982.

So, for two decades prior to the decision in *Mabo (No. 2)*,[9] there was a real possibility that the High Court might declare the common law of Australia in terms different from the decision of Blackburn J. in the *Gove Land Rights* case. Legislatures, however, for the most part, proceeded in happy reliance on the old assumptions and the decision in the *Gove Land Rights* case. Land rights Acts were drafted on the assumption that statutory title was the only means by which the indigenous relationship to land might be recognized.

Two broad approaches are evident in the several land rights Acts. Some proceeded on the assumption that the indigenous relationship to land was a reality, deriving from the laws of the particular peoples concerned, so that the primary function of the legislation was to provide recognition of, and protection for such rights and interests under Australian law. The path-breaking *Land Rights (NT) Act* based on the recommendations of Justice Woodward,[10] is of this nature, particularly in its provisions for land claims. Two negotiated South Australian Acts also vest ownership of lands in Aboriginal peoples on the basis of their traditional rights in respect of those lands.[11] Statutory land rights under such legislation appear likely to sit quite comfortably with native title under the common law principles declared by the

High Court in *Mabo (No. 2)*,[12] and with Native Title legislation, Commonwealth, State or Territory.

Other land rights Acts were not (or not necessarily) predicated on the survival of traditional rights and interests. In the longer settled parts of Australia, this was not surprising. Such legislation tended to speak in terms of *grants* of title rather than *recognition* of pre-existing rights. The *Aboriginal Land Rights Act* 1983 (NSW) followed the Northern Territory model by transferring remaining reserves into the ownership of local Aboriginal Land Councils. It also followed the Northern Territory model by establishing a claims process but one which was much more closely circumscribed. More significantly, an Aboriginal Land Council claiming 'claimable Crown land' is not required to establish any sort of basis for such a claim, let alone ownership under Aboriginal law. In Queensland the *Aboriginal Land Act* 1991 (Qld) and the *Torres Strait Islander Land Act* 1991 (Qld) both established a claim process which required claimants to prove traditional affiliation, or historical association, or economic and cultural viability. Some grants under the claims process may, therefore, reflect rights under Aboriginal law; others may not. Claims based on traditional affiliation are given priority over claims made on other bases.

Statutory Title and Native Title at Common Law

The question has already arisen for judicial consideration whether such legislative provision for Aboriginal ownership or occupation of land is consistent with native title or inconsistent so as to extinguish any native title. In *Mabo (No. 2)* the majority Justices spoke in terms of a presumption that native title is not extinguished unless there is evident in legislation a 'clear and plain intention' to the contrary.

Reserves

Prior to the Aboriginal Land Trust model established by the *Aboriginal Land Trusts Act* 1966 (SA) (a model subsequently followed in several other jurisdictions such as in New South Wales) the sole basis acknowledged in Australian law for Aboriginal or Torres Strait Islander occupation of land was the designation of 'Crown land' as reserves for the purpose. The reserve system had continued in Queensland until it began to be replaced by Deeds of Grant in Trust (DOGIT titles) vested in Aboriginal or Island Councils.[13] Murray Island (Mer), the subject of the *Mabo* litigation, was a reserve and the plaintiffs were resisting the possible imposition of DOGIT title.

Brennan J. (with whom Mason C.J. and McHugh J. agreed) saw no inconsistency between the designation of land as a reserve and the survival of native title:

> A clear and plain intention to extinguish native title is not revealed by a law which merely regulates the enjoyment of native title or which creates a regime of control that is consistent with the continued enjoyment of native title. *A fortiori*, a law which reserves or authorizes the reservation of land from sale for the purpose of permitting indigenous inhabitants and their descendants to enjoy their native title works no extinguishment.[14]

After analysing the history of the reserve status of Murray Island, Brennan J. continued:

> Native title was not extinguished by the creation of reserves nor by the mere appointment of 'trustees' to control a reserve where no grant of title was made. To reserve land from sale is to protect native title from being extinguished by alienation under a power of sale. To appoint trustees to control a reserve does not confer on the trustees a power to interfere with the rights and interests in land possessed by indigenous inhabitants under a native title. Nor is native title impaired by a declaration that land is reserved not merely for use by the indigenous inhabitants of the land but 'for use of Aboriginal Inhabitants of the State' generally.[15] If the creation of a reserve of land for Aboriginal Inhabitants of the State who have no other rights or interests in that land confers a right to use that land, the right of user is necessarily subordinate to the right of user consisting in legal rights and interests conferred by native title.[16] Of course, a native title which confers a mere usufruct may leave room for other persons to use the land either contemporaneously or from time to time.[17]

Clearly, the particular Crown lands legislation in each jurisdiction would have to be considered. But the indications are that, generally speaking, the status of land as an Aboriginal or Islander reserve is unlikely to extinguish any native title.

Statutory Title

Whether native title is extinguished by the vesting of statutory title (freehold or leasehold) in a state-wide Aboriginal Land Trust, or in a more localised Land Trust or Council, will also depend on an analysis of the particular legislation. Again, such analysis will be guided by the necessity for there to be evidenced a 'clear and plain intention' for native title to be extinguished.

The *Mabo* plaintiffs had two particular motivations for resisting the possible imposition of DOGIT title. As a matter of principle they insisted that their title should be seen as deriving from Meriam law, not Queensland law. They also were concerned that title be defined in accordance with Meriam law as encompassing individual and family ownership, whereas, under DOGIT title, ownership would be vested in the Island Council as trustee with power to grant leases which might cut across individual and family title.

On these grounds the plaintiffs asked for a declaration that it would be unlawful for the Queensland Government to grant DOGIT title as it would extinguish native title and would, thus, be ineffective or invalid because of the *Racial Discrimination Act* 1975 (Cth) (hereinafter referred to as the *R.D.A.*) as applied by the High Court in *Mabo (No. 1)*.[18] Such a declaration was refused on the basis that there was no evidence that the Governor-in-Council intended to grant DOGIT title.[19]

This left open the question whether grant of such a title would be sufficiently inconsistent with native title as to extinguish it. No analysis was offered on this issue. The judgments of Deane and Gaudron JJ. and of Toohey J. did agree that if a grant of DOGIT title was inconsistent with native title then the *R.D.A.* would come into play as a form of protection to require treatment of the native title holders on the same terms as required for the holders of other forms of title.[20]

Brennan J., however, questioned whether the protection of the *R.D.A.* would be available as a basis for an order that a grant of DOGIT title would be unlawful.

> Secondly, s.10 of the *Racial Discrimination Act* may not have an effect on the granting of a deed of grant in trust similar to the effect which s.10 had upon the *Queensland Coast Islands Declaratory Act*

1985. It will not have a nullifying effect if the action taken under the relevant State laws constitutes a special measure falling within s.8(1) of the *Racial Discriminatjon Act* and thereby escapes the operation of s.10 (*Gerhardy v. Brown* (1985) 159 C.L.R. 70). Whether the granting of a deed of grant in trust would constitute a special measure is a question which cannot be answered without an examination of all the relevant circumstances; it involves findings of fact. In the absence of findings which determine whether a deed of grant in trust would constitute a special measure, no declaration that the granting of such a deed would be "unlawful" can be made. There is no need to determine whether s.9 of the *Racial Discrimination Act* is inconsistent with the relevant provisions of the *Land Act* 1962, for there is nothing to show that those provisions will be used to affect interests which the plaintiffs seek to protect.[21]

Section 8(1) of the *R.D.A.* provides:

> This Part does not apply to, or in relation to the application of, special measures to which paragraph 4 of Article 1 of the Convention applies except measures in relation to which sub-section 10(1) applies by virtue of sub-section 10(3).

The Convention is the *International Convention on the Elimination of All Forms of Racial Discrimination.* Article 1(4) of the Convention says:

> Special measures taken for the sole purpose of securing adequate advancement of certain racial or ethnic groups or individuals requiring such protection as may be necessary in order to ensure such groups or individuals equal enjoyment or exercise of human rights and fundamental freedoms shall not be deemed racial discrimination, provided, however, that such measures do not, as a consequence, lead to the maintenance of separate rights for different racial groups and that they shall not be continued after the objectives for which they were taken have been achieved.

The suggestion by Brennan J. was that grant of DOGIT title (or, presumably, title under the *Aboriginal Land Act* 1991 (Qld) or *Torres Strait Islander Land Act* 1991 (Qld)), would be a special measure. It would follow that, if a grant of statutory title *were* inconsistent with surviving native title, then the native title would not be protected by the *R.D.A.* The High Court had upheld the validity of the *Pitjantjatjara Land Rights Act* 1981 (SA) as a special measure, so as not to offend the *R.D.A.*, in *Gerhardy v. Brown*.[22]

It is suggested that there is a crucial difference.[23] In 1981 the proposition generally accepted by lawyers was that the sole legal basis for continued Pitjantjatjara occupancy of their traditional lands was the status of those lands as Crown land reserved for Aboriginal occupation. As noted earlier, the decision of Blackburn J. in the *Gove Land Rights* case[24] was widely accepted as indicating that Aboriginal people had no land rights except for those granted by governments. In *Gerhardy v. Brown*[25] Deane J., in particular, strongly emphasised this factor.[26] So an Act vesting ownership under South Australian law was seen as a special measure helping to secure equal enjoyment or exercise of human rights or fundamental freedoms.

The principal holdings in the 1992 *Mabo* case itself turn this situation about. If Aboriginal people already hold 'native title', how can it be a special measure to extinguish that and to substitute some form of statutory title?

In *Gerhardy v. Brown*[27] Brennan J. himself saw four *indicia* of a special measure:

> A special measure (1) confers a benefit on some or all members of a class, (2) the membership of which is based on race, colour, descent or national or ethnic origin, (3) for the sole purpose of securing adequate advancement of the beneficiaries in order that they may enjoy and exercise equally with others human rights and fundamental freedoms, (4) in circumstances where the protection given to the beneficiaries by the special measure is necessary in order that they may enjoy and exercise equally with others human rights and fundamental freedoms.[28]

On the third point he insisted that the 'wishes of the beneficiaries for the measure are of great importance (perhaps essential) in determining whether a measure is taken for the purpose of securing their advancement'.[29] His fourth point was that a special measure needs also to be 'necessary'.

The consequence is that the *R.D.A.* could apply to protect the native title. But the issue arises only if the statutory title is inconsistent with native title. As noted, the High Court did not consider this issue in the Queensland context in *Mabo (No. 2)*.

The issue subsequently arose for judicial determination in the context of the *Land Rights (NT) Act* in *Pareroultja v. Tickner*.[30] The full Federal Court held that the grant of statutory title to a Land Trust under that Act is not inconsistent with the continuance of native title so as to extinguish it, and is not in breach of the *R.D.A.*

In the Lake Amadeus land claim[31] the Aboriginal Land Commissioner had found that the applicants and the second respondents were 'traditional Aboriginal owners' of the land, and he recommended a grant of title to a Land Trust. The first respondent, the Minister, was preparing to recommend to the Governor-General a grant of statutory title. The applicants opposed the making of the grant on the basis that it would be 'an unlawful extinction, impairment, interference with or reduction of their native title to the land'.

Lockhart J. (with whom O'Loughlin and Whitlam JJ. agreed) first analysed the scheme of the *Land Rights (N.T.) Act*, in the course of which he restated his own description of the Act in *Attorney-General (NT) v. Hand, Minister for Aboriginal Affairs*:

> The *Land Rights Act* is beneficial legislation, recognizing the importance of traditional land to the Aboriginal people and their spiritual affinity with it. It is an Act designed to return to the Aboriginal people so much of their traditional land as Australian society can make available to them. The Act recognizes the tension between the religious affinity of Aboriginal people to their traditional lands and the demands of a modern western society, between an ancient people and a cosmopolitan society. It is an attempt to do justice to the Aboriginal people consistent with the good government and progress of Australia for all its people.[32]

After considering the nature of 'native title' in light of the judgment in *Mabo (No. 2)* Lockhart J. concluded that a grant of land, to which there is native title, to a Land Trust under the *Land Rights (NT) Act* does not extinguish the native title and is not inconsistent with the continued existence of native title. The purpose of the *Land Rights (NT) Act* is to further the interests of traditional owners and is not inconsistent with their interests. The use by the *Land Rights (NT) Act* of Land Trusts and Land Councils 'is essentially a modern adaptation of traditional

Aboriginal decision-making processes through their communities',[33] and the terms of the Act make it clear that a grant of land in fee simple to a Land Trust 'does not prevent Aboriginals having the benefit of native title from continued occupancy, use or possession of their land to the extent that it is in conformity with Aboriginal tradition governing the rights of the relevant Aboriginals with respect to that land'.[34] Lockhart J. went on to state 'the grant of land, to a Land Trust does not extinguish native title; it protects it'.[35]

> When one examines the *Land Rights Act* and the rights that it confers upon persons who have the benefit of a land grant, it is apparent that, although the rights and obligations enjoyed or suffered by Aboriginal people entitled to the benefit of native titles will vary as between clans or groups and areas of land, it is the interests of the relevant Aboriginal people that are necessarily taken into account by the exercise of the various mechanisms established by the *Land Rights Act* for their benefit.[36]

After reference to a number of statements in the judgments in *Mabo (No. 2)* instancing grants of interests which would not extinguish native title, Lockhart J. said: 'land is granted to Land Trusts under the *Land Rights Act* to preserve native titles and Aboriginal interests and is not inconsistent with the continued enjoyment of native title'.[37]

The Federal Court was dealing with two Commonwealth Acts — the *R.D.A.* and the later *Land Rights (NT) Act*. Its overall decision was that if the *Land Rights (NT) Act* had been subject to the *R.D.A.* (which it was not), and even if it had been contrary to that Act (which it was not), it would still have survived as a 'special measure' within section 8(1).

Counsel for the applicants seeking special leave to appeal to the High Court advanced four main lines of argument:

(1) that the *Land Rights (NT) Act* properly construed, simply does not apply to land in respect of which there is valid and subsisting common law native title; alternatively,

(2) that the provisions of the *Land Rights (NT) Act* for the vesting of statutory title in a Land Trust and the conferral of management powers on a Land Council contravene the *R.D.A.* section 10(3) (about non-

consensual management of the property of Aboriginal people) to which the 'special measures' exemption in section 8 does not apply; alternatively,

(3) that the provisions of the *Land Rights (NT) Act* which authorise grants of statutory title over land which is subject to native title contravene the *R.D.A.* section 10(1), and that the *Land Rights (NT) Act* cannot be regarded as a 'special measure' since the High Court determined, in *Mabo (No. 2)*, that Australian common law recognises and protects native title; and

(4) that the effect of the *Native Title Act* 1993 (Cth) gives the common law holders of native title a choice whether to hold that title themselves or to have it held for them in trust by a prescribed body corporate; accordingly, the earlier *Land Rights (NT) Act* must now be read as permitting a similar choice.

The case for the applicants was argued on 12 April 1993. On the following day, the Chief Justice announced that the High Court proposed not to hear from counsel for the respondents. His Honour continued:

> What I am about to say represents the views of the majority of the Court, Justices Deane and Gaudron dissenting.
>
> This is an application for special leave to appeal from a unanimous judgment of the Full Court of the Federal Court answering questions in a case stated. Having considered the detailed arguments presented in support of the application, the Court has come to the conclusion that, in relation to the first three grounds of appeal, the proposed appeal does not enjoy sufficient prospects of ultimate success to warrant the grant of special leave.
>
> In saying that, we are not to be taken as necessarily agreeing with the conclusion of the Full Court that the grant of an estate in fee simple to a Land Trust under the *Aboriginal Land Rights (Northern Territory) Act* 1976 (Cth) is consistent with the preservation of native title to the land the subject of the grant.
>
> With respect to the further ground based on the *Native Title Act* 1993 (Cth), we do not consider that it would be appropriate, in the circumstances of this case, to grant special leave on this ground alone when the Court lacks the advantage of any consideration of the ground by the Federal Court, that aspect not being before the Federal Court. In addition, there is the circumstance that, although the

validity of the *Native Title Act* is common ground between the parties, there is a pending challenge to the validity of the Act. The application for special leave is therefore refused.

So, while the decision of the Full Federal Court stands as the final determination of the particular case, the High Court expressly reserved its position on the relationship between native title and statutory title under the *Land Rights (NT) Act*. It also declined to consider arguments about the relationship between the *Land Rights (NT) Act* and the *Native Title Act* 1993 (Cth).[38]

As noted, the High Court has also not ruled on the issue under Queensland legislation. The relationship between native title and statutory title under other land rights legislation also awaits consideration.

If the Federal Court was correct in holding in *Pareroultja*[39] that a land grant under the *Land Rights (NT) Act* would not have the effect at common law of extinguishing native title, then in agreement with Richard Bradshaw[40] the same conclusion ought logically to follow in relation to some other land rights Acts. It would certainly apply to the *Pitjantjatjara Land Rights Act* 1981 (SA) and the *Maralinga Tjarutja Land Rights Act* 1984 (SA) and also to pre-1994 grants made on the basis of 'traditional affiliation' under the *Aboriginal Land Act* 1991 (Qld) and the *Torres Strait Islander Act* 1991 (Qld).

The vesting of land under the *Aboriginal Lands Trust Act* 1966 (SA) may not have extinguished native title. But it seems likely that pre-1994 grants under the *Aboriginal Land Rights Act* 1984 (NSW) would extinguish any native title, unless the native title was saved by force of the *R.D.A.*[41] The effect of section 10(1) of the *R.D.A.*, as applied in *Mabo (No. 1)*, is to 'top up' any racially differential diminution or extinguishment of native title so as to equate with the rights and interests of others. Accordingly, the effect of section 10(1) may be to preserve the native title interest as co-existing with the statutory title. Alternatively, the native title holders would be entitled to compensation for any loss of native title rights.

The above discussion deals with the relationship between statutory title and native title at common law, as underpinned by the *R.D.A.* Native title at common law is now underpinned more specifically by the *Native Title Act* 1993 (Cth) most of the provisions of which commenced operation on 1 January 1994 (some retroactively to 1 July 1993). Also relevant is State and Territory legislation on native title, some complementary to the *Native Title Act* 1993 (Cth),[42] but that of Western Australia in opposition to it.[43]

Statutory Title and Native Title Legislation

Past Acts

The validation provisions in the *Native Title Act* 1993 (Cth),[44] authorised to be enacted by State or Territory legislatures,[45] operate only in respect of 'past acts' of governments which (as defined in section 228) were invalid because of the existence at the time of native title in relation to the land or waters in question. Presumably, the only source of any such invalidity would have been the *R.D.A.* The *Native Title Act* 1993 (Cth) section 7, which provides that nothing in the Act affects the operation of the *R.D.A.*, is subject to the proviso that this does not affect the validation of past acts by, or in accordance with the *Native Title Act* 1993 (Cth).

Accordingly, if by reason of the *R.D.A.* any State or Territory land rights Acts, or acts done pursuant to such Acts, were invalid, they may now be validated. The effect on native title of validation of past acts is spelled out in section 15 as extinguishing native title, when the past act falls within Category A as a grant of freehold or of many forms of leasehold title or a public work.[46] One exception is made where a grant of a freehold estate is 'a grant made by or under legislation that grants freehold estates only to or for the benefit of Aboriginal peoples or Torres Strait Islanders' or 'a grant of a prescribed kind to or for the benefit of Aboriginal peoples or Torres Strait Islanders'.[47] Another exception is made where a grant of a lease is 'a grant made by or under legislation that grants leases only to or for the benefit of Aboriginal peoples or Torres Strait Islanders' or 'a grant of a prescribed kind to or for the benefit of Aboriginal peoples or Torres Strait Islanders' or 'a grant over land or waters that, on 1 January 1994, are Aboriginal/Torres Strait Islander land or waters'.[48] Similar exceptions are made in regard to the validation of other forms of leases which would fall within

Category B, the effect of which would otherwise be to extinguish native title to the extent of any inconsistency.[49]

The phrase 'Aboriginal/Torres Strait Islander land or waters' is defined as meaning land or waters held by or for the benefit of Aboriginal peoples or Torres Strait Islanders under three listed Commonwealth land rights Acts,[50] three listed South Australian land rights Acts[51] 'and any other law prescribed for the purposes of the provision in which the expression is used'.[52]

The intention is clearly to protect native title from any extinguishment effect that would otherwise flow from the validation of the pre-1994 grants of statutory title under land rights Acts. If such grants of statutory title do not fall within Category A or Category B they will come within Category D as to which (together with Category C — the grant of a mining lease) 'the non-extinguishment principle' applies.[53] However, the native title is subordinated to the extent of, and for the duration of the validated interest.[54] In other words, the statutory title under a land rights Act would prevail over any native title considerations. Of course, none of the provisions will operate if the grant of statutory title under a land rights Act is not invalid by reason of the *R.D.A.*

Future Acts

Would it be open to governments after 1 January 1994 to grant statutory title over land which is subject to surviving native title? Some such grants may fall within the definition of 'past acts' so as to be covered by the preceding discussion. A 'past act' within the *Native Title Act* 1993 (Cth) section 228 may apply to post-1993 acts which constitute options or renewals etc., under pre-1994 past acts including 'exercise of a legally enforceable right created by' legislation or other acts which are 'past acts'. Bradshaw points out, correctly I believe, that the interpretation given to the *Aboriginal Land Rights Act* 1983 (NSW) is such that a post-1993 grant of statutory title would qualify as a 'past act'. This would not, however, seem to apply to post-1993 grants made under other land rights Acts, even grants based on claims heard and determined before 1994.

Would a grant of statutory title after 1 January 1994 under a land rights Act, in respect of land subject to native title, constitute a 'permissible future act'? The *Native Title Act* 1993 (Cth) definition of permissible future acts[55] generally requires an equivalence of treatment for native title as for 'ordinary title'. 'Ordinary title' is defined in section 253 as a freehold estate in fee simple (or, in the case of the Australian Capital Territory or Jervis Bay territories, a lease). Freehold and leasehold titles may not be granted by governments over freehold (or leasehold) titles without the prior acquisition of such titles, so the same would apply to grants over native title land.

The definition of 'future act' in the *Native Title Act* 1993 (Cth) includes the requirement that it 'affects native title in relation to the land or waters' in question.[56] But the definition does not apply to 'an act that causes land or waters to be held by or for the benefit of Aboriginal peoples or Torres Strait Islanders' under land rights Acts.[57] So such a grant of statutory title would seem simply not to fall within the definition of 'future act' so as to be either 'permissible' or 'non-permissible' within the terms of the *Native Title Act* 1993 (Cth). However, the requirement of equivalence of treatment of native title and other forms of title would seem still to be applicable on the basis of the *R.D.A*. If a grant of statutory title under land rights Acts may not be made over freehold land, it could not be made over native title land.

Land rights Acts in New South Wales and Queensland have been amended by the State native title legislation so as to clarify the relationship between post-1993 grants of statutory title and native title.[58] The new provisions provide, simply, that a grant of statutory title will be subject to any native title rights and interests existing immediately before the grant. Similar amendments are probably needed for the *Land Rights (NT) Act*.

Conclusion

To attempt to pull these complex threads together, the following tentative summary is offered:
1. Legislation needs to display a 'clear and plain intention' before courts will conclude that its effect is to extinguish native title.
2. Land rights legislation conferring title on the basis of traditional rights in relation to land will not be so

inconsistent with native title as to extinguish the native title.
3. Land rights legislation conferring title other than on the basis of traditional rights will almost certainly extinguish native title if the grantees are people other than the native title holders. If the grantees are the native title holders, the legislation may still extinguish native title if the terms of the grant are inconsistent with native title.
4. The protection against extinguishment of native title offered by the *R.D.A.* may not operate in respect of land rights legislation under 3 (above) if the legislation can be described as a 'special measure' within section 8(1) of the *R.D.A.* For this purpose, the criteria enumerated by Brennan J. in *Gerhardy v. Brown*[59] need to be considered. But the 'special measures' exception may not avail against native title holders after 3 June 1992, the date of the High Court decision in *Mabo (No. 2)*.
5. The validation provisions in native title legislation in respect of 'past acts' operate only where such grants etc., are invalid because of the existence at the time of native title. In any case, validation provisions expressly provide that any extinguishment of native title that would otherwise flow from validation does not apply in respect of grants under land rights legislation. Native title is not extinguished but is overlaid by the statutory title.
6. Post-1993 grants of statutory title may simply not fall within the definition of 'future acts' in the native title legislation. As a result, a grant of statutory title could not be made over land subject to native title because of the effect of the *R.D.A.* Land rights Acts need to be amended to clarify that future grants of statutory title will be subject to native title. This has been done in Queensland and New South Wales land rights legislation but not in relation to the Northern Territory legislation.

There is little doubt that these issues will arise for further judicial consideration. There will be a need for close analysis of the specific legislative context in each jurisdiction in which the issue may arise. Analysis in advance may help to avoid litigation, either by clarifying the position or else by establishing the need for amending legislation to overcome difficulties.

Reconciliation of statutory title and native title will not be possible where the grantees of statutory title are not those who would hold the native title. But issues of competing claimants can arise even when one is dealing solely within the context of a land rights Act, or solely within native title law. The issue will simply not arise in respect of land for which no group has been able to maintain the traditional connections necessary to support native title. Otherwise the ideal outcome should clearly be that statutory title and native title are reconciled to the greatest extent that is possible.

Notes

1. (1971) 17 F.L.R. 141.
2. For an overview of such land rights legislation, see H. McRae, G. Nettheim and L. Beacroft, *Aboriginal Legal Issues: Commentary and Materials* (Sydney: Law Book Co., 1991), Ch.5. For fuller accounts, see *The Laws of Australia* 1. Aborigines and Torres Strait Islanders (Sydney: Law Book Co., 1993), *Halsbury's Laws of Australia* 1. Aboriginals and Torres Strait Islanders (Sydney: Butterworths, 1991).
3. McRae, Nettheim and Beacroft, *supra* note 2, 155–158.
4. *Administration of Papua v. Daera Guba* (1973) 130 C.L.R. 353, 397 per Barwick C.J.
5. (1979) 53 A.L.J.R. 403.
6. *Id*. 408 per Gibbs J.; see also 411 per Jacobs J. and 412 per Murphy J.
7. (1985) 159 C.L.R. 70.
8. *Id*. 149.
9. (1992) 175 C.L.R. 1.
10. Aboriginal Land Rights Commission, First Report (1973), *Second Report* (1974) (Canberra: A.G.P.S.).
11. *Pitjantjatjara Land Rights Act* 1981 (SA); *Maralinga Tjarutja Land Rights Act* 1984 (SA).
12. (1992) 175 C.L.R. 1.
13. Brennan S.J., *Land Rights Queensland Style* (Brisbane: University of Queensland Press, 1992).
14. (1992) 175 C.L.R. 1, 64–65.
15. Assuming that that term relates to all indigenous inhabitants of the State whether having any connexion with the particular reserve or not: see *Corporation of the Director of Aboriginal and Islanders Advancement v. Peinkinna* (1978) 52 A.L.J.R. 286.
16. On the basis of these remarks, it is arguable that the Supreme Court of Queensland was right and the Judicial Committee of the Privy Council was wrong in *Corporation of the Director of Aboriginal and Islander Advancement v. Peinkinna* (1978) 52 A.L.J.R. 286.

17. (1992) 175 C.L.R. 1, 66–67. To similar effect see 111 per Deane and Gaudron JJ., 196 per Toohey J.
18. (1988) 166 C.L.R. 186.
19. (1992) 175 C.L.R. 1, 74 per Brennan J., 119–20 per Deane and Gaudron JJ.
20. *Id.* 119–120 per Deane and Gaudron JJ., 214–216 per Toohey J.
21. *Id.* 74.
22. (1985) 159 C.L.R. 70.
23. G. Nettheim, "'Native Title", Statutory Title and "Special Measures"' (1993) Vol. 3 No. 63 *Aboriginal Law Bulletin* 4.
24. *Milirrpum v. Nabalco Pty. Ltd.* (1971) 17 F.L.R. 141.
25. (1985) 159 C.L.R. 70.
26. *Id.* 149–150. See also 87 per Gibbs C.J.
27. (1985) 159 C.L.R. 70.
28. *Id.* 133.
29. *Id.* 135.
30. (1993) 117 A.L.R. 206, and Casenote (1993) Vol.3 No.64 *Aboriginal Law Bulletin* 29.
31. *Ibid.*
32. (1989) 25 F.C.R. 345, 357; 90 A.L.R. 59, 66.
33. (1993) 117 A.L.R. 206, 214.
34. *Id.* 215.
35. *Id.* 214.
36. *Id.* 217.
37. *Id.* 218.
38. *Pareroultja v. Tickner* No. S156 of 1993, 12–13 April 1994; Casenote (1994) Vol.3 No.68 *Aboriginal Law Bulletin* 28.
39. *Ibid.*
40. Bradshaw, 'Relationship of Native Title and Native Title Legislation to Land Rights Legislation' in R. Bartlett and G. Meyers (eds.), *Native Title Legislation in Australia* (Perth: Centre for Commercial and Resources Law, University of Western Australia and Murdoch University, 1994).
41. Bradshaw, *supra* note 39.
42. *Native Title (Queensland) Act* 1993; *Validation of Titles and Actions Act* 1994 (NT); *Native Title (New South Wales) Act* 1994.
43. *Land (Titles and Traditional Usage) Act* 1993 (WA).
44. *Native Title Act* 1993 (Cth) (hereinafter referred to as *N.T.A.*) s.14.
45. *Id.* s.19.
46. *Id.* s.229.
47. *Id.* s.229(2)(b)(ii) and (iii).
48. *Id.* s.229(3)(d)(ii), (iii) and (iv).
49. *Id.* s.230(d)(ii), (iii) and (iv).
50. For the Jervis Bay Territory, for Lake Condah and Framlingham Forest in Victoria, and for the Northern Territory.
51. The *Aboriginal Lands Trust Act* (SA) 1966 and the *Pitjantjatjara Land Rights Act* 1981 (SA); *Maralinga Tjarutja Land Rights Act* 1984 (SA).
52. *N.T.A.* s.253.
53. *Id.* s.15(1)(d).
54. *Id.* s.238.
55. *Id.* s.235.
56. *Id.* s.233(1).

57. *N.T.A.* s.233(3)(a). Section 233(3) was added as a Government amendment during the course of the Senate debate on the *N.T.A.* It also excludes from the definition of 'future act' '(b) any act affecting Aboriginal/Torres Strait Islander land or waters', defined in s.253 *N.T.A.* by reference to land and waters held under Land Rights Acts.
58. *Aboriginal Land Act* 1991 (Qld) ss.3.06, 5.08 and *Torres Strait Islander Act* 1991 (Qld) ss.3.06, 5.08 as amended (respectively by ss.161 and 162, and ss.169 and 170 of the *Native Title (Queensland) Act* 1993); *Aboriginal Land Rights Act* 1983 (NSW) s.36(9) and (9A) as amended by s.107 and Schedule 1, *Native Title (New South Wales) Act* 1994.
59. (1985) 159 C.L.R. 70.

Index

Aboriginal
    approach to land holding, 40
    hunting, fishing, and gathering rights, 43
    reserves, *see* Reserves
    rights and interests, 4, 168
    rights to natural resources, 43
    sacred sites, 128
    special attachment to the land, 4, 41, 53, 148–49, 176
    traditional relationship with the land, 172
Aboriginal and Torres Strait Islander Commission
    amendment, *see* ATSIC Amendment
Aboriginal and Torres Strait Islander Social Justice Commissioner, 2
Aboriginal Land Act 1991 (Qld), 157, 161, 185, 188, 193
    Land Tribunal role, 160
    result of successful claims, 160
Aboriginal Lands Rights Act 1983 (NSW), 185, 195
Aboriginal Land Rights (Northern Territory) Act 1976, 5, 63, 84, 89, 184, 190, 191, 192, 196
    role of Aboriginal Land Commissioner, 160
Aboriginal Land Trusts Act 1966 (SA), 185
Aboriginal/Torres Strait Islander bodies, 86
Acquisition of property
    see also Compulsory Acquisition Act; Compensation
    by Commonwealth, 42, 122
    by State and Territory Governments, 42
Acquisition of sovereignty 37, 168
    see also Terra nullius
Act, 121, 128
    attributable to Commonwealth, State or Territory, 127
Acts of sovereignty, 120, 121, 122, 123, 125

A.C.T.V. v. Commonwealth (1992), 33
Agricultural lease, 2, 7
Amodu Tijani v. Secretary, Southern Nigeria (1921), 29
Applications *Native Title Act* 1993 (Cth), 89, 132
    see also Native title claims
    application procedures, 89, 90, 103, 132
    compensation, 1, 89, 132
    consent applications, 91
    material to accompany applications, 93, 94
    native title, 1, 9
    non-claimant, 56–58, 60, 64, 137
    onus of researching the title history, 95–97
    opposed, 91
    party to application, 90, 91
    party whose interests are affected by the application, 91
    Registrar's power to accept or reject application, 93, 94
    rejection of application, 90
        appeals from Registrar's rejection of application, 90
    right to negotiate, 89
    special inquiries, 89
    unopposed, 91, 142, 192
Approved determination of native title, 77
Arbitral body, 8, 9, 72, 130, 131
    judicial functions of, 131–32
Assessor, *see* Federal Court; National Native Title Tribunal
ATSIC Amendment (Indigenous Land Corporation and Land Fund) Bill 1994, 1
Attorney-General (NT) v. Hand, Minister for Aboriginal Affairs (1989), 190
Australia Act 1986, 112
Australian Railways Union v. Victorian Railways Commissioners (1930), 30, 31

Body corporate (holding native title), 2, 5

Category A past act, *see* Past acts
Category B past act, *see* Past acts
Category C past act, *see* Past acts
Category D past act, *see* Past acts
Charter of the United Nations, 40
Coe v. The Commonwealth (1993), 12, 96
Coe v. The Commonwealth (1979), 184
Comalco Act 1957, 10
Commencement of the *Native Title Act* 1993 (Cth), 1
Commercial lease, 2, 7
Commissioner for Aboriginal Planning, 19
Common law
    see also Racial discrimination
    the force of law of the Commonwealth, 26, 53
    native title, recognition of, 4, 33
Common law native title, see Native title
Commonwealth of Australia Constitution Act 1900, 127
Commonwealth v. Tasmania (1983), 32, 127
Compensation, 6, 10, 14–15, 28, 31, 43, 51, 73, 75, 86, 122, 124, 126, 128, 129, 135–53
    see also Just terms
    after unopposed determination of native title, 142
    application procedures, 89
    breach of fiduciary duty, 149
    criteria, 10
    discussion in Mabo (No.2), 135–36
    extinguishment of native title, 138, 140, 141, 143
    future acts, 141–43
    impairment of native title, 138–39, 142, 143
    liability of grantees of interests for, 140
    past acts, 6, 21, 28–29, 122, 127, 138–39, 140
    payable by the Commonwealth, 140, 143
    payable by State or Territory, 21, 31, 127, 143
    Racial Discrimination Act and, 136, 139
    similar compensable interest test, 129, 139, 142, 145
    time limits for, 129, 140–41
Compulsory Acquisition Act, 8, 10, 128, 129, 142, 144
Constitution
    "characterisation" of Act, 27, 29, 30
    express prohibitions, 30–31
    fettering the legislative capacity of State Parliaments, 33
    head of power, 26–30, 120
    implied prohibitions, 31–34
    limitation on the exercise of Federal judicial power, 160
    section 51, 120, 123, 126, 131
    section 51 (xxxi) (external affairs power), 27, 122, 123, 135, 140, 143
    section 51 (xxvi) (race power), 26–31, 124, 126, 127, 131
    State Constitutions, 30, 31, 33
Constitutional law
    constitutional validity of *Native Title Act* 1993 (Cth), 26–34, 88, 120, 126
    inconsistency, 26, 27, 33, 87, 88, 125, 136
Convention for the Protection of the World Cultural and Natural Heritage, 127
Crown
    compensation payable by the, 127, 149
    fiduciary duty to indigenous title holders, 10–12, 29, 135, 149
    see also Wik claim
    grants of land, 6, 14
    ownership of colonial land, *see* Crown ownership of land
Crown ownership of land, 27, 29, 30
Crown ownership of natural resources, 51

Deed of grant in trust titles (DOGIT), 186, 187, 188

Delgamuukw v. British Columbia, 98, 106
Determination(s)
  see also Applications
  approved determinations of native title, 77, 162
  arbitral body, 9
  claims filed, 85
  claims procedures, 89
  Federal Court, 9
  in terms of agreement, 91
  National Native Title Tribunal, 9, 91, 132
  of native title, 132
  overruling, 10, 78
  registration of, 77
  revocation, 86
  variation, 86
Discrimination, 3, 7, 13, 27, 33, 37, 40
  see also Racial discrimination
Draft Declaration on the Rights of Indigenous Peoples, *see* United Nations

Evidence, 54, 55, 56–64, 129, 133, 165
  expert evidence, 58–64
  hearsay, 57
  lay evidence, 57–58
  material to accompany claims applications, 93, 94, 95
  Native Title Tribunal, 163
  onus of researching title history, 95–97
Expedited procedure, 8, 39, 78, 130
Extinguishment of native title, 26, 28, 36, 56, 120, 128, 142, 168, 171, 180, 185, 193, 194, 195
  see also non-extinguishment principle
  clear and plain intention required, 174–75
  deed of grant in trust, 186, 187
  grants in trust, 5
  grants of freehold, 6, 121, 122
  land rights legislation, 4
  lease grants, 6, 94, 97–98, 106, 122, 125
  mineral and petroleum tenements, 6, 51
  mining lease, 6
  pastoral leases, 6, 94, 97–98, 104, 105, 106
  reservations permitting continued Aboriginal access, 5, 97–98, 105
  revival, 125
  statutory title, 187, 190, 191, 193, 194
  to extent of inconsistency, 120, 121

Federal Court, 54, 130, 132
  see also Determinations; National Native Title Register; National Native Title Tribunal
  assessor assisting, 9
  determination of, 162
  evidence, 93, 132, 133
  jurisdiction of, 9, 93
  matters to be considered, 54, 132
  onus of proof, 93
  parties, 93
  proceedings, 93
  representation, 130
Federal Court of Australia Act 1976, *see* Federal Court, assessor assisting
Fiduciary duty of Crown, *see* Crown
Fishing rights, 4, 8, 22n2, 24
  see also Native title
Freehold grants, 6
Future acts, 28, 73, 76, 86, 128, 195, 196, 197
  see also Compensation
  act attracting the expedited procedure, 8
  compensation for future acts, 141–44
  dealings, 2, 4, 7, 39, 128
  definition, 128
  impermissible, 7, 26, 28, 31, 128
  invalidity of, 75, 128, 130
  low impact, 7–8
  permissible, 7–8, 26, 28, 31, 117, 128, 130, 196
  similar compensable interest test, 142

Gerhardy v. Brown (1985), 15, 27, 184, 188, 189, 197
Gove Land Rights Case, *see Millirrpum v. Nabalco*
Guerin v. R (1984), 135

High water mark, 2

Index

Hunting rights, 4

Impermissible future acts, *see* Future acts
Inconsistency, *see* Constitutional law
Indigenous Land Corporation and Land Fund (ATSIC Amendment) Bill 1994 (Cth), 1
Injunctions
 available to protect native title, 76
 Canadian authorities, 76
International Covenants
 International Covenant on civil and political rights, 40
 International Covenant on economic, social and cultural rights, 40
International Convention on the Elimination of all Forms of Racial Discrimination, 37, 38, 40, 188
International Labour Organisation (ILO), 41
 Convention on Indigenous and Tribal Peoples in Independent Countries, 41–43, 44–46
International Law, 36–47
 see also United Nations; International covenants
 duty on States to identify and protect indigenous peoples' land, 41–42
 international human rights standards, 38
 protection from alienation, 42–43
 recognition of indigenous ownership on indigenous terms, 42
 rights of indigenous peoples to natural resources, 43
 special significance of land, 41
Invalid acts and grants, *see* Past acts; Future acts; Validation regime

Joint Committee on Native Title, *see* Parliamentary Joint Committee on Native Title
Jurisdictional limits, 80
Just terms, 6, 8, 33, 42, 122, 123, 128, 129, 139, 142, 143, 144, 145–46, 148–49
 see also Acquisition of property

Koowarta v. Bjelke-Petersen (1982), 32

Land
 see also National Aboriginal and Torres Strait Islander Land Fund
 title searches, 95, 96, 97
Land Act 1910 (Qld), 108
Land Act 1898 (WA), 113
Land Act Amendment Act 1934 (WA), 114
Land fund, 1, 40, 43, 84
 see also National Aboriginal and Torres Strait Islander Land Fund
Land rights legislation — States, 183–200
Land (Titles and Traditional Usage) Act (WA) 1993, 17–21, 40, 72, 87, 168, 169–81
 challenge to validity of, 180
 compensation for native title, 171, 172, 175–78
 extinguishment of native title by, 171, 172, 175, 176
 substitution of statutory rights of traditional usage, 17, 172–75, 178, 179
 uncertainty for resource management, 181
 violation of R.D.A., 179–81
Leases, 74, 104–17
 see also Agricultural lease; Commercial lease; Mining lease; Pastoral lease; Renewal of leases; Residential lease
 arguments for dealing with reservation clauses, 109–113
 discussion in *Mabo* (No. 2), 94, 106
 examples of reservation clauses, 113–15
 extinguishment of native title by, 6, 74, 94, 97–98, 105–106
 renewal of, 2, 7, 117
 reservation clauses, 5, 104, 105, 107–13
 validity of, 6, 104
Low water mark, 2, 80

Mabo v. Queensland (No. 1) 1988, 38, 39, 40, 121, 124, 180, 187, 193
Mabo v. Queensland (No. 2) 1992, 11, 15, 18, 29, 34, 36, 38, 39, 41, 43, 49, 50, 51, 54, 58, 63, 64, 71, 84, 89, 94,

96, 97, 106, 107, 108, 109, 111, 120, 122, 126, 129, 132, 135, 136, 156, 157, 168, 179, 184–87, 189, 192, 197
Maralinga Tjarutju Land Rights Act 1984 (SA), 193
Mediation, 9, 92, 130, 132
Melbourne Corporation v. The Commonwealth (1947) (the State Banking Case), 31–33
Milirrpum v. Nabalco (1971), 36, 183, 189
Mining
   application for mining tenement procedure, 51–53, 76–77, 79
   decision of Tribunal in relation to mining, 52
   granting of exploration permit, 78–80
   granting of mining tenements, 51–52, 72, 75–77, 79–80
   in Western Australia, 51–52
   mineral and petroleum tenements native title, whether extinguished, 6
   mining industry, 43, 168–69
   renewal of mining tenement, 52–53
   right to negotiate, 53, 78–80, 130
   shift of power from States to Commonwealth, 73
   time to process mining tenement claim, 76, 78, 79, 80
   validity of mining titles granted, 2, 80
Mining Act 1978 (WA), 18–19
Mining lease
   invalidly issued, 6, 75
   non-extinguishment rule, 51
   renewal of, 2–3, 7, 52–53, 80
   validly issued, 6
Mining Wardens Court, 9, 54, 73, 88
Minister
   Commonwealth
      right to overrule Tribunal, 10, 52, 78
      powers regarding mining tenement, 73, 74
   State
      right to overrule Tribunal, 10, 52, 78
      right to overrule Mining Wardens Court, 72

Minister for Aboriginal and Torres Strait Islander Affairs, 1
Muduwongga claim, 95

National Aboriginal and Torres Strait Islander Land Fund, 1, 40
National Native Title Register
   contents, 9, 77
   registration of claims, 77, 90
   significance of absence of entry, 77
National Native Title Tribunal
   see also Queensland Native Title Tribunal
   appeals to Federal Court, 54, 90, 160
   applicants' guide, 1
   applications to, 9, 90
   appointment of members, 158, 159, 163
   assessor, 55, 133
   consent applications, 91, 92
   determination of, 91, 92, 160, 161, 162
   evidence, 93, 94, 133
   functions, 9, 132
   joint appointments to Queensland Native Title Tribunal, 163
   matters to be taken into account on determination NT, 79
   mediation, 9, 92
   membership, 55, 158
   opposed applications, 91, 92
   President, 55, 158
   questions of law, 92
   referral to Federal Court, 92, 160
   Registrar, 9, 89, 90, 92, 132, 133, 164
   registration of determinations in Federal Court, 9
   regulations, 1
   relationship with Queensland Native Title Tribunal, 158
   review of Registrar's rejection of claim, 93, 94
   royalty arrangements, 91
   time limits, 52
   unopposed applications, 54, 91, 92, 160
Native title, 4, 28, 36, 126, 169
   see also National Native Title Register; National Native Title

Tribunal; Native Title
Registrar
common law recognition of, 33,
169
determination of, 9, 132
extinguishment of, *see*
Extinguishment of native title
fishing, hunting, gathering, 2, 4, 29
future acts *see* Future acts
gardening rights, 29
holder, 127
holders in Western Australia, 20
nature and incidents of, 125, 126
   continued acknowledgment of
      traditional laws and customs,
      125
   spiritual attachment, 41, 171
   statutory recognition of, 17–20
   statutory title and, 193
   traditional connection with land,
      28, 85, 125, 129, 174
   traditional sustenance for
      hunting, gathering and
      fishing, 4, 174
   unique, 170
   varies according to traditional
      law, customs and usages,
      170–71
pragmatic compromise of *Johnson v. McIntosh*, 169
protection of, 170
recognition of, 4–5
rights of user, 110
titles exchanged for, 64
Native Title Act 1993 (Cth)
amendments needed, 56
commencement, 1
constitutional challenge to, 26–34, 88, 126
Native Title (Notices) Determination No 1 1993, 86
Practice directions, 86
   compensation, 86
   material to accompany claim
      applications, 94, 95
   need for, 92
   variation of approved
      determination, 86
regulations, 85
ultra vires, 86

Native title claims
   see also Applications; Expedited
      procedure
adjudication of claims, 53–56
Burri Gubbi claim, 51
Carpentaria claim, 93, 95, 97
claims procedures, 89–94, 103, 133
compensation, 89–90
consent applications, 91, 92
effect of no entry of native title
   claimant on register, 77
flowchart, 89, 103
material to accompany claims
   applications, 93, 94
Muduwongga claim, 95
native title determinations, 89–90
Ngaluma Ingibundi claim, 95
onus of researching title history, 95–97
opposed applications, 91, 92
party to application, 90, 91
procedural amendments, 56
referral to Federal Court, 54, 92
Registrar's power to accept or reject
   claims, 93, 94
review of rejected claims, 94
unopposed applications, 54, 91
Wannyi claim, 63–107
Wik claim, 10–12, 51, 54, 62, 97, 135, 149
Native Title Act 1994 (ACT), 21n62
Native Title (New South Wales) Act 1994, 21n62
Native Title (Queensland) Act 1993, 20–21, 155–65
   see also Queensland Native Title
      Tribunal
amendment of, 156
appeals, 160, 161
commencement of, 156n6
determination, 160
determinations of native title, 161
effect of approved determination of
   native title, 162
evidence, 163, 165
joint appointments to Queensland
   Native Title Tribunal and
   N.N.T.T., 163
objectives of Act, 156
recognised State/Territory body, 161

Registrar, 164
relationship with *Native Title Act 1993* (Cth), 156–158
Native Title Register, *see* National Native Title Register
Native Title Registrar
　see also National Native Title Register; National Native Title Tribunal
　application to, 9, 89, 90, 132–33
　duties of, 9, 90
　notice by, 90
　notification by person wishing to be party, 90
　powers of, 133
　power to accept or reject claim, 93, 94
　review of rejection by, 94
Native Title Tribunal, *see* National Native Title Tribunal
Natural resources, 43, 51 *see* Right to negotiate
Negotiation regime
Ngaluma Ingibundi claim, 95
N.N.T.T., *see* National Native Title Tribunal
Non-discrimination principle, 7, 18
Non-extinguishment principal, 7, 75, 125, 138, 195

Offshore, 139, 142
Onshore, 7, 139, 142
Ordinary title, 128

Pareroultja v. Tickner (1993) (The Lake Amadeus land claim), 5, 21, 190–93
Parliamentary Joint Committee on Native Title, 2
Past acts, 6, 11, 28, 52, 73, 80, 121–25, 194, 195
　see also Extinguishment of native title
　Category A, 6, 28, 121, 194
　Category B, 121, 195
　Category C, 122, 125, 139
　Category D, 98, 122, 125, 139
　compensation, 138–41
　need to validate, 28, 104, 124
　similar compensable interest test, 139
　validity of, 5, 6, 14, 74, 104, 105, 122, 123, 141
Past grants, *see* Past acts
Pastoral Land Act 1992 (NT), 114
Pastoral Land Management and Conservation Act 1989 (SA), 115
Pastoral lease, 94–95, 97–98, 104–67
　Aboriginal reservation or access clauses in, 97, 98, 104–17, 113–15
　arguments for dealing with reservation clauses, 109–13
　extinguishment of native title by, 74, 105, 106, 107
　impact of, upon native title, 97
　mining over, 115
　native title claimable over, 115
　N.N.T.T. guidelines, 108
　rejection of claim over, 94
　renewal of, 7, 27, 117
　validation of, 116
　validity of, 2, 6, 104–105
Pearling Act (WA) 1969, 18, 173
Permissible future acts, *see* Future acts
Petroleum Pipelines Act 1969 (WA), 18, 173
Petroleum (Submerged Lands) Act 1967 (WA), 18, 173
Petroleum (Submerged Lands) Act 1982 (WA), 18, 173
Pitjantjatjara Lands Right Act 1981 (SA), 15, 16, 188, 193
Political Broadcasts and Disclosures Act 1991 (Cth), 33
Profit á prendre, 29
Property
　　see Acquisition of property
　right to own, 40
Public Works Act 1902, 18

Queensland Coast Islands Declaratory Act 1985, 136, 176
Queensland Electricity Commission v. The Commonwealth (1985), 27, 32
Queensland Native Title Tribunal, 20, 158–64

Racial discrimination, 3, 32, 38–39, 169–70, 179, 181
　limit to future dealings in land, 2

limit to legislative power over native title, 8
non-discrimination principle, 34
Racial Discrimination Act 1975, 2–6, 13–15, 17–18, 20–21, 26–27, 38, 39, 40, 43, 51, 88, 104, 105, 113, 122, 123, 124, 136, 139, 141, 168, 169, 170, 175, 178, 179, 187, 191, 193, 194, 197
    question of invalid grants, section 9, 14; section 10, 18, 20, 21
    violation of, 179–81
Racial Discrimination Convention, 126
Radical title, 28, 29, 31
Recognised State/Territory bodies, 73, 130, 131, 133, 159, 161, 165
    see also Arbitral body
Register of Native Title Claims, *see* National Native Title Register
Registrar, *see* Native Title Registrar
Renewal of leases, 2–3, 7–8
    Commercial, agricultural, residential and pastoral, 2–3, 7–8
    Mining, 2–3, 7
Reserves, 185–186
Residential lease, 2, 6, 7
Revival of native title, *see* non-extinguishment principle
Right to negotiate, 2, 7–9, 10, 22, 40, 41, 52, 53, 73, 74, 78–80, 86, 89, 92, 115, 130
    see also Applications

Section 51(xxxi), Constitution, *see* Constitution
Second Uniform Tax Case, see Victoria v. The Commonwealth (1957)
Similar compensable interest test, *see* Compensation; Future acts; Past acts
Social Justice Commissioner, *see* Aboriginal and Torres Strait Islander Social Justice Commissioner
Sovereignty, 120
    acquisition by Crown, *see* Acquisition of sovereignty
    original, of Aboriginals, 96
Special matter, 92
Special measure, 13, 15, 16, 27, 124, 126, 188, 189, 191, 192
    see also Racial discrimination

State(s)
    see also State and Territory legislation
    acts attributable to, *see* Future acts; Past acts
    agreements with native title holder, 7
    crown land, 3, 4
    jurisdictional limits, 11
    land rights legislation, 183–200
    licensed activities, 8
    ownership of natural resources, 51
    residual powers, 28
    validation of acts, *see* Validation regime
State and Territory legislation, 17–22, 40, 87–89, 124, 126
Statutory title to land, 187, 190, 193, 194, 196, 197
Suspension of native title, *see* non-extinguishment principle

Tasmanian Dam Case (Commonwealth v. Tasmania) (1983), 32, 127
Terra nullius, 37, 51
Territory, 40
    see also State & Territory Legislation
    acts attributable to, *see* Future acts; Past acts
    validation of acts, *see* Validation regime
Title searches, 95–97
Torres Strait Islander Land Act 1991, 156, 185, 188, 193
    Land Tribunal (Qld) role, 160
Traditional title, *see* Native title
Tribunal, *see* National Native Title Tribunal

United Nations, 40, 46–47
    Draft Declaration on the Rights of Indigenous Peoples, 41–43
Universal Declaration of Human Rights, 39, 40
Usufructuary rights, 29

Valid grants and acts, 5
Validation of Titles and Actions Act 1994 (NT), 21n62
Validation regime, 5, 6, 13, 15–17, 39,

73–75, 104, 116, 122, 123, 126, 128, 130, 141, 195, 197
  see also Past acts
Valuation of native title, 137–38, 144–49
  circumstances valuation required, 137
  criteria, 146–48
  date of valuation, 141
  special attachment, 148
Victoria v. The Commonwealth (1957), 30

Waanyi claim, 63, 107

Wardens Courts, *see* Mining Wardens Courts
Waters, 2, 8
Western Australia
  approach to *Mabo*, 171
  State Act, *see* Land (Titles and Traditional Usage) Act 1993 (WA)
Wik claim, 10–12, 51, 54, 62, 97, 135, 149
World Heritage Properties Conservation Act 1983 (Cth), 32